SOCIAL
CONTEXT
AND
RELATIONSHIPS

UNDERSTANDING RELATIONSHIP PROCESSES

Series Editor
Steve Duck, *University of Iowa*

This series of books on the theme **Understanding Relationship Processes** provides a coherent and progressive review of current thinking in the field. Uniquely organized around the notion of relational competence, the six volumes constitute a contemporary, multidisciplinary handbook of relationship research for advanced students and professionals in psychology, sociology, communication, family studies, and education.

Volumes in the Series

1. INDIVIDUALS IN RELATIONSHIPS
2. LEARNING ABOUT RELATIONSHIPS
3. SOCIAL CONTEXT AND RELATIONSHIPS
4. THE DYNAMICS OF RELATIONSHIPS
5. RELATIONSHIP CHALLENGES
6. UNDERSTUDIED RELATIONSHIPS

EDITED BY
STEVE DUCK

SOCIAL CONTEXT AND RELATIONSHIPS

UNDERSTANDING RELATIONSHIP PROCESSES SERIES
VOLUME 3

SAGE Publications
International Educational and Professional Publisher
Newbury Park   London   New Delhi

For information address:

  SAGE Publications, Inc.
2455 Teller Road
Newbury Park, California 91320

SAGE Publications Ltd.
6 Bonhill Street
London EC2A 4PU
United Kingdom

SAGE Publications India Pvt. Ltd.
M-32 Market
Greater Kailash I
New Delhi 110 048 India

Printed in the United States of America

Library of Congress Cataloging-in-Publication Data

Main entry under title:

Social context and relationships/edited by Steve Duck.
    p. cm.–(Understanding relationship processess: v. 3)
    Includes bibliographical references and indexes.
    ISBN 0-8039-5377-1 (cloth).–ISBN 0-8039-5378-X (pbk.)
    1. Interpersonal relations. 2. Social networks. 3. Social structure. I. Duck, Steve. II. Series: Understanding relationship processes series: v. 3.
    HM132.S5665   1993   93-5197
    302dc20

93 94 95 96 10 9 8 7 6 5 4 3 2 1

Sage Production Editor: Diane S. Foster

Contents

Series Preface

This short series **Understanding Relationship Processes** rsponds to recent calls for an attention to process in relationships. A close look at the nature of processes in relationships will reveal that, over and above the importance of change, temporality, and an orientation to the future, beneath most process thinking on relationships lies the implicit notion of competent use of knowledge across time. For example, this assumption is true of many elements of the work on relationships, such as the (competent) transition to marriage, (skilled) conflict management, (appropriate) self-disclosure in relationship development, and (orderly) organization or (satisfactory) maintenance of relationships diachronically. The assumption also is contained in discussion of intimacy assessment of couple creation (by which authors evaluate the degrees of intimacy or progress that are adequate, allowable, suitable, or competent) and is latent in discussion of relationship breakdown where discussions treat breakdown as failure or incompetence, contrasted with skill or competence.

Such competence is evident in, and constrained by, a variety of levels of influence on behavior. In focusing on some of these topics, this series moves conceptually outward; that is, the series begins with the contributions of individuals and their developmental experiences to relationships, and moves toward the social context and interpersonal interaction. Individuals bring into relationships their individual characteristics and factors that reflect their point in the life cycle and their developmental achievements. Individuals are influenced by the social setting (situational, cultural, linguistic, and societal) in which the relationship takes place; they are constrained and influenced by the structural, transactional, behavioral, and communicative contexts for their relationships; and they sometimes conduct the relationships in dysfunctional environments or disrupted emotional contexts. The series takes the contextual themes in sequence and deals with the latest research and thinking that address these topics.

Accordingly, each volume focuses on a particular context or arena for relationship activity. The first three volumes of the series deal respectively with the following topics:

Individuals in Relationships. Volume 1 deals particularly with the ways internal or intrapersonal context is provided by structures of the mind or of knowledge that are prerequisite for success in relationships; however, rather than focusing on such things as if they were the end of the story, the chapters place such knowledge styles and structures in context by referring frequently to behavioral effects of such structures.

Learning About Relationships. Volume 2 covers especially the skills and experiences in childhood that lay the groundwork for competence as a properly functioning relater in adult life; the volume emphasizes the wide range of social sources from which development of competence is derived and the richness of the social sources from which developing minds acquire their sense of relationship competence.

Social Contexts and Relationships. Volume 3 focuses especially on the social structural constraints within which relationships are located and the ways the two partners must negotiate and deal with the dialectical and interior pressures created by such contexts.

Other volumes in the series deal with the dynamics of relational transactions, challenging contexts for relating, and overlooked elements of relating.

STEVE DUCK

Volume Preface

The first two volumes in this series, **Understanding Relationship Processes,** have outlined the contribution of individual knowledge to the conduct of relationships, whether from the point of view of cognitive structure or of the learning that takes place in childhood. Volumes 3 and 4 explore the relational contexts provided by various social, cultural, structural, network, or dynamic transactional processes.

This volume considers the forces on dyadic relationships that are exerted by people other that the partners themselves. Social influences arise from membership of networks and groups, from the impact of culture on the forms of relationships, and from the structuring effects of a daily life carried out in a place and time. These influences constitute the tensions and guidance, difficulties and resolutions, advice and reproach, created by simultaneous membership in several reference groups beyond any particular dyadic relationship in which one is a member. They are summarized in the volume's title as the *social context* of relationships between individuals or, to put it another way, the ways in which a developed individual fits into the social structures, the cultural structures, and the contextual realities of relational life for a human being in a Western society.

This volume thus deals with some of the large tentacles against which individuals may struggle or against whose background activities their personal relationships take on a special meaning. Culture and society, social structure, the embeddedness of relationships in a social network all affect individuals by creating needs to deal with dialectical pressures as the individuals work their own personal and relational requirements into the patterns created by joint activity in relationships. Also present in social relationships, however, both in form and in definition, are the gossamer strings of various puppeteers, such as the influence of gender on relationships as well as the role of time and daily routines.

In brief, the volume confronts those issues that affect the individual and the pair in transacting their relationship. It then makes the point once again that forces creating and shaping relationships are not purely individual or dyadic. It also argues the position that competency in relating is in part assessed in terms of exterior societal criteria as well as those based on individual satisfaction or desire. To be judged competent, relaters need to juggle various competing and conflicting demands, to adhere to customary guidelines and structural forces within the society (both at large and in the smaller scale), and to manage their relationship in a way that manages the "organizational framework" of the relationship itself in a given context.

As more than one contributor notes, even dyadic relationships, which are traditionally conceived by some scholars to be the result of emotional activity or to be "caused" by cognitive operations or attitudinal change, are embedded not only in a social context but also in an economic one. As such, they present not only individual emotional, attributional, or cognitive problems but predicaments of practical management. Much research takes for granted the social cultural practices that influence, overshadow, and command relationship activity, and very little attends to the socioeconomic thread that makes many relationships in reality quite different than the ones idealized in the writing of many researchers. In real life, far from the sunlit choices and bracing freedoms of well-off college students on well-endowed American campuses, the huge majority of members of all cultures, including our own, conduct their relationships in a climate of restriction and submission, clouded by restraints on freedom, limits on opportunity, the compulsions of coercive family norms, the encumbrances of responsibility, and perhaps even the smell of poverty and the disgusting enactment of racial, religious, political, sexual, and economic bigotry. Volumes 5 and 6 will spend more time on the practicalities of such matters; the current volume alerts us to their causal force and invites theorists to open the windows of their ivory towers and look out at the scurrying beings cutting through the intricacies of their real lives against a background of constraints.

Although economic factors impinge on all our lives, it is a rum thing that the so-called science of relationships has based much of its theorizing on an economic theory in one form or another (exchange theory, equity theory, investment theory, interdependence theory) yet paid little attention to the wider socioeconomic influences on relationships beyond the dyadic bartering of costs and rewards. Yet the dyadic is strongly influenced by the sociocultural (Milardo & Wellman, 1992), and the sociocultural is to some extent predetermined by its economic underpinnings. This volume foretells that the *context* of the currently disembodied activities of sequestered cognitive structures will be the ground to which theory and research ineluctably turns in the next millennium.

Graham Allan's chapter begins the volume by explicating some of these points in relation to a wide literature in sociology. Taking issue with the recent popularity of a culturally reflective style of research that treats dyadic relationships as discrete units isolated from the wider influences in which they are embedded, Allan's chapter attends to the structures in which they occur, whether social, economic, cultural, or biographical. By considering the ways in which cultural practices for relationships are taken for granted and accepted as obvious and natural, Allan highlights the different ways in which structural features influence personal ties and the expectations that people have about them. A close consideration of friendship, courtship, marriage, parent-adult child ties, and divorce rounds out the case that relationships are fashioned by structural constraints that are a balancing force against pure voluntarism.

In the second chapter, Julia T. Wood examines cultural practices that promote generalizable (though not universal) differences
in women's and men's ways of communicating and interpreting the
relational communication of others. The chapter traces the manner
in which individuals' embodiments of cultural prescriptions reverberate throughout the ongoing processes that make up social
and personal relationships. The chapter then explores how
gender-associated differences in communication may enrich or
endanger relational satisfaction, depending largely on partners'
abilities to recognize, respect, and employ each other's perspective and style. The chapter discloses gender's reflection in styles
of interacting, ways of expressing affection, use and abuse of
power, and feelings of responsibility for relationships. Wood
concludes that intimacy is a culturally patterned arrangement as
well as a personal choice.

Chapter 3, by Renate Klein and Robert M. Milardo, deals with
the impact of social networks on the management of personal
relationships, specifically their development and maintenance.
The authors argue that outsiders affect the feelings of the relational partners and constrain, influence, or develop the sort of
relationships that they are able to create and enjoy. By focusing
on those points in relationships where conflict is likely to occur,
Klein and Milardo point up places where competence is challenged and where the influence of others on the relationship
may be significant for its future development. Not only do
partners refer their feelings about the relationship to standards
present in the network, but they also occasionally refer the
relationship itself to outsiders for intervention. Third parties
affect relationships by applying their own perspectives of judgment, and to some extent their own standards, to relational
behavior. In so doing, they modify partners' views of themselves
and the relationship and so create a frame for interpretation. In
emphasizing the social construction of relationships, rather than
an individual skills interpretation, the authors emphasize the
elements of relationship competence that accord not only with
idiosyncratic but also with conventional wisdom.

Catherine H. Stein deals with "felt obligation" in adult family
relationships and outlines the ways in which the partners' sur-

rounding network of associates provides resources, support, and opportunities for growth in the relationship. She balances that against consideration of the negative consequences of such network membership and emphasizes the special demands and needs for skillful conduct that such a situation creates. She argues that adult relationships with kin exist as (and within) a unique context of previous history and future involvement that influences the ways in which partners deal with one another. In such an analysis, the untrammeled freedoms of choice in relationship form, relationship behavior, or interdependent activity seem overrepresented in present-day research. The chapter deals with the rights and duties that are embedded in long-term relationship with kin across the life cycle. Felt obligation is a strong social force that shapes the conduct of personal relationships.

Another hidden force constraining relationships is discussed by Niall Bolger and Shannon Kelleher in a chapter dealing with daily life in relationships. Daily routines of relating (and other spheres of life) have impact upon the relationship and affect the ways in which it is interpreted and experienced by the partners within it. The chapter addresses the issue of management of daily routines and confrontations over minor daily hassles, showing that relationship effects cannot be understood without reference to larger social structures and contexts such as the workplace.

Carol M. Werner, Irwin Altman, Barbara B. Brown, and Joseph Ginat follow this with a chapter that looks at other social contexts that frame relationships, namely, the special events that occur in the context of relationship: celebrations in personal relationships. This chapter examines how couple and family celebrations contribute to relationship viability. The authors focus on four contextual themes: Social units are embedded in social and physical environments; relationships contain inherent temporal qualities; embeddedness involves dialectical tensions between social units; and celebrations reflect the temporal qualities and are one method of coping with and reflecting the dialectical tensions. The emphasis of the chapter is on the ways in which physical environment and social contexts are *integral* to relationship, emphasizing that they occur in physical environments and that people use objects and settings as relationship symbols.

Celebrations are not just oddities that happen during relation-ships, they are central ways in which people provide a context for relationships and structure them. The authors argue the case that exploration of the social, physical, temporal, and environ-mental contexts of relationships is an essential part of our fullest understanding of how they work.

In the final chapter, Leslie A. Baxter rounds out the discussion of the ways in which the personal relationship is embedded in a web of sociality that extends beyond the boundaries of the dyad. She argues the fundamental significance of the fact that personal relationships are embedded in the broader social order, and she explores the ways in which this social exigency poses three fundamental dialectical tensions for relationship parties: (a) the dialectic of integration versus separation (the extent to which a couple withdraws from interaction with others), (b) the dialectic of private versus public (the extent to which parties keep private between themselves their relationship status), and (c) the dialectic of uniqueness versus typicality (the extent to which a couple replicates traditional forms of intimacy).

Taken as a set, the chapters in this volume make a compelling case for a modest redirection of research on relationships away from the over application of an individual perspective and more toward the inclusion of contextual features against which the struggling individual and dyadic lusts and preferences are wres-tled out. This is more than the interdisciplinary argument that there are more things in relationships than are dreamed of in social psychology or communication. It is the practical argument that relationships have to be *enacted* in a time, place, and context, by persons embedded in societies and networks and invested with the raiment of their historical time or cultural conventions. Personal relationships are practical things with practical implications, not merely "outcomes" produced by cog-nitive gymnastics. As indicated above, this book promotes the idea that the time is now ripe for personal relationships research to recognize this fact more explicitly and more generally than before. We must move toward the next millennium with the issue of social context ever before us. As Milardo and Wellman (1992) noted, the personal is also social.

STEVE DUCK

1

Social Structure
and Relationships

Graham Allan

Over the last 15 years, new approaches have come to dominate the study of personal relationships. In particular, a concern with personality, attitudes, and other essentially individualistic theoretical constructs has been replaced by a fuller focus on interactional and relational processes (Duck, 1990b). Yet to a large degree this new focus has itself tended to analyze dyadic relationships as discrete units, isolated from the wider contexts in which they are embedded (Milardo, 1988; Milardo & Wellman, 1992). To this extent, the new approach echoes the dominant cultural understanding of personal relationships as voluntaristic ties that those involved construct according to their own private agendas. Within this approach, in other words, there is an emphasis on agency over and above structure.

Yet, dyadic relationships are clearly not just personal constructions. Agency, of course, does matter. Relationships are actively developed and sustained through the strategic decisions and immediate responses those involved make. At the same time,

1

structure plays its part. The options people recognize and the choices they make are patterned by the social, economic, cultural, and biographical contexts in which they act. Moreover, while personal relationships are not static, either individually or culturally, many are routinely sustained through a process of "non-decision making" (Delia, 1980). That is, they are sufficiently embedded in socioeconomic relations and sociocultural practices for their form to be taken for granted and accepted as obvious and "natural" even while still being seen as personally constructed in their detail. Thus personal relationships as diverse as courtship and neighboring have been transformed under conditions of modernity as wider social and economic change alters the overall configuration of people's dependencies on one another (Giddens, 1991). This simple point is widely recognized in long-running debates about the impact of industrialization on family and community life but is often ignored when the focus is on more recent orderings of personal relationships. But these new orderings, despite their tendency to emphasize "the relationship" as a personal construction, are as much a product of their socioeconomic time as earlier forms.

This third volume in the series Understanding Relationship Processes is concerned primarily with exploring the ways in which these wider contextual and structural aspects impinge on and shape personal relationships. More narrowly, its focus is on how social and economic rather than individual or dyadic constraints influence what is judged at an everyday level to be competent relational behavior. This chapter sets the scene for those that follow by highlighting some of the different ways in which structural features influence personal ties and the expectations people have about them. It cannot do this comprehensively but will attempt to indicate the necessity of locating dyadic relationships within broader structural contexts if they are to be understood satisfactorily. In making its arguments, the chapter draws heavily on British studies; the underlying issues being addressed, though, apply to the construction of relationships in any society.

Structure, Competence, and Rules

Personal relationships are actively sustained through the endeavors of those involved, but not, to paraphrase Marx, necessarily in ways of people's own choosing. Individual relationships—whether friendship, marriage, collegiality, or whatever—are developed and managed by reference to socially and economically sustained models of what these relationships should be like. In other words, the general forms taken by different types of relationship have an independence from any particular existing dyadic example, though the forms themselves are at the same time underpinned through the continued production of the individual dyadic ties.

In most, if not all, instances, acting competently within relationships—"doing" the relationship satisfactorily—involves at least an implicit knowledge of the dominant models of those types of relationship. Individuals engage with these models in their everyday interactions with others through their reflective monitoring of other people's ties and via media representations of different forms of relationship (Prusank, Duran, & DeLillo, in press). Talk—analysis, discussion, and gossip within social networks—is itself a key mechanism through which knowledge about cultural models of different relationships, and the behavior considered legitimate within them, is routinely channeled. It is with these socially and economically grounded models as a context that people routinely cultivate their own, apparently individual, relationships. Competence in this sense means broadly following a set of socially sanctioned guidelines and acting out a socially sustained script.

Yet here, of course, we run into potential difficulties, for such terms are not entirely appropriate characterizations of relationship accomplishment. For example, to talk of relationship *rules* or of socially agreed *scripts* runs the risk of becoming overly deterministic. The rules that relationships follow are not as well specified as most forms of rules, nor so tightly framed. Similarly, the *scripts* that *actors* follow are rather freer, open to far more improvisation, than the dramaturgical analogy sometimes implies. So, too, to talk of relationships being premised on cultural forms or models, which themselves can be seen as rooted in prevailing socioeconomic organization, can imply an oversocialized perspective on social action as well as overemphasizing the extent of normative consensus at the expense of subcultural variations.

Notwithstanding these difficulties, in examining the way in which personal relationships are patterned and structured by circumstances and processes outside the influence of those directly involved in the tie, some form of conceptualization based around the idea of "rules" or "guidelines" is difficult to avoid. To adopt a spatial analogy, personal relationships can be seen as bounded areas or "fields" of permissible action within which people construct their individual ties. The largeness or smallness of the "field" will differ between different types of personal relationship, some being less tightly specified and allowing greater freedom than others. The boundaries here can be conceived broadly as the parameters of socially accepted behavior and exchange within the given form of relationship. They are the "rules of relevance" (Allan, 1979; Paine, 1969) applied to, and consequently patterning, these ties. To carry the analogy a little further, the point of this chapter is to specify in some measure the way in which factors external to individual dyads shape the boundaries, topography, and landscape of the social "fields" in which different relationships are located.

If it is accepted that the form taken by different types of personal relationship is influenced by social "guidelines," that the boundaries of what we construct as relevant to them is at least in part socially and economically fashioned, then an important set of questions concerns the nature of those external influences. What range of factors shape and pattern adult relationships? What affects and alters the boundaries of competent, acceptable behavior within them? What are the parameters within which individuals are "free" to construct these "personal" adult ties? Providing answers to such questions is not at all straightforward, for the social development of different types of relationship will be patterned by rather different configurations of external factors. Thus, for example, the location of marriage within the social formation is quite distinct from, say, that of neighboring, and in turn neighboring is structured by a different constellation of social and economic influences than friendship.

In this chapter, it will be possible only to give a broad indication of the structural factors and processes that pattern the forms taken by different personal relationships. To highlight the different elements involved, the chapter will focus on three types of relationship: friendship, parent-adult child ties, and marriage. These three types of relationship have been selected because they are each, in their different ways, of quite major consequence within individuals' personal networks. They are ties that matter to people and to which they commonly devote a good deal of time, energy, and care. More important within the context of this chapter, they represent relationships that are structurally embedded to differing degrees and in different ways. Thus friendship appears to be the epitome of a voluntaristic and unstructured personal tie. There seems to be a great deal of freedom over who friends are and what they do together. On the other hand, marriage, notwithstanding contemporary visions that emphasize its freely negotiated character, is generally recognized as being patterned more by convention and as more integral to social order. Parent-adult child ties lie somewhere in between, being seen as nonvoluntary in some respects but open to individual determination. To explore the different ways in which personal relationships are structured, this chapter will focus first on the least embedded of these ties, friendship, then consider parent-adult child ties, and finally turn to marriage.

Friendship

As noted, within modern culture, friendship is generally seen as one of the least institutionalized of all relationships. While some researchers have sought to specify the "rules" governing it (Argyle & Henderson, 1984; Ginsburg, 1988), culturally friendship is taken as largely a matter of personal decision. Though there may be a greater degree of choice in friendships than in many other relationships, these ties are still patterned by contextual and situational factors lying outside the direct control of those involved. Even though the friends themselves may not necessarily be aware of the external influences there are on their friendships, these ties are created and sustained within the overall configuration of social and economic relations structuring their lives. This section of the chapter will focus in particular on two issues—the opportunities people have to develop friendships and the form that those friendships take—and examine some of the ways in which these are patterned by wider influences.

Before doing so, it is necessary to say a little about friendship as a cultural construction. In particular, it is important to recognize that "friendship" is a relational label rather than a categorical one (Allan, 1979). That is, the existence of the tie is not defined by an individual's position within a specific social organization, as, for example, "colleague" or "uncle" are within workplace and kinship domains, respectively. Rather, it depends on the judgments the individual makes about the quality of the tie and whether it matches the generally implicit criteria taken to signify friendship. Moreover, these criteria, as well as being implicit, are imprecise and variable; they not only differ between individuals but also vary with context. Thus one may feel it is appropriate to refer to someone as a friend in one situation but not in another. Because of this, the analyst can easily get into difficulties over exactly which sociable relationships should be included under the rubric *friend*. The position taken here is that the detailed specification of friendship matters less than the patterning of sociability in general. Consequently, the focus will be on the broad range of relationships that are generally accepted as being within the realm of *friendship,* widely defined.

A key issue in analyzing the social basis of friendship from the viewpoint of this broader perspective is that friendships are dynamic. More specifically, while most friendships persist over some period of time, friendship circles overall are not particularly stable. In other words, friendships tend to wane as well as wax as people's circumstances alter and their lives develop in new directions. A small minority of friendships—those generally characterized as "real" or very special friendships—do endure over the long run. More "everyday," run-of-the-mill friendships tend not to be so long lasting, however. Most tend to be active for a period, possibly quite lengthy, but then gradually fade, in practice becoming passive if not moribund. The processes involved in these transformations are important and reveal a good deal about the factors that structure friendship relations.

It is particularly noticeable that people's friendship circles tend to change as their life circumstances alter. For example, when people leave college, when they begin courting, when they move from their homes or change jobs, when they divorce, it is likely that aspects of their existing patterns of sociability will come to be modified, sometimes radically, generally more subtly. Put simply, the reason for this is that most friendships, in whatever form they take, require "servicing." They need contact; they need involvement; they need in a sense to be "worked at," whether this is achieved through occasional phone calls or more frequent conversations and shared activities (Duck, Rutt, Hurst, & Strejc, 1991). When, through change of circumstance, the opportunities for interaction and consequently for sustaining the relationship diminish, then the friendship itself is effectively, though generally not deliberately, undermined and begins to lapse. While culturally this is sometimes interpreted as an indication that the relationship was somehow deficient, that is, not a "proper" friendship, in reality it is an entirely routine and unexceptional process. What it highlights is the importance of context within the majority of friendships.

The contexts in which friendships, as defined here, are serviced vary quite widely. As already indicated, there are a small number of friendships that do not seem to require a great deal of active attention. These ties remain significant to those involved even though there is little contact, direct or indirect. The sense of solidarity is sustained through the friends' shared history and becomes almost inalienable. The majority of friendships, though, are not like this; with them, a degree of more active involvement is central to their continuation. Some, no matter what the original point of contact, are developed and sustained through involvement in a variety of shared sociable activities, often including spontaneous or prearranged visits to one another's homes. Other friendships are located more firmly within particular contexts, for example, work settings, sports clubs, leisure activities, though often labels other than friendship, such as *mate* or *buddy*, may be used to depict some of these latter, contextually grounded ties. Now, if the majority of friendships do require servicing within some or other contexts, it follows that continued access to those contexts, whether work, the home, or a club, is important in sustaining the ties. Where circumstances alter so that participation in the established setting(s) becomes more tenuous, then often contact is diminished and the relationship itself undermined (see Werner, Altman, Brown, and Ginat in this volume).

In addition, it follows that access to appropriate social settings is also important in the generation of friendships and the development of friendship networks. This is not to say that all friendships arise from specifically sociable settings, for this is clearly not the case. Friendships develop in myriad ways. Yet, if individuals are to form personal ties of friendship, then they normally do need opportunities to meet with others and get to know them informally. Crudely, the more integrated people are into formal and semiformal social arenas, the easier it will be for them to develop and sustain informal sociable relationships and to replace ties that, for whatever reason, fade. Conversely, of course, those who for whatever reason have less access to such arenas are likely to find it harder to conserve their friendships and replace those that become inactive. So, for example, some of the gender differences that are found in friendship patterns at various stages in the life course may, at least in part, be a consequence of the different involvement that males and females have in both employment- and leisure-oriented organizations (Allan, 1989; O'Connor, 1992) as well as their different resources (Oliker, 1989). Similarly, some of the difficulties that divorced and widowed people report having in sustaining friendships can be linked to the "couple" orientation of many adult sociable settings, though other factors are also important here including the problems of reciprocity in asymmetrical couple-individual ties (Bankoff, 1981; Rands, 1988).

Unemployment provides a particularly good example of the processes that can operate here. Numerous studies have pointed to the social isolation that unemployment generates for both men and women (Allen, Waton, Purcell, & Wood, 1986; Fineman, 1987). It is clear that for many people unemployment limits the structured opportunities for social interaction in their daily routines as well as reducing the resources they have available for sociability. The consequence is a gradual displacement and withdrawal from the contexts of interaction that normally sustain sociable ties and the reduction of friendship circles, both for the individuals directly affected and for other household members (McKee & Bell, 1987). It is interesting to note though that such an outcome is not inevitable. In particular, studies of groups who have experienced chronic unemployment indicate that mechanisms may be found to maintain active sociable networks with others in a similar position (see, for example, Binns & Mars, 1984; Liebow, 1967). In these instances, the absence of resources requires that the developed forms of sociability do not involve very much reciprocal expenditure.

While others may not be so limited in this respect, the activities they engage in with friends will be influenced by the level of material resources they have free to devote to sociability. Other features of an individual's class position also play a part in shaping their patterns of friendship, though not in a simple or mechanistic way, nor necessarily with similar effects in different societies. For example, research has suggested that class location, along with other structural characteristics, especially gender (O'Connor, 1992), influences the way in which friendship ties develop, with those having fewer resources being more likely to restrict interaction to specific contexts (Allan, 1979; Hunt & Satterlee, 1986). Similarly, there are arguments linking class and marital organization to the use of the home for entertaining and the involvement of friends in the private, domestic sphere (Allan, 1989; R. G. A. Williams, 1983). So, too, Wellman's (1985) work in Toronto has indicated very clearly how people's work situations pattern their friendship networks and the nature of their sociable interactions (see also Wellman & Wellman,

1992). The general point here is that class location is a core element within people's social and economic environment and as such inevitably plays a part in fashioning friendship behavior.

The impact of social structure and social division on friendship can be seen in other respects, not least in the broadly similar structural locations that friends usually occupy. While there are plenty of individual exceptions, in the main friends tend to be homogenous in terms of their social and economic characteristics. This is hardly surprising given that friendship is culturally perceived as a relationship of equality based around common interests. Yet its implications are of some consequence, for, as writers like Hess (1972) and Jerrome (1984) have argued, friendship plays a significant role in cementing social identities while often seeming not to. That is, on the one hand, friendships allow the expression of individuality by appearing to be separate and distinct from people's established social roles and responsibilities. Yet, because friends tend to be in essentially similar social positions and share equivalent worldviews and values, in practice they actually tend to provide legitimation and support for these roles.

Thus, in Jerrome's study, friends evidently used their relationships to express a side of themselves that was not so apparent in other contexts. Here they could distance themselves from the various role positions they occupied, for example, complaining to each other about their marriages or about their work, and express themselves apparently quite freely. Yet the "selves" they were being in these interactions still clearly reflected their wider social location. For instance, the value they placed on style and accomplished entertaining when they met informally derived directly from their position as established and relatively wealthy, older, middle-class women (Jerrome, 1984).

What is important here are the subtle ways in which social identity patterns and shapes friendship interactions. The way we are with our friends, the personas we present, are clearly not just amalgams of the role set we occupy now or have occupied in the past. To some degree, we are free to accentuate one element over another or to attempt to leave aspects of our lives aside from our friendships. Yet, generally, our activities and interactions with friends will mirror, to a greater or lesser extent, the social identities we establish outside the ties. In the process, friends play their part in molding these identities and reinforcing commitment to social roles. At the same time, by so often being premised around wider social identities, friendship circles also reveal the status divisions and boundaries of social closure that exist within the larger social order (O'Connor, 1992).

As Milardo and Wellman (1992) argue, relatively little attention has been paid to the ways in which informal ties like friendship have impact on issues of social division and political advantage. Indeed, because of the heavy concentration in relationship research on isolated dyadic bonds, the collective impact of different relationships is often ignored. Yet relationships are clearly not developed in isolation from one another. In particular here, other people are routinely incorporated into the various contexts within which individual friendships are enacted. For example, friends sometimes meet as dyads, but they also often engage with one another in more collective social settings. More important, whatever the dominant pattern of their interactional contexts, the nature and content of their relationship is likely to be influenced by other ties within their social networks. The strength of this point can be recognized without needing to embrace any particular stance to the configurational properties of different networks. For example, the ways in which the respective spouses regard one another may well influence the path that a friendship takes; conflict developing between other members of one's friendship circle may make it difficult to sustain one's own ties with these people; over time, a new friendship may generate further introductions, which diminish involvement with an existing set of friends; and so on. While these issues are of a different order than those raised earlier, they do indicate again the importance of a structural perspective for analyzing friendships.

Parent-Adult Child Ties

The relationships that parents have with their dependent children can be recognized as being quite highly institutionalized and tightly framed. There are many social and legal obligations that parents have to their children as well as an immense quantity of popular, professional, and academic guidance about the best ways of managing these relationships. The form that these relationships take when the child becomes adult is, however, much more idiosyncratic and less socially regulated. Thus, while parent-adult child ties are usually viewed as less "voluntary" than the friendships discussed in the previous section, they are still open to a good deal of individual "negotiation" and are not tightly governed by well-specified or institutionalized frameworks. Indeed, while there is a strong cultural expectation that the relationships will continue to be sustained in some form, there is an equally powerful pressure for children to be socially and economically independent as adults. In consequence, there is variation in the nature of the ties that develop in adulthood. Nonetheless, contextual and structural factors, as well as individual choices, play a part in patterning these ties.

The variation there is in these relationships, between people and over time within relationships, makes it difficult to characterize them. In general, however, there appears, as mentioned above, to be a normative consensus that these relationships should be maintained at least at some minimal level. Unlike, say, friendships and more distant kin ties, they are not usually allowed to lapse altogether. Contact is maintained by phone, visits, and letters; information about general well-being and significant changes in circumstance is provided. Research from different countries suggests that the only significant exceptions to basic maintenance of this form of relationship arises in some single-parent families where the nonresidential parent was effectively absent from the child's life. (The numbers of such instances are, of course, likely to grow, given the increasing incidence of single-parent families.) Many parent-adult child relationships, however, involve more than the continuation of limited contact, so the important questions concern the factors that structure greater involvement.

Geographic mobility and physical separation are obvious factors placing constraints on the interaction possible between the generations. It would also appear that gender is a significant influence, with females generally being more active in servicing these ties than males (see Wood's chapter in this volume). Other influences are more subtle, however. For example, time is an important element in the construction of these relationships, not just in the obvious sense of the time given over to them but also in two other ways (Blieszner & Adams, 1992). First, these relationships are not static, either biographically or historically. Historical shifts are largely outside the scope of this chapter, but changes over the life course are not. Central to this are the ways in which the commitments, obligations, and responsibilities of the two generations, in both public and private spheres, alter over time in ways that impinge on their relationships. Second, time is important because each relationship brings with it a history and assumed future that pattern its current form. How the relationship is defined, in other words, depends in part on its character in previous periods and, at some stages at least, on the expectations there are about its future development.

Thus there is a dynamic within these relationships that is fashioned through the interplay of, on the one hand, their enduring, though diffuse and sometimes shallow, commitment (D. M. Schneider, 1980) and, on the other, the shifting configuration of other influences—personal, familial, social, and material—that at any time shape their lives. So, for example, leaving home, becoming adult, being geographically mobile are all going to influence the relationships young adults have with their parents, though not in uniform or consequently entirely predictable ways. It is generally the overall constellation of circumstance that matters rather than any particular element. Equally, the younger generation's own family formation often alters the parent-adult child relationship, though again the exact form of influence is affected by factors lying outside the tie.

In particular, while marriage itself will have some bearing on the relationship between the generations, the birth of (grand) children is likely to be particularly significant. Again, the degree of variation should not be underestimated, but generally the presence of grandchildren gives a different focus to the parent-adult child relationship and allows grandparents a greater justification for intervening in their children's lives without contravening independence. Contextual factors are, of course, always important in the details of that intervention, but one issue to note is the impact that increased labor force participation, combined with the demographic characteristics of childbirth, has had on the social position of grandmothers especially. The typical grandmother to dependent children is now relatively young, that is, in her early fifties, likely to be in employment and to have domestic and other responsibilities. Such factors have led to these relationships having a rather different exchange basis than that predominating in earlier decades.

There are, of course, numerous other structural features that pattern the contours of these intergenerational relationships. One, for example, is the material dependencies that exist between the younger and older generations. Although for most people waged labor generates economic independence, in some instances, such as family businesses, some farming communities, and the like, the second generation's well-being depends on access to material property controlled by the first generation. In these circumstances, the element of economic dependence can have a direct impact on the dynamics of the relationship by influencing the personal independence and freedoms of the adult child(ren) involved (Allan, 1982; Delphy & Leonard, 1992). Similarly, in situations of chronic poverty, mothers with young children often come to depend on their own parents for small-scale material and familial support to a greater degree than is otherwise the case (Brannen & Wilson, 1987; Stack, 1974).

Another important factor, though one that has received rather little attention, stems from the fact that parent-adult child ties are usually part of a network of kin relationships, so that other relationships influence the form that any given tie takes. Generally speaking, there are three major sets of relationships within family networks that are likely to be of consequence here. The spouse/parent-in-law tie and the grandchild(ren)-grandparent tie will clearly be patterned by the character of the intermediary parent-adult child bond, but so too the dynamics of these other relationships will have an impact on the contours of the parent-adult child tie. Equally, the relationships that siblings have with parents can mutually influence each parent-adult child tie, though not necessarily in ways that are always apparent. At issue here is not some particular outcome from a given network configuration but that the presence of others who participate in a common social domain, in this case primary kinship, is likely to have some bearing on the construction of each constituent relationship and on the way its performance is judged.

The research area where these types of issues have received most attention in recent years concerns care provision for elderly parents who have become disabled. Despite popular claims about the failure of families to provide support, the research literature demonstrates that in the great majority of cases adult children feel a sense of responsibility for the welfare of their parents. Many factors affect the ways in which this sense of responsibility is translated into action—some quite directly, others more subtly. Prime among these are the dominant systems of welfare within the society and the ability of the parent(s) to gain access to adequate levels of nonfamilial support. Within most modern societies, recent fiscal crises combined with a significant aging population have led to an emphasis on "community care" and/or private market policies, which in practice can often leave adult children with much responsibility for primary care provision.

The forms of support that adult children are able and willing to give to their parents as need arises will be shaped contextually by the circumstances of the different parties involved. Aside from the detail of the (changing) care required and the sometimes delicate management of the transition from independence to dependence, factors like residential proximity, gender, and the existence of other responsibilities influence the pattern of provision that emerges. Another significant contextual element is the availability of support from other sources, including other siblings. Again, here it is important to recognize the influence of both biographical and network effects. In particular, recent research has argued that decisions about care arrangements, along with other aspects of filial obligation, often emerge through protracted, though implicit, "negotiations" involving the family as a network (Finch & Mason, 1993). In other words, the stances taken by different members of the primary kin network over time can mean that "decisions" about care provision are not necessarily made in an explicit way; rather, responses to current care dilemmas are structured by previous patterns of involvement, with the outcome being "obvious" to all given the actors' different circumstances. Thus, while support for dependent parents is recognized in the abstract as the responsibility of all children, it appears rare that the weight of caring is borne equally by all. Often, practical considerations are important in this—the readier availability of one sibling or the difficulty of rearranging social and medical services appropriately—but it is a good illustration of the way in which contextual and structural factors can mediate individual choice in parent-adult child ties. Qureshi and Walker's (1989) suggestion, based on their study of carers in Sheffield, England, that a significant minority of children caring for dependent parents have long-standing negative feelings about them is clearly pertinent here. (Also see Lewis & Meredith, 1988.)

Marriage, Courtship, and Divorce

The final type of relationship to be considered in this chapter is that of marriage, including routes into and out of that state. It is widely recognized that the form that marriage takes varies significantly between different cultures and, to a lesser degree, between cohorts. Within present-day industrial societies, those characterized by late modernity, there is, however, an increasing emphasis on marriage as a "pure relationship," individually constructed principally to meet the emotional and personal needs of the two individuals involved (Giddens, 1992; Morgan, 1991). Under conditions of modernity, the place of marriage within the wider social order appears to be culturally undermined, with the relationship being defined as an end in itself.

Yet, just as in other societies and other epochs marriage is patterned by social conventions and material relations that lie well outside the dominion of individual couples, so in modern society the different transformations there have been in the ideology and reality of marriage—captured quite neatly by the linguistic shift from *spouse* to *partner*—are themselves framed within a much broader canvas. Despite the popularity of the view that couples each fashion their own marriage, in reality the couple's construction of their tie is undertaken within a social and economic context that is highly likely to influence not only the decisions they take but also the issues they do not negotiate. That is, some areas of activity are sufficiently constrained by aspects of social and economic organization rooted outside the marriage that decisions tend not to be made about them. For most couples most of the time, the arrangement of these activities is so taken for granted, perhaps even defined as so natural, as to make discussion of them largely redundant. Yet, these activities may, of course, vary over time; what is taken for granted at one time later becomes contentious as social and economic conditions shift. For example, while most couples continue to prioritize husbands' employment over wives', the division of domestic labor and child-care tasks has become an issue of some debate, even if overall responsibility in most households is little altered.

Love and Courtship

Within modern discourses of marriage, it is evident that notions of love and personal commitment now hold the ideological high ground. Love not only is taken by most people to legitimate selection of a marriage partner but has also come to be seen as the rationale for the relationship's continuation. Within legal frameworks as well as common culture, the absence of "love" is increasingly taken as indicative of the irretrievable breakdown of the relationship and is thus of itself reasonable grounds for ending the union. Love is of course normally characterized as a peculiarly individual experience and as one over which those affected have rather little control. If not usually a bolt out of the blue or passion at first sight, you are supposed to be caught in its web without too much contrivance on your part. Yet it is quite evident that no matter how it is experienced, love is a social construction, and one into which a good deal of cultural "work" is crammed (Cancian, 1987; Sarsby, 1983). Most obvious, and perhaps most important, putative adults are systematically exposed to messages about the normality of falling in love and given guidelines as to how it is achieved. From well before puberty, romantic visions and "careers" are fostered both through the bombardment of media representations in music, television, and fiction and through the actions of friends, siblings, and other direct contacts (Prusank et al., 1993). In similar ways, the different modes of love seen as appropriate for people in different life stages are culturally conveyed, whether developing in a new relationship or within an existing attachment.

But, if falling in love can be recognized as an activity for which individuals receive extensive, if informal, preparation, other factors play their part in patterning the transition to marriage. Aside from there being an element of normative agreement about the "right" age for (first) marriage (Finch, 1987)—a consensus that varies somewhat between groups and over time—there is also a notable degree of social homogeneity between those who choose to marry one another. Although less uniform than in the past, most marriages still involve people from similar class positions, similar age cohorts, similar educational backgrounds, and with similar religious beliefs (Surra, 1990). In part, of course, this is because for most people the pool of eligibles they meet tend to be involved in activities and settings similar to theirs and are thus already socially and economically "sorted." The way in which eligibility is constructed, however, is itself important here. Love is generally not so blind as to inveigle people who have radically different social horizons. Moreover, parents and friends are active in promulgating appropriate notions of eligibility and, where necessary, may work hard in subtly or otherwise discouraging those romantic/sexual attachments they see as unsuitable.

It is also worth noting here how patterns of courtship have altered in recent years, and especially the role that cohabitation now plays in the transition to marriage, for again this illustrates the significance of the "social" in what appears to be an individual concern. In many Western countries, there have been dramatic shifts in patterns of cohabitation generally and cohabitation prior to marriage especially (Haskey & Kiernan, 1989; Thomson &

Colella, 1992). The degree of change represents a significant shift in courtship behavior. The acceptance of cohabitation, the belief across the generations that it is reasonable, indeed sensible, to live together in a trial form before full commitment in marriage, contrasts strongly with the moral position dominant a generation or two previously. The concept of "living in sin" has all but vanished from present-day discourse. The reasons for this change have, as yet, received surprisingly little attention from sociologists and other social scientists. The readier control of conception, increases in the experience of divorce, and changes in the housing market, however, have all been of some importance. Yet, whatever the factors at play in this, the issue to emphasize here is that a couple's decision to set up home together outside marriage is more than just an individual decision. It is a decision grounded in a moral order that no longer considers cohabitation to be unreservedly shameful.

Marriage

As already suggested, with modernity, marital ideologies have increasingly emphasized intimacy and personal attachment above economic or instrumental cooperation. Traditionally in other types of society, with their different domestic economies, the dominant marital "blueprints" (Cancian, 1987) have attached greater weight to practical than emotional compatibility (Medick & Sabean, 1984). Indeed, even when personal attraction has been a significant element in marital selection, the emotions behind such attachments appear to have been framed quite differently than the emotional construction of contemporary love (Bauman, 1990; Sennett, 1977). Yet marriage in modern societies, for all the emphasis there is on individual choice and freedom, is still shaped by structural characteristics embedded in other features of social organization. The most obvious factor influencing marital relationships is the gender order, though the class system also plays its part. In particular, the structured access males and females have to material resources within the wider social formation strongly influences the division of responsibilities and tasks within marriages.

In Britain, for example, despite 20 years of equal opportunity
legislation, the labor market continues to be highly segregated
to the disadvantage of females. Women tend to be employed in
a small number of female-dominated occupational categories
that typically pay significantly less than most men's jobs. Moreover, unlike in America, married women's increased participation in the labor force over the last two generations has largely
been through an increase in part-time employment, where hourly
rates of pay are generally lower than full-time rates (Beechey &
Perkins, 1987). As a result of this gender order within employment,
little inroad has been made into the overarching division of labor
within marriage, especially after the birth of any children (Brannen
& Moss, 1991; Martin & Roberts, 1984). While many other factors
augment this situation, including lack of child-care facilities and
differential socialization, in the great majority of marriages, wives
continue to take responsibility for the bulk of domestic organizing, servicing, and tending. In comparison with previous generations, there may be more discussion and negotiation of the
details of what counts as a fair share of labor within the home,
but essentially for most couples the basic division of responsibility is not too contentious as the realities of the labor market make
the decision "obvious." Each couple, in responding thus to the
structural pressures that encourage a conventional division of
primary responsibility, in turn helps make that very division
appear the more compelling and orthodox. It is within this
context that images of what counts as a successful marriage are
constructed both by those involved in the marriage and by
outsiders.

In other cultures, and at other times, the routine pattern of
activities and responsibilities considered normal within a marriage may differ, but their general form will still be framed by both
material and social relations external to the relationship. For example, in North America the predominance of full-time employment
for married women over part-time labor appears to facilitate a
greater opportunity for flexibility within the domestic sphere,
especially for well-educated, middle-class wives. Equally, research
has indicated how chronic male unemployment and inadequate
welfare systems combine to discourage stable marital unions and

foster extensive domestic exchanges between networks of female kin and friends (Jencks & Peterson, 1991; Stack, 1974).

In a quite different setting, Matthews (1984), in her brilliant study *Good and Mad Women,* analyzes the social and economic processes that were important in structuring definitions of femininity and normal marriage in Australia in the interwar and postwar periods. She highlights the ways in which changes in, inter alia, demographic characteristics, domestic production and consumption, employment, and the state's involvement in health and child care recast ideologies of femininity and created a marital environment in which women's options were tightly constrained and their creativity often stifled. She depicts how some of those women who resisted these conventions, including those governing a marriage system in which wives' main responsibility lay in servicing their households, were consequently judged to need psychiatric treatment. While Matthews's study illustrates particularly well how structural and contextual elements influence social definitions of relational competency, the general point being made here is that the organization of marriage is social as much as it is individual and so is patterned by external social and economic configurations.

From a rather different perspective, the interplay between the structural and the personal within marriage can also be recognized in the changing order of the domestic environment and the symbolic and material standing of the home in people's lives. One element within this complex has been the developing cultural representation of the home as private space, distinct and separate from the public realm (Allan & Crow, 1989). Although the details of this will vary from one society to another, in Britain the drive for domestic privacy can be traced to at least the last century, when the propertied middle class began to screen their homes behind walls and hedges (Davidoff & Hall, 1987) and working-class "respectability" became centered upon domestic order (Daunton, 1983; Pahl & Wallace, 1988). But just as social, economic (and technological) changes in Victorian Britain led to altered perceptions of the home, so too changes during the course of this century have resulted in further transformations in the significance attached to the home (Wellman, 1992). In particular, without downplaying the importance of social and economic divisions within the housing market, the notion of people exercising an increased control and autonomy over the home, and indeed of the home providing them with a sense of "ontological security" (Saunders, 1990), has a popular resonance (Crow & Allan, 1990).

In line with this, and facilitated by technological developments and the growth of owner occupation, the style and ambience of the home has come to be regarded as a significant means of personal expression. Thus, for many, the active construction of the home, the decisions that are made about its ordering and decoration, the buying of appropriate furnishings and furbishments, and the creation of a desired ambience have become an important aspect of the way in which couples construct and express their "coupledom" and indeed of the way in which other people "read" this identity (Mansfield & Collard, 1988; Werner et al., 1992). Again the point to stress about this is that, despite the apparent emphasis on the home as a personal project, not only are the choices that people make about domestic styles social (and economic) ones, but moreover the centrality of the home within a marriage, and the use of the domestic ambience as a vehicle for expressing aspects of conjugal solidarity, are themselves phenomena that are rooted in the developing sociohistorical conditions of late modernity.

Divorce and Remarriage

Finally, it is worth considering briefly the impact of structural issues on patterns of divorce and remarriage. Certainly over the last 30 years there has been a change in moral climate so that divorce is seen as an acceptable solution to marital difficulties that in previous generations would have been defined as tolerable. While the decision to terminate a marriage is normally perceived as a private matter, it can never be just this. These apparently individual decisions are rooted in the same social and material conditions that have allowed present-day marriage to be viewed as a personal matter; the readier availability of divorce is itself a component of the shifts in the marital blueprint discussed above. Yet, interestingly, despite 30 years of high divorce rates throughout the modern world, social responses to the personal problems that divorce generates are only slowly being institutionalized. The legal process of divorce has generally become simpler, but, for example, socially sanctioned practices for creating new social identities as "singles," for coping with the emotional upheavals of divorce for adults and children, and even for sustaining and developing social networks after divorce are taking time to establish. Such matters, however, are now more openly on the social/political agenda than in the past, as the recent debate around the television show *Murphy Brown* in the United States illustrated. As personal experience feeds into public expression, culturally approved responses to the dilemmas of divorce are likely to emerge more fully.

Similar issues are faced by many stepfamilies (see the Coleman and Ganong chapter in Volume 5 of this series). Despite the increasing prevalence of this family form, there are very few socially accredited or sanctioned "rules" that people can draw on in ordering these relationships. While a growing research literature, not least within family therapy, demonstrates the common structural tensions that "reconstituted" families experience, cultural solutions have not yet emerged. For instance, expectations about the stepparent role remain ill-defined and contradictory; there is little guidance on the developing dynamics of reconstituted families; mechanisms for addressing the mixed feelings of children about a new marriage and a new household are largely absent. Without socially accredited responses, the dilemmas that people face after either separation or remarriage are often defined as essentially personal; the strains and difficulties are interpreted as individual failings, as due to personal inadequacy or incompetence rather than to structural tension. No doubt with time, fuller social guidelines will emerge to provide models of competent performance and make the management of these family transitions less problematic.

Conclusion

This chapter has been a scene-setting one. Its aim has been to indicate some of the ways in which structural and contextual influences pattern what is regarded as competent relationship performance. Because of this, it has necessarily been limited, in terms of both the relationships it has considered and the depth of analysis produced. It has also been ethnocentric in relying disproportionately on research about one part of the world— Britain. To some degree, these weaknesses will be compensated for in later chapters, which scrutinize specific issues more fully and from different angles. Nonetheless, the chapter has demonstrated the need to take a more structural perspective on personal relationships if they are to be understood and analyzed satisfactorily. The scope of the arguments that have been developed, though not their detail, applies to personal relationships in general. Despite the tendency in much social research to view many as voluntary, as choice driven, and as essentially dyadic, in the end, all relationships are embedded within structural contexts that govern their patterning, including, of course, the degree to which they appear to be voluntaristic and free floating.

The alternative here does not involve an overly deterministic view of personal relationships. While some relationships are more constrained by wider social and economic relations than others, in all there is an element of individual freedom. To use the spatial analogy introduced earlier, the boundaries of different personal relationships may be more or less tightly drawn, but within each there is still a "field" or "area" of discretion. But, equally, within each, influences outside the direct control of the individuals involved pattern the relationships that they construct. As has been indicated in the foregoing, the structuring of relationships occurs through a variety of mechanisms, some social, some economic, some cultural. The interplay between these different structural processes is itself emergent rather than determined and consequently liable to change over time rather than be static. But no matter what the structural features that combine to set the boundaries of relationships, individuals engage with them through their actions and words in the everyday production of their various personal relationships. For this reason, it is necessary that analysts pay sufficient heed to the contexts in which relationships are fashioned and the structural constraints that serve to frame competence in the conduct of relationships.

2

Engendered Relations: Interaction, Caring, Power, and Responsibility in Intimacy

Julia T. Wood

The misunderstandings between women and men on matters of love and intimacy are often funny, but they are no joke.

Tavris (1992, p. 149)

As open systems enmeshed in a larger society, human relationships inevitably reflect not just personal choices but also values, expectations, roles, and lines of interpretation that organize the communities within which individuals and relationships exist. Among ordering

AUTHOR'S NOTE: I am grateful to Michelle Violanti and Chris Inman, who assisted me in tracking down research germane to this chapter and whose responses to earlier drafts were most instructive to me. I also benefited from insightful comments from Steve Duck and Donna Vocate, who read early drafts of this chapter.

principles salient in Western culture is gender, which is primary to collective and individual life. In this chapter, I explore how relationships are affected by gender, a social-symbolic category that prescribes identities for women and men. After examining social and psychodynamic influences on the formation of masculine and feminine identity, I trace the way individuals' embodiments of cultural prescriptions reverberate throughout the ongoing processes that make up personal and social relationships.

Four interlinked topics compose my inquiry. First, I distinguish between sex and gender, concentrating on the latter as culturally and historically variable constructions of masculinity and femininity. Next, I consider present-day American views of gender, probing what these entail and how they are passed along to new members of the culture. I then demonstrate how gender is evident in four key processes in personal relationships. Woven throughout my discussion of these topics is critical reflection on some troublesome assumptions that invite both researchers and relational partners to (mis)interpret interactional patterns and processes.

Gender as a Basic Social Category: Construction of Masculinity and Femininity

While increasingly scholars distinguish between sex and gender, terminology is inconsistent. What I refer to as *gender,* others label *gender role, sex role,* or *psychological sex role.* My preference for the term *gender* is informed by West and Zimmerman's (1987) persuasive argument that gender is not a role, because we perform roles only at specific times and in situated moments, while we "do gender" all the time, every day, in every context. Like race and class, gender is so basic to identity that it must be understood as a primary aspect of selfhood, not a mere role.

Sex refers to biological, genetic, and physiological characteristics, including, for example, differential hemispheric specialization in the brains of women and men and hormones and genitalia distinctive of the sexes. While this seems a straightforward category, what fits within it can be ambiguous. For instance, Hines (1992) recently reported that the splenium, a bundle of nerves and fibers connecting the two hemispheres of the brain, which is thought to account for women's generally greater capacity to cross from one lobe to the other, changes in response to experience. Findings such as this suggest tentativeness in what we designate as sexual, that is, permanent, qualities.

Gender is a considerably more complex concept. Often gender is differentiated from sex by noting the former is learned while the latter is innate. Although perhaps technically accurate, this distinction obscures the profoundly systemic and cultural nature of gender, which consists of historically and culturally variable systems of belief that invest meager anatomical differences with major social significance. Woven throughout public and private life, prescriptions for masculinity and femininity attempt to organize individuals' understandings from a collective perspective (Goldner, Penn, Sheinberg, & Walker, 1990; Janeway, 1971; Lorber, 1989, p. 61; J. Scott, 1986) and thus to perpetuate that perspective and the illusion that its arbitrary prescriptions are natural. Through participation in social life, most individuals become engendered, that is, they come to understand what it *means* to be female and male within a particular culture. Simultaneously, they learn men's and women's positions within a culture, relation to each other, and "appropriate" ways of thinking, acting, and feeling. Fox-Genovese (1991, p. 120) notes that "when the [socialization] process is successful, gender appears to both women and men as the seamless wrapping of the self. To be an 'I' at all means to be gendered." Consequently, individuals who accept cultural constructions of gender act to sustain the contemporary conventions, while those who reject prevailing prescriptions "disturb the order" and sometimes provoke revisions in gender ideologies. Thus presumptive cultural views of gender are attenuated by their susceptibility to change in response to individuals' resistance and capacity to legitimize alternatives.

Gender is culturally variable. Consensually regarded as far more extensive than sex differences, gender reflects what a particular society at a given time defines as masculine and feminine. Considerable variety in cultural meanings for gender is evident in comparative data on the division of labor in sundry societies (Murdock, 1937). Further, some cultures consider an individual's gender changeable (Kessler & McKenna, 1978), while other cultures recognize and celebrate more than two genders (Garbarino, 1976; Olien, 1978). My personal experience living in a Tamang village in the hill country of Nepal revealed vast differences between gender there and in America. Both Tamang men and women nurture children, cook, tend crops, and carry 75 pounds of gear for foreign trekkers. In addition to differing among cultures, gender is temporally variable, as even cursory acquaintance with its evolution in the Western world reveals.

Gender is also relational; masculinity and femininity are defined largely in relation to one another. Yet Western constructions of gender have not always been as rigidly dichotomized as they are today. Prior to the industrial revolution, family life and work life were intertwined in ways that fostered agentic and communal qualities in both men and women (Bellah, Madsen, Sullivan, Swidler, & Tipton, 1985; Cancian, 1987, 1989; Cancian & Gordon, 1988; Degler, 1980; Douglas, 1977; Goode, 1963; Hanson, 1989; Shorter, 1975; Stone, 1979; Welter, 1966). Within this composite life, Ryan (1979, p. 24) noted, "Domestic affection, like sex and economics was not segregated into male and female spheres." More than any other single event, the industrial revolution gave birth to the ideology of separate spheres in which life was divided into distinct realms: men and work, and women and relationships. As men entered into "productive" labor outside of the home, women increasingly assumed nearly exclusive responsibility for the "reproductive" labor of caring for home and family. Concurrent with the public-private bifurcation of life were reconstructions of each gender. Femininity came to be defined by nutritiveness, deference, nurturance, and purity, while masculinity was equated with aggressiveness, independence, self-control, ambition, and lack of emotionality.

As women and men increasingly developed perspectives and skills required by their distinct domains, dichotomous images of the sexes arose: Each came to be viewed as by nature possessing the qualities, interests, and abilities required by the respective realms they inhabited (Collins, 1989; Harding, 1991; Ruddick, 1989). As Cancian (1989, p. 18) explains, "With the split between home and work and the polarization of gender roles, love became a feminine quality." Simultaneously, love and, more generally, relationships were sundered from public life and masculinity. Relationships became the essence of what women did and who they were. So rigid were the associations of men with work and women with home that, even when a man's salary was inadequate for a family, respectable wives did not work. In her autobiography, Emma Goldman (1931, p. 23) recounts stopping work when she married, because "it was considered disgraceful for a married woman to go to the shop" even though on her husband's meager earnings "life became insupportable."

This necessarily broad historical sketch reveals that gender is not accurately regarded as synonymous with sex, constant across time and cultures, or a trait of individuals. Rather, because gender is a constructed system that is deeply ingrained in social structures and practices, it is both as malleable and as intractable as other cultural phenomena. Recognizing the constructed character of gender highlights its status as a basic analytic category that organizes social life, individual identities, and interpersonal relationships.

Once gender deposed sex as a focus of research, empirical and theoretical advances resulted. One consequence was resolution of puzzling apparent contradictions in prior findings regarding sex differences in friendships. For example, D. G. Williams (1985) found that *both males and females* with high levels of feminine qualities also reported higher levels of intimacy in friendships while Jones and Dembo (1989) reported that only sex-typed boys, that is, those with masculine orientations, were significantly lower than girls in intimacy. Similarly, Fischer and Narus (1981) found gender to be an important attenuating factor with a feminine orientation closely related to intimacy in friendships. Other researchers (Kaye & Applegate, 1990; Risman, 1987, 1989) reported that men who are primary caretakers develop high degrees of nurturance more generally associated with femininity. In a particularly illuminating study of violence between intimates, Thompson (1991) showed that aggressiveness is more closely linked to gender than sex, and both women and men with masculine orientations are more aggressive than women and men with less masculine and/or more feminine orientations. Gender appears to be more powerful than sex in explaining interpersonal phenomena.

Gendered Socialization

At least within Western culture, gender is a central organizing principle for social life. Fox-Genovese (1991, p. 162) observes that "gender has always constituted a 'master' discourse, a primary interpretive map for participants in a culture." Like other matters important to social order, instruction in gender begins early and is reinforced throughout life by a multitude of cultural practices. The fact that the majority of men and women conform to broadly held cultural views of masculinity and femininity, respectively, testifies to the strength of socialization.

Lest we overestimate the power of socialization, however, an important caveat needs to be entered. Noting that most individuals conform to gender prescriptions implies neither relentlessly deterministic socialization nor a monolithic view of gender. The extent to which a given individual embodies cultural definitions for gender depends on myriad factors: parents, who may reproduce or depart from conventional codes; interactions with peers, teachers, siblings, and others, each of whom varies in the extent to which she or he subscribes to prevailing gender prescriptions; and ongoing interactions throughout life that affect the way individuals define themselves. In addition, as Mead (1934) reminds us, we must never overlook the "I" aspect of self—the innovative, mischievous, creative, rebellious spark in individuals that is never fully socialized. Elsewhere (Wood, in press) I probe ways individuals dispute social constructions of gender and, in so doing, sometimes alter those constructions. Keeping these qualifications in mind, we may proceed to ask how most individuals do fit within prevailing views of masculinity and femininity.

From birth—and some argue earlier—the sexes are engendered in conspicuously distinct ways that typically, though not invariably, construct feminine women and masculine men. Initial engendering with the primary caretaker is elaborated and sometimes modified through interactions with peers (Maltz & Borker, 1982), teachers (Hall & Sandler, 1982, 1984; Sadker & Sadker, 1984; Sandler & Hall, 1986; Wood & Lenze, 1991a), media (Tavris, 1992), as well as through general participation in a culture that prescribes masculinity and femininity and designates the prerogatives and restrictions inherent in each. A sizable body of research demonstrates that boys and girls are regarded and treated distinctly, encouraged to think differently and about disparate things, and reinforced for discrete goals, behaviors, values, attitudes, achievements, and feelings (e.g., Chodorow, 1978; Lorber, 1989; Miller, 1986; Safilios-Rothschild, 1979). This early socialization and its reinforcement throughout life encourage biological males to become masculine, currently defined as being strong, self-reliant, invulnerable, emotionally controlled, and competitive. Biological females are urged to be feminine, currently constructed as including sensitivity to others, cooperativeness, emotional expressiveness, deference, and being relationally oriented. It is important to remember, however, that, while socialization aims to feminize women and masculinize men, neither sex nor socialization invariably determines gender: Females can be masculine and males can be feminine.

Summaries of specific differences in socialization processes and outcomes for boys and girls have been provided by others and need not be reiterated here. It should prove more enlightening to sketch a conceptual framework that illuminates early developmental processes influential in forming gender identity. When these processes are "successful," females adhere to cultural constructions of femininity, and males conform to cultural codes of masculinity, although clearly some of us are more compliant students than others in acquiescing to cultural teachings.

The past decade has yielded extensive insights into how individuals learn gender and particularly into the crucial role of the family, which typically provides the first and arguably the most powerful instruction in gender. Thought to become consolidated between 1 and 3 years of age, a child's sense of gender is acquired concomitantly with the acquisition of selfhood, or personal identity. Pivotal in developing gender identity is a child's relationship with the primary caretaker, usually the mother. A girl develops in relation to someone like her, that is, a female, while a boy evolves in relation to someone not like him. Theorists, particularly clinically trained ones, argue that a daughter's experience of likeness with mother leads her to define her self and her gender *within relationship,* while the gender difference between mother and son propels him to define his self and his gender by *differentiating from relationship* (Chodorow, 1978, 1989; Miller, 1986). In Goldner et al.'s (1990, p. 348) words, "The boy constructs his sense of himself out of a negative: 'I am not like my Mother; I am not female.' "

The different genesis of identity for most boys and girls profoundly affects the ways in which they view themselves and interact with others. Formed within relationship to another, feminine identity typically manifests permeable ego boundaries, which blur lines between self and other so that a feminine individual tends to know herself within and through connections with others. In turn, this fosters qualities such as empathy, sensitivity to nuanced relational dynamics, loyalty, responsiveness to others' needs, and a tendency to experience others' feelings as her (or his) own. By contrast, masculine identity, erected through separation from the primary caretaker, rests on the titular issue of autonomy. Intense closeness can be uncomfortable because it potentially jeopardizes autonomy and recalls what was sacrificed when the boy had to give up closeness with his mother to define his own identity and gender (Chodorow, 1978; L. Rubin, 1985).

Whether identity initially arises through connection or separation predisposes individuals to feel safe with distinct relational orientations and interactional patterns. Masculine individuals typically accord priority to preserving independence, even within intimacy, while feminine persons tend to prioritize connection (Chodorow, 1978, 1989; Gilligan, 1982; Riessman, 1990; Schaef, 1985). When these asynchronous orientations converge—or clash— the stage is set for contradictory expectations, conflicting interaction patterns, and a wealth of resulting misunderstandings. Such discordance is, in fact, virtually encoded into heterosexual relationships if partners skillfully perform what the culture deems "appropriate" gender.

Enacting Gender in Personal Relationships

With this general understanding of how socialization attempts to engender individuals, we may proceed to consider how gender resonates throughout adult relationships. Specifically, I wish to trace gender's impact on four key processes in personal relationships: interaction patterns; the dialectic of autonomy and connectedness and, relatedly, responsibility for relationships; ways of expressing care; and uses and abuses of power. Two qualifications presage my analysis. First, because most research is restricted to heterosexual relationships, that is the focus of my analysis. Second, understanding the influence of gender is complicated by the tendency of researchers, especially those prior to the 1990s, to define participants according to sex differences, that is, biological qualities. Because sex and gender are closely linked, however, most males in Western culture adopt masculine gender and most females adopt feminine gender. Thus it seems reasonable to infer that what are reported as sex differences roughly reflect gender differences. In what follows I make the inference that empirical sex differences translate generally to gender differences.

Engendered Interactional Preferences/Patterns

Motivated to preserve independence, masculine individuals tend to stress competition, maintaining some distance from others, operating by rules, interacting in groups, and *doing* things as the primary way to engage in relationships (Bakan, 1966; Balswick & Peek, 1976; R. R. Bell, 1981; Reisman, 1981; L. Rubin, 1985; Swain, 1989; L. Weiss & Lowenthal, 1975; Wright, 1982). Femininity, reflecting its genesis in relationships, inclines individuals toward cooperation, making and sustaining connections with others, being responsive to particularities of different relationships, participating in close, dyadic friendships, and—centrally—relying on talking as the primary way to *be* with others (Chodorow, 1978; Gilligan, 1982; Goldner et al., 1990; Miller, 1986; Riessman, 1990). Growing out of these interpersonal orientations are engendered communication pat-

terns. Consistent with masculine priorities, masculine individuals generally use communication to compete for the talk stage,
to gain and hold attention and status, and to assert themselves
(Maltz & Borker, 1982; Swain, 1989). The communicative patterns associated with femininity involve using talk to collaborate
and cooperate with others, to encourage others' participation,
and to express and respond to feelings as a way of building
relationships with others (Maltz & Borker, 1982; Wood & Lenze,
1991a, 1991b).

Not a surprise, these differences lay foundations for misunderstandings and conflicts in interactional patterns. Expecting conversation to provide support, understanding, and a connection
with another, feminine individuals typically attune closely to the
relationship level of messages. Given this, they tend to be frustrated by what masculine people are most likely to offer in a
genuine effort to help: advice on solving problems, judgment,
and information, all of which are typical of what Tannen (1990)
calls male "report talk." Resolving a problem ends conversation,
and information and judgment fail to address relationship issues
nestled in all communication. A contrasting scenario informs
masculine orientations toward interaction. Preferring not to
make themselves vulnerable by disclosing fears and weaknesses
and trained to be instrumental, masculine individuals tend to
focus on the report, or command, level of communication. When
they voice problems, typically they want practical help—problem solving, information, and advice. Thus the understanding
and support of "rapport talk," in which feminine persons tend
to specialize, may be unsatisfying to masculine partners because
"processing feelings" fails to resolve problems.

Differences in fundamental interactional orientations promote
not only frustration but misconstruals of motives, involvement, and
efforts. Recognizing the disparity in what tends to be confirming
to masculine and feminine persons, Schaef (1985, p. 150) noted
that "women are often hurt in relationships with men because
they totally expose their beings and do not receive respect and
exposure in return . . . knowing and being known are of the
utmost importance." Thus feminine individuals may perceive
advice and analysis in response to stated problems as patronizing

displays of superiority and insensitivity to feelings involved in the matter under discussion. In parallel fashion, typically feminine displays of emotional support and empathy often strike masculine partners as intrusive and oblique to the topic at hand.

Another aspect of gendered interactional orientations is captured in the process versus product distinction. A number of years ago Schaef (1985) observed that an instrumental focus typical of masculinity begets a view of intimacy itself as a goal that is achieved and then remains settled. This may explain research findings as well as abundant anecdotal evidence that the attentiveness men often demonstrate during courtship tends to wane precipitously following commitment. Femininity, in contrast, inclines individuals toward processual orientations in which relationships are conceived as "a series of passages, or a series of interlocking cycles" (Schaef, 1985, p. 123). From this perspective, a relationship is not a "done deal" once commitment is clinched, a point Duck made (1990b) in discussing relationships as "unfinished business." Similarly, the purpose of a conversation is not so much to achieve some concrete result as it is to sustain a relationship through daily interactions that connect the small and large comings and goings of two lives (Wood, 1993).

Rapport talk in a processual mode and report talk in a results-oriented vein represent different languages and distinct understandings of what interaction is about. Each language seems mystifying to nonnative speakers. Processual, feeling-focused talk may seem pointless to masculine people, while structured, outcome-bent conversation may inhibit the nuances and spontaneity that *are* the point of feminine communication. These basic differences undergird misunderstandings between partners and are implicated in other relational processes to be discussed next.

Engendered Needs:
Autonomy, Connection, and Responsibility

The autonomy-connectedness dialectic. Both academic researchers (Baxter, 1990; Thorbecke & Grotevant, 1982; Wood, Dendy, Dordek, Germany, & Varallo, in press) and clinicians (Bergner &

Bergner, 1990; Goldner et al., 1990; Napier, 1977; Scarf, 1987; Thompson & Walker, 1989) identify autonomy and connectedness as basic and positive human needs, which interact dialectically. Because the two appear contradictory, satisfying both can be difficult, especially in personal relationships, which require coordinating frequently different senses of a "proper balance."

While all humans seem to seek both autonomy and connectedness, the relative amount of each that is preferred appears to differ rather consistently between genders. Defined largely by independence and emotional control, masculine identity generally prefers a higher degree of autonomy than connectedness. In contrast is feminine identity, whose emphasis on relationships typically generates a desire for greater connectedness than autonomy. While the genders agree in valuing both autonomy and connection, they tend not to agree on how much of each is ideal. Gender-differentiated emphases accorded to connection and autonomy have been repeatedly confirmed by research (Gilligan, 1982; Hatfield & Rapson, 1987; Kaplan, 1978; Napier, 1977; Sherrod, 1989; Thompson & Walker, 1989; Wood, 1986). Because, of course, there is no absolutely "right" balance of autonomy and connection, neither gender's typical preference for amounts of each is more correct or constructive. For this reason, prescriptive models emphasizing disclosures, open communication, and so forth, while not uncommon (see Reis & Shaver, 1988), seem imprudent.

More constructive perhaps is to realize certain implications of the incongruity between the proportionate amounts of autonomy and connection generally preferred by masculine and feminine individuals. Understanding this sheds light on two related tensions recurrently found in heterosexual couples. Bernard's (1972) classic discussion of "his" and "her" marriage has repeatedly resurfaced in findings that women invest more in and report caring more about close relationships than do men (Hatfield, Traupmann, Sprecher, Utne, & Hay, 1984; Thompson & Walker, 1989; D. G. Williams, 1985, 1988), and women are often dissatisfied with the amount of closeness their partners want and allow, while men frequently feel smothered by the amount of intimacy their partners seek (Christensen & Heavey, 1990; Napier,

1977; Peplau & Gordon, 1985; L. Rubin, 1985; Thompson & Walker, 1989).

Growing out of disjunctive preferences for autonomy and connection is a conundrum recurrently documented in marriages. Variously labeled "intrusion-rejection" (Napier, 1977), "demand-withdraw" (Christensen & Heavey, 1990), and "pursuer- distancer" (James, 1989), the pattern arises when a feminine partner demands emotional closeness to be achieved through mutual self-disclosure and intimate talk, and a masculine partner withdraws from what he (or she) perceives as stifling intimacy. Feminine attempts to enhance connections through talk contend with masculine quests to retain personal independence. Seeking closeness, the feminine partner promotes intimate talk, which precipitates withdrawal by the masculine partner, who feels deprived of the autonomy he (or she) needs to be comfortable. As the masculine partner retreats to create distance, the feminine partner feels anxious that closeness is in jeopardy and she (or he) is being rejected. Discordant preferences for degrees of autonomy and connection often escalate into what Hatfield and Rapson (1987, p. 21) describe as "a destructive tug-of-war" in which each partner intensifies efforts to achieve what he or she needs, which paradoxically fuels counterefforts by the other. The more a feminine partner tries to enhance closeness with her partner, the harder the masculine partner has to work to create the distance needed to feel safe; the more the masculine partner moves toward autonomy, the harder the feminine partner pursues connection. Disparate desires for autonomy and connection invite misunderstandings of partners' motives. For instance, a feminine partner may attribute quests for distance to lack of commitment; a masculine partner may regard efforts at closeness as disrespect of independence.

Women as relationship specialists. Gender-differentiated weightings of autonomy and control are reflected in women's well-documented role as "relationship specialists." Arising within relationships, femininity tends to be involved with and attentive to interpersonal dynamics. Masculine identity, carved through separation, is generally less aware of and skilled in interpersonal processes, which may be obscure and unfathomable to someone not socialized to decode nuances of interaction. Wamboldt and Reiss (1989, p. 321) report: "Women, as relationship specialists, appear more finely attuned to the subtleties of communication within intimate relationships." Because most women internalize feminine gender, they are generally more sensitive to interpersonal dynamics and thus see themselves and are seen by others as the experts at keeping relationships healthy (Cancian & Gordon, 1988; Tavris, 1992). Summarizing extensive research, Thompson and Walker (1989, p. 849) concluded that wives "have more responsibility than their husbands for monitoring the relationship, confronting disagreeable issues, setting the tone of conversation, and moving toward resolution when conflict is high."

The association of femininity with taking care of relationships, which is widely endorsed by both genders, potentially cultivates problems. First, it unfairly burdens one partner with primary responsibility for relational maintenance, which can lead to stress, perceptions of inequities in commitment, and resentment (Cancian, 1989; Hochschild, 1989; Miller, 1986; Tavris, 1992; Thompson & Walker, 1989). Compounding this burden is the difficulty of meeting the responsibility to manage the relationship when that clearly requires at least passive involvement from a partner who is less willing and/or less able to attend to the relationship. Thus disparity between feminine and masculine attentiveness invites another "tug-of-war" in which one partner feels frustrated that "he won't talk to me or about us" while the other wishes "she would quit analyzing the relationship to death!" The feminine partner is likely to be perceived as nagging, about which Tavris (1992, p. 265) wryly notes: "It is her *job* to know how everyone is feeling in order to head off problems at the pass. Naturally she's motivated to talk; she needs to know if anything in the relationship needs fixing, because she will be blamed if she doesn't fix it." The masculine partner is likely to be perceived as disinterested and/or uncommitted. Such (mis)perceptions lay fertile ground for pain, dissatisfaction, and decline in the quality of relationships.

In summary, feminine socialization predisposes individuals toward desiring a greater degree of closeness than autonomy and, relatedly, toward feeling responsible for maintaining relationships. Masculine socialization, on the other hand, promotes precisely opposite tendencies in which more autonomy than closeness is preferred and relational processes are less salient. Scholarly documentation of the feminine role of relationship specialist and discordant, gender-linked views of the dialectic of distance and closeness, then, reflect the stunning consistency with which the majority of males and females are persuaded to enact their "appropriate genders" and, with that, to embrace quite different understandings of the way to engage in relationships.

Engendered Modes of Expressing Care

Among therapists and researchers, there is widespread agreement on three matters pertinent to caring in close relationships. First, almost universally, expressions of care (affection, love) are recognized as important to satisfaction. There is also broad consensus on what embodies expressions of care (Christensen & Heavey, 1990; Hatfield & Rapson, 1987; James, 1989; Napier, 1977; Peplau & Gordon, 1985; Thompson & Walker, 1989). Finally, women are regarded widely as more skilled in communicating caring (Goldner et al., 1990; Rusbult, 1987; Tavris, 1992; Tognoli, 1980; Winstead, 1986), and some argue that women in general actually *are* more caring, or intimate, than men (Bernard, 1972; Chodorow, 1978; Gilligan, 1982; Lewis, 1978; Miller, 1986; Sherrod, 1989; Traupmann & Hatfield, 1981).

Close inspection of evidence for these premises suggests they merit unequal confidence. The first claim is warranted by ample clinical and empirical data: Expressing care is integral to intimacy. The second and third claims, however, rest on more precarious footing. Research on intimacy is characterized by a persistent conflation of expressing care and a *particular way* of expressing care. There is no convincing evidence that women exceed men in the degree to which they care or love, nor is there persuasive support for the more moderate claim that women exceed men in the extent to which they express care. Existing data demonstrate only that there are gender-linked distinctions in how care is expressed. This hardly grounds inferences either that women care more or that women express caring more than men.

The feminization of love: Take two. Masculine and feminine socialization leads to generalizably different ways of communicating closeness (Jones & Dembo, 1989; Swain, 1989; Thompson & Walker, 1989). Within our society, however, only one of these ways—the feminine style—is granted legitimacy in broad understandings of what intimacy is. Referring to this as the "feminization of love," Cancian (1987, 1989) argues it yields restrictive conceptions of caring, which, in turn, encourage misperceptions by both researchers and intimate partners.

As earlier sections of this chapter demonstrated, socialization processes are deeply engendered. Training for femininity cultivates a markedly processual and verbal orientation in which relationships are understood to be ongoing and sustained primarily through communication and personal revelations. Individuals inculcated into femininity tend to be skilled at and interested in talking about relational issues, openly stating feelings, disclosing personal information, and using conversation to sustain a sense of connection. In contrast is masculine socialization, which teaches that relationships consist of things done for and with a partner, and commitment does not require—and may be diminished by—explicit talk. Thus masculinity highlights shared activities, instrumental action, and concrete forms of assistance as ways of caring. From a masculine perspective, talking about feelings and self-disclosing are not preeminent ways to show care and may be unsatisfying, uncomfortable, and not particularly contributory to feelings of closeness (Bergner & Bergner, 1990; Bronstein, 1988; Riessman, 1990; Swain, 1989).

While researchers recognize distinctions between masculine and feminine styles of intimacy, they do not generally confer equal validity on each. Instead, these two modes of expressing affection have been conceived hierarchically and accorded differential value. The feminine style is routinely used as the primary or sole measure of *real* intimacy. For instance, White, Speisman, Jackson, Bartis, and Costos's (1986) study of "intimacy maturity" unambiguously privileged expressing feelings so that the "most mature intimacy" was equated with the most verbal and emotional forms of expression. Behaviors—favors done, activities shared—did not count as indicators of closeness. Similarly, L. Weiss and M. Lowenthal (1975) viewed greater disclosures of personal information by females as evidence that they are more emotionally mature and interpersonally competent than males. Reis and Shaver's (1988) model defines intimacy as a process sustained by progressive expressions of and responses to personally revealing feelings or information. Such feminized views of caring not only devalue the ways masculine people show care but also diminish the likelihood they will get the kind of caring they value. Research indicates masculine individuals particularly appreciate instrumental demonstrations from others (Cancian, 1986; Riessman, 1990; Swain, 1989; Wills, Weiss, & Patterson, 1974). Yet a feminine model of intimacy obscures understanding, and, therefore, providing a kind of care masculine people regard as gratifying.

The feminine bias carries over into (mis)interpretations of responses to breakups, where the criteria used to assess depression reflect feminine, but not masculine, expressions of distress: crying, talking about unhappiness, eating disorders, expressing misery, and feeling sad (Riessman, 1990, pp. 156-157). Because socialization discourages men from openly expressing emotion and vulnerability, those who adhere to the code of masculinity are frequently (mis)judged to be less affected and to feel less hurt when intimacy ends (Peplau & Gordon, 1985; Stapley & Haveland, 1989). Mental health professionals, argues Riessman (1990, p. 159), have "set up women's modes of expressing distress as the standard against which men are evaluated—and found wanting."

Studies of friendship are similarly flawed by conflating feminine modes of expressing closeness with closeness itself. Friendships between men have been widely devalued as not intimate, because typically they do not emphasize explicit expressions of affection and personal disclosure (Balswick & Peek, 1976; R. R. Bell, 1981; Buhrke & Fuqua, 1987; Caldwell & Peplau, 1982). Mazur and Olver (1987, p. 553) assert that "men, as a group. . . feel threatened by intimacy," a conclusion based on the finding that male participants scored lower on expressiveness than did female participants. Aukett, Ritchie, and Mill (1988) reported that friendships between women are more affectionate, loving, and accepting than those between men, an inference derived from equating emotional expressiveness with feelings of closeness. Meanwhile, D. G. Williams (1988, p. 588) quite bluntly claims men's friendships lack "mutual self-disclosure, shared feelings, and *other demonstrations of closeness* which are thought to characterize women's friendships" (italics added). In their widely cited study of friendship, Caldwell and Peplau (1982, p. 725) began with a priori definitions of "intimate friend" as a person with "whom one can confide about feelings and personal problems" and a more casual friend as a person with "whom one enjoys doing things and talking about important interests, but not a person with whom one discusses very personal thoughts." Relatedly, feminine views of closeness lead to recurrent criticisms of men's "failures" and "deficiencies" in intimacy (Balswick & Peek, 1976; R. R. Bell, 1981; Tognoli, 1980). Consistently men are faulted for not valuing emotional closeness, yet evidence does not indicate that women have any monopoly on closeness as a goal for intimacy. When feminized forms of intimacy are the only ones counted, is it any surprise that men are found to be less intimate than women?

Feminized conceptions of caring similarly distort analyses of sexuality. The masculine orientation toward doing and the feminine orientation toward talking as distinct routes to emotional closeness lead to quite different understandings of what sexual activities mean. Riessman (1990, p. 46) explains: "Instead of viewing sex as women tend to—as a way to express intimacy already established by talking and sharing—men expected to become intimate with their wives through sex," that is, through doing an activity together. Psychologists such as Bergner and Bergner (1990, p. 464) extend this by noting an "empirically common pattern of marital dysfunction . . . comprises male and female partners attaching different central significances to the act of sexual intercourse." Yet, once again, a feminized orientation toward sex is elevated so that sex as a way *to become intimate* is not accorded legitimacy (Schaef, 1985; B. E. Schneider & Gould, 1987). Sex, like other intimate interactions, has been feminized in ways that exclude or devalue masculine meanings for sexual activity.

Men are indicted for not living up to a standard that from the start ignored masculine modes of experiencing and expressing closeness. Riessman (1990) reported that both women and men seek emotional closeness in marriage; what differs is what each understands closeness to be and therefore what each counts and offers as demonstrations of closeness. For women, emotional closeness is identified with "communicating deeply and closely . . . warmth and sharing. . . . Talk with a spouse is how women think emotional intimacy ought to be realized" (p. 24). For men, however, "talk is not the centerpiece. Rather, men . . . want a variety of physical and other concrete demonstrations of intimacy . . . physical, not verbal, manifestations of emotional closeness" (pp. 37-38). Yet, because prevailing conceptions discount the latter ways of caring, men continue to be indicted for not caring and/or not showing that they care. Parallel criticism is not levied at women for not according priority to instrumental assistance, shared activities, copresence without words, and other masculinized forms of caring.

Pervading research on closeness are the insufficiently supported assumptions that (a) verbal expressiveness is more indicative and facilitative of intimacy than instrumental or physical expressiveness and (b) men are therefore "deficient"—what Balswick and Peek (1976) labeled the "tragedy [sic] of the inexpressive male" (p. 55). And, indeed, masculinized individuals (thus most men) are less skilled at specifically feminine ways of expressing care. Yet only feminine ways are recognized as valid: "Men's behavior is measured with a feminine rule" criticizes Cancian (1987, p. 74), so that "social scientists rarely recognize men's practical help as a form of love" (p. 76). A concurring opinion comes from Tavris (1992, p. 253), who points out that the feminization of love means "men rarely get credit for the kinds of loving actions that are more typical of them."

Caring is misconstrued by its persistent association with only one mode of expression, and this misrepresentation has substantial pragmatic and scholarly ramifications. An abridged conception of intimacy diminishes our ability to see, much less appreciate, a range of ways that individuals create and express closeness. For researchers, this invites continuing inattention to instrumental and other masculinized ways of creating intimacy. By extension, theories based on truncated views of caring are impoverished by their failure to reflect all of the people whom they claim to represent and to whom they are applied. Fully a decade ago Gilligan (1982) noted that conventional theories of moral development are systematically biased, because women were excluded from the data base on which the theories were erected. She argued that it is inappropriate and misleading to apply theories to those not represented in their formulation. The same reasoning suggests that excluding masculinized ways of demonstrating intimacy falsely restricts understandings of what caring is and how it may be felt, created, and communicated.

The intent of this discussion is not, of course, to devalue verbal expressiveness and self-disclosure as means of expressing intimacy: Obviously these can enhance closeness for those who value and are comfortable engaging in them. Yet, for individuals who find other modes more meaningful and/or comfortable, alternative measures are needed. A comprehensive, accurate conception of intimacy and its expression would include and equally value both verbal, disclosive interaction and "closeness in the doing" (Swain, 1989, p. 77). Just as traditional moral theories have been justly critiqued for excluding patterns of moral development empirically more associated with women than men and conventional models of narration have been reproached for ignoring styles of storytelling more typical of women than men (Hall & Langellier, 1988), so are prevalent theories of intimacy flawed by their exclusion of masculine styles of creating and expressing closeness. This suggests that an important challenge for researchers is to develop inclusive theories of intimacy that are able to identify and respect differences without invoking hierarchical judgments.

Engendered Power, Influence, and Responsibility

Gender distinctions appear not only in styles of closeness but also in orientations toward power, which resound in interaction between intimate partners. Masculinity's emphasis on competitiveness, control, gaining and protecting status, taking action, and repressing feelings predisposes direct and active efforts at influence. In striking contrast is feminine socialization, which prioritizes cooperativeness, affiliation, responding to others' needs, and feeling and talking with intimates and inclines feminine individuals toward indirect, bilateral (or deferential), and verbal strategies of power and control.

Gendered power. Research confirms the engendered orientations toward power including the well-established finding that women are perceived and expected to be less powerful than men (Christensen & Heavey, 1990; Janeway, 1971; Lakoff, 1990; Miller, 1986; Peplau & Gordon, 1985; B. E. Schneider & Gould, 1987). Profoundly entrenched social practices and structures define femininity as decidedly subordinate to masculinity. Writing as recently as 1990, Riessman pointed out: "Traditional marriage is a gendered institution—not just because women and men participate in it, but because the gender-based division of labor in it, in turn, creates inequality between women and men" (p. 15), and, "although there has been some change . . . the institutionalized roles of husband and wife continue to provide a general blueprint for marriage, situating men's work primarily in the public sphere and women's in the private sphere" (p. 51). Men's placement in the public realm is also placement in the arena esteemed by Western culture, which requires but demeans work in the private context of home and family. In short, masculinity is in substantial measure defined by powerfulness in the activities and contexts that have currency; femininity is not. This structured difference in roles and identities undergirds and illuminates the gendered basis of many power dynamics within close relationships.

Power is often indicated by whether the husband's or the wife's preferences prevail. Repeatedly, studies find husbands' preferences count more than those of wives on matters from how often to engage in sex (B. E. Schneider & Gould, 1987; Szinovatz, 1984; Thompson & Walker, 1989) to how to divide up household chores and child-care responsibilities (Hiller & Philliber, 1986; Hochschild, 1989; Okin, 1989; Paul & White, 1990). Indicative of the relationship between interpersonal power and public status is the finding that only when spouses perceive the wife as a coprovider who is successful in work do they even approach relative equality in contributions to homemaking and child care (Ferree, 1988; Thompson & Walker, 1989). As long as spouses perceive the husband as the primary wage earner (regardless of whether this perception is empirically grounded), his preferences hold sway, and the female partner does the overwhelming bulk of child care and homemaking.

Not only is the overall power balance influenced by gender, but also attempts at influence are parsed consistently along gendered lines. As we would expect, research reveals that masculinity's emphasis on independence and deemphasis on talk predispose masculine individuals toward unilateral power and avoidance strategies. Importantly, gender, not sex is the stronger predictor: The association is between people who hold traditional views of masculinity and reliance on unilateral strategies both to address and to avoid conflict (Snell, Hawkins, & Belk, 1988). Equally significant is the finding that women who hold traditional views of masculinity and men's roles report using indirect strategies to confront problems with male partners and compliance and acquiescence strategies to avoid or defuse conflict. These findings reveal that both women and men rely on techniques that reflect belief in the "masculine prerogative to be the leader and initiator" (Snell et al., 1988, p. 47). Other research (Belk & Snell, 1988; Howard, Blumstein, & Schwartz, 1986; Vuchinich, 1987) further confirms the relationship between power strategies and gender by reporting women disproportionately compromise, submit, and defer while men tend to bully, assert, and issue fiats. Consistent with these accounts is B. White's (1989, p. 103) report that men tend to assume coercive stances and women are inclined to adopt affiliative ones in dealing with conflict, because "in resolving conflict men could be expected to proceed by seeking distance while women have as a first priority maintaining communication in relationships," thus reiterating Miller's (1986) observation that men use power to gain control whereas women rely on pleasing others as a route to the same end.

Finally, consider the impressive line of research on responses to dissatisfaction in close relationships. From a series of studies,

Rusbult (1987) concludes that the responses consistently most characteristic of women are voice (initiating talk about problems) and loyalty (standing by during times of trouble without actively intervening), both of which enact the feminine injunction to sustain connections. The responses more typical of men are exit (leaving physically or psychologically) and neglect (denying or minimizing problems), both of which reflect masculine ideals of protecting self, not being too connected to another, and exercising control especially by refusal to talk with others. Viewing three of these responses in ways consistent with Rusbult's definitions, Hirschman (1970) earlier argued that the options are not discrete but are interactive in significant ways. The possibility of exit attenuates motivation to employ voice to improve a relationship. Ironically, and for quite different reasons, when exit is not perceived as a viable option, the likelihood of using voice also ebbs because the possibility of exit enhances the persuasiveness of voice. Even loyalty loses meaning when there is no alternative to staying put. In effect, Hirschman argues, whenever exit is not perceived as a real option, voice becomes ineffectual. Thus a primary means to redress inequity and/or dissatisfaction within a troubled relationship erodes. Loyalty remains the only possible option, yet, in the absence of alternatives, it tends to embitter the person exercising it and to be depreciated by the one receiving it.

Another gendered aspect of power dynamics is the pursuer/distancer pattern discussed earlier in which women consistently occupy the pursuer role and men consistently inhabit the distancer role. While cursory consideration of this pattern might suggest women's role is dominant, further reflection yields a different interpretation. Because women almost universally assume principal responsibility for relational maintenance and define relationships as central to their lives, and especially because women typically hold inequitable positions in close relationships, they are likely to see problems and to seek changes. Men, who generally notice and attend less to relationship processes and who benefit from the inequities institutionalized in heterosexual relationships, have much to gain by maintaining the status quo and resisting changes. Women's and men's respective assumption of pursuer and distancer roles, then, may reflect their inequitable positions in the power structure of both society and relationships. As Thompson and Walker (1989, p. 849) noted, "Many of the qualities that women display in marital conversation and conflict are traceable to their subordinate position." Extending this, Stark (1991) reported that men adhere more to sex stereotypes than do women, which he reasoned reflects men's greater fears of what they would lose if traditional masculine prerogatives diminished. My review of gender's relation to power foreshadows attention to violence and abuse in intimacy.

No exit: Engendered violence. Physical violence, or abuse, is strongly linked to gender. Perhaps the most useful conceptualization of abusive relationships comes from Goldner et al. (1990, p. 344), who drew on both original clinical work and existing research to argue that "relationships in which women are abused are not unique but, rather, exemplify in extremis the stereotypical gender arrangements that structure intimacy between men and women generally." Elaborating gender's association with violence, the authors reported that "gendered premises about masculinity are rigidly adhered to in the families of men . . . who are violent toward women" (p. 351) while women's staying in abusive relationships is "as an affirmation of the feminine ideal: to hold connections together, to heal and care for another, no matter what the personal cost" (p. 357). In other words, staying fulfills the prime directives of femininity: to care for others and to sustain relationships.

Further evidence of the connection between gender and physical abuse comes from Thompson's (1991) study of violence in dating relationships. Based on reports from 336 undergraduates, Thompson reported that the expected sex differences were not present: Men were not more physically aggressive than women. The data, however, resoundingly supported a relationship between gender and violence, indicating that more masculine and less feminine men *and women* were more likely to be violent toward intimates than less masculine and more feminine women *and men*. From this study, Thompson concluded that physical aggression is consonant with traditional views of masculinity, making gender "quite important to understanding both men's and women's involvement in dating violence" (p. 274). Other research underlines the link between physical abuse and masculinity (Dobash & Dobash, 1979; Gordon, 1988; Ptacek, 1988; Thompson & Walker, 1989).

Existing academic and clinical evidence consistently demonstrates the gendered nature of many facets of power and its abuse in intimacy. While sex is no longer widely regarded as a particularly strong predictor of power dynamics, increasingly gender is recognized as centrally implicated in the entire power structure of close relationships. Gendered beliefs and identities undergird the most compelling and robust explanations of how power is allocated and deployed, what strategies individuals adopt in attempts to exert power, the roles intimates assume in lobbying for and resisting changes, responses to others' power strategies, and the attitudes and identities that sustain abusive cycles. A focus on gender, rather than sex, has decisively advanced understanding of patterns of power use and abuse in intimacy, and this is a particularly important focus for continuing research that might illuminate ways of preventing or—that failing—intervening in relationships where violence exists.

Chapter Summary and Implications

A gendered society fosters gendered individuals, who, in turn, create gendered relationships. This chapter discloses gender's reflection in styles of interacting, ways of expressing affection, use and abuse of power, and feelings of responsibility for relationships. Emerging from this review are three broad conclusions and related recommendations for future thinking, teaching, scholarship, and clinical practice.

Gender as a Primary Focus of Study

Research consistently demonstrates that gender is a more useful focus than sex for studying relationship processes. Sex is a biological, personal quality while gender is a basic social-symbolic category prescribing identities of and relations between women and men. Yet, recognizing gender's centrality to relationship dynamics only foreshadows the need to rethink and refine how we conceive gender and, by extension, how we study and incorporate it in teaching and therapy. Most of the work reviewed here demonstrates tendencies in some masculine and some feminine individuals to think and act in various ways at specific times in their lives and the life of the society. What it does not and cannot tell us is how gendered identities evolve over time and what ramifications flow from changes in them.

Fuller understanding of the vital nexus among gender, individual identity, human relationships, and cultural life is vital. To move toward this, we need far more dynamic conceptualizations of gender. It is not, as much existing research tacitly assumes, a standard component inserted into essentially passive individuals at an early point in their lives that then remains relatively stable over time and experience. It will probably be more generative to conceive gender as dynamic and to explore how social meanings and individual embodiments of it vary situationally and temporally. The micro-structural approach advocated by Risman and Schwartz (1989) is promising in defining gender as a changing aspect of culture and identity. Viewing gender as a sociological rather than a psychological phenomenon, they argue the need to take "into account the impact of adult life experiences on men's and women's self conceptions and actions" because men and women "are continuously re-created." They further suggest that gender differences in intimacy are continually constructed in and through interactions between partners.

Following Duck (1990b) and Duck and Pond (1989), a more fluid conception of gender would direct attention toward the *process* of relationships, that is, how relationships are continuously created in interaction. We need to move beyond treating gender as a dependent or independent variable and probe the way it interacts with patterns in close relationships in systemically influential ways. Among the questions that spring from such a processual approach are these: How do the embodiments of gender initially embraced by individuals change over time and interaction? How do changes in gendered identities of partners influence interactional patterns as well as relational satisfaction? How do partners' enactments of gender within personal relationships reflect and shape their enactments of it in social and professional relationships? Do partners' embodiments of gender evoke genderized behaviors in each other, and how do these change? Tracking questions such as these would enrich understandings of how gender arises and is continually reconfigured in ongoing relational processes.

Inclusive Views of Closeness

A second issue emergent from my review is the need to reflect seriously on how we conceive closeness—interactional processes, goals, behaviors, and attitudes. At least in some areas, notably views of what constitutes expressions of care, intimacy seems to be defined by phenomena more characteristic of and valued by feminine individuals than masculine ones. Pervading scholarship and clinical reports are assumptions, generally unstated and perhaps widely unrecognized, that there is a single "right" or "best" way to be close. Typically what is advanced as the "right" way to be intimate reflects feminine orientations toward relationships and concurrently excludes or devalues masculine ways of relating. This ubiquitous bias needs to be rectified.

Developing more inclusive models of intimate processes requires rethinking the questions we ask, the methods by which we pursue them, and the lenses through which we interpret findings. For instance, measuring the amount and intimacy of talk to gauge emotional closeness, which has been repeatedly done, entails an a priori feminized view of closeness as verbal. A more inclusive view of intimacy would incorporate both characteristically masculine and feminine modes of expression and measure not only talk but also shared activities and practical assistance. Doing and talking would be represented as parallel, equally legitimate ways of achieving and expressing closeness.

Yet, inclusive views of closeness require more than acknowledging masculine styles. Because my focus in this chapter is gender, I have confined my discussion to masculine and feminine styles. Truly comprehensive views of personal human relationships between humans, however, demand attention to race, class, sexual preference, and perhaps other factors that influence the ways humans express and experience closeness. Reports by Ting-Toomey (1991) and VanYperen and Buunk (1991), for instance, indicate that many findings about intimacy do not generalize to non-Western cultures. Thus an important challenge for future study of personal relationships is expanded views of how diverse people in varied situations form, sustain, and communicate closeness.

Resisting Being "Goaded by Hierarchy"

The foregoing two suggestions foreshadow a third pertinent to stances assumed and goals sought in teaching and counseling. Currently, pedagogical and therapeutic practice emphasize differences between genders, attach unequal value to masculine and feminine styles, and strive to teach students or clients to enact the "better" mode. Limitations inherent in this viewpoint need to be recognized and evaluated critically. Identifying differences between genders may expand understanding of perspectives distinct from one's own. Yet that alone does not necessarily provoke change or enhance partners' coordination and satisfaction. Similarly, designating "better" forms of intimacy can be counterproductive because it depreciates how some individuals establish and enact closeness and diminishes appreciation of the range of attitudes, behaviors, and orientations constitutive of intimacy. Perhaps a more constructive approach would aim to increase individuals' fluency in the many languages of caring and commitment. Continuing the linguistic metaphor, we might try to teach students and clients how to translate partners' languages (e.g., to understand that washing a car may translate as a demonstration of love; Wills et al., 1974). A compelling longer term goal is to increase individuals' actual fluency in languages other than their native one so that they develop skills in multiple ways of feeling and expressing intimacy.

Intimacy is not only a personal choice governed by individual desires and capabilities. It is also a culturally patterned arrangement, infused with the values and beliefs legitimized by the surrounding society. A particularly important dimension of contemporary Western culture is its gender system, through which masculine and feminine identities are constituted, and appropriate ways of thinking, acting, and relating are designated. Through socialization, most individuals acquire gendered identities that profoundly influence interaction patterns, preferences for autonomy and connectedness, modes of expressing care, strategies of power and abuse, and responsibility for relationships. In each of these respects, intimacy may be seen to be engendered.

3

Third-Party Influence on the Management of Personal Relationships

Renate Klein

Robert M. Milardo

This chapter explores the impact of social networks on the development and maintenance of personal relationships. Our central objective is to analyze how network structure and specific relationships with network members influence the management of personal relationships. We will argue that (a) the structure of partners' social networks affects the nature, availability, coordination, and timing of influence attempts by network members, or what we collectively refer to as "third parties," and (b) that the influence of third parties rests, at least in part, on their ability to define relational competence. We see the concept of competence as consisting of three elements: the task that has to be accomplished or the problem needing a solution, a set of behaviors that are appropriate in response to the problem, and criteria that indicate whether the task has been accomplished successfully.

In line with the objectives of this series, and this volume in particular, we will take a closer look at how social networks affect relational competence. Our analysis will concentrate on critical phases in personal relationships; that is, where conflicts occur and where some efforts at resolution are required. It is in these phases that the partners' relational competence is challenged and the influence of others on the relationship may be significant for its future development. We draw upon work on third-party influence in formal settings (e.g., labor-management negotiations) to develop a model of third-party influence in informal settings (e.g., close relationships).

Our use of the term *third party* will include interventions by network members collectively and individually, a broader interpretation than is typical in the literature on formal third-party influence (e.g., J. Z. Rubin & Brown, 1975). Conceptualizing the impact of social networks as third-party influence draws attention to the fact that network members do not represent passive environmental constraints on a couple's behavior nor do they necessarily display a consensus of values. Members may actively pursue interpersonal goals based upon their own evaluations of a target relationship in addition to generalized normative beliefs regarding such relationships (e.g., beliefs in monogamy or the appropriate distribution of household labor). The respective networks of each partner may differ considerably with regard to the availability of other network members, their consensus of values, and the type and scope of support or interference each partner can expect (see M. P. Johnson, Huston, Gaines, & Levinger, 1992; Wellman & Wellman, 1992).

For instance, network members who are highly interconnected and share similar values and interests may collectively attempt to influence partners as in the case of a wedding ceremony, or they may channel their influence through a particular network member such as a parent or sibling. On the other hand, network members may act independently without coordinating their attempts at influence. We consider both types of third-party influence and the conditions under which they are likely to occur.

Our general model of third-party influence on relational competence is depicted in Figure 3.1. We will discuss how network structure affects the nature, availability, coordination, and timing of informal third-party influence and how this influence affects the definition of the task that has to be accomplished, the recommendation of appropriate behaviors, and the evaluation of successful relationship management.

The Social Construction
of Relational Competence

Satisfying personal relationships, particularly close and intimate ones, are important determinants of overall life satisfaction (A. Campbell, Converse, & Rogers, 1976; Klinger, 1977). The notion of relational competence is especially alluring because it promises the key to personal fulfillment and happiness through one's relationships (Carpenter, in press). Once you know how to manage your relationships successfully, a prosperous and perhaps a very profitable life will result. This view of competence implies that the necessary skills can be learned, otherwise we would not be talking about relational competence but about inherited resources, talents, or giftedness.

The demand for training in relationship management seems to be insatiable, provoking a substantial industry in self-help books and social skills programs. The emphasis of this industry on individual behavior change reflects the second promise of relational competence: Not only is there a key to happiness but you can hold it in your own hands. Far from discouraging these approaches to self-empowerment, we want to take a different look at relational competence.

As we mentioned above, we view competence as composed of three critical elements: task definition, behavioral repertoire, and evaluative standards. By *task definition* we mean the interpretation of the relational problem: for example, how people interpret relationship problems, how they account for them, and the attributions they make in coming to understand the problem at hand (e.g., Burnett, McGhee, & Clarke, 1987; Fletcher & Fincham, 1991; Ginsburg, 1988; Harvey, Agostinelli, & Weber, 1989). By *behavioral repertoire* we mean the set of behaviors

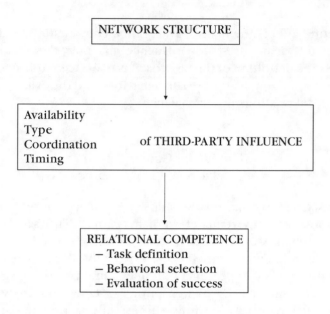

Figure 3.1. Network Structure and Relational Competence

that are selected to cope with the problem: for example, how people react in terms of the conflict tactics they employ and the responses they regard as appropriate in a given situation (e.g., Schaap, Buunk, & Kerkstra, 1988; Scott, Fuhrman, & Wyer, 1991). By *evaluative standards* we mean the criteria that are used to assess whether the behavior was successful in addressing the problem. For example, what constitutes a successful resolution: actions that promote individual satisfaction or actions that ensure the longevity of the relationship?

The components of relational competence are neither fixed nor absolute but are socially constructed, and we will analyze the role third parties play in this process. By *socially constructed* we mean competence based on the idiosyncratic preferences of partners or some degree of social consensus, as opposed to immutable, timeless, and objective fact. This approach anchors relational competence in the social organization and distinguishes our approach from conceptualizations that view competence as a set of particular social skills (e.g., McFall, 1982) or as a set of stable personality attributes (e.g., Carpenter, in press). For individuals or their relationships, this distinction between idiosyncratic preference and social consensus may be irrelevant in that socially constructed rules can exert as powerful an influence on daily life as biological or physical forces. But socially constructed rules are still a product of the social organization, no matter how overwhelming the consensus on an issue might be, and the fate of partners is not independent of human affairs but intertwined with the concerns, motives, and fears of this social organization.

More specifically, third parties affect each element of relational competence by applying their own perspectives and standards to the target relationship, including values, beliefs, experiences, needs, interests, and objectives. In doing so, they may modify the interpretation of a problem, directly or indirectly suggest appropriate responses, or impose evaluative standards. For example, to the extent that "peacefulness" is valued by family and friends alike, conflict avoidance or denial of one's own interests might constitute a competent solution to the problem. To the extent that partners' self-assertion is valued, these behaviors would be regarded as incompetent, whereas lengthy discussions or fights might seem appropriate. The influence of third parties on relational competence in terms of the interpretation of interpersonal problems, the selection of appropriate responses, and the definition of evaluative standards is illustrated in a study of husbands, their families, and coworkers.

Kemper (1968) examined how family members prescribe the behavior of husbands/fathers in nonfamilial settings, particularly work, and the extent to which employers and coworkers prescribe their behavior in family settings. Wives, children, and parents of spouses were actively involved in both familial and nonfamilial settings through their prescriptions of appropriate role behavior for husbands. In a complementary fashion, members of the work setting, especially colleagues, offered prescriptions for the behavior of husbands/fathers in nonfamilial and familial settings. At times the prescriptions of wives and colleagues concerning appropriate action were not in agreement. In this example, third parties—coworkers and family members—apply their notions of competent behavior and put pressure on the target person—husbands—to comply with their prescriptions. The messages sent may differ between different network sectors (family versus colleagues), possibly reflecting different interests or beliefs of network members. They also cut across social settings, with family prescribing behavior in nonfamilial settings and colleagues prescribing behavior in familial settings, demonstrating third-party influence beyond mere role assignment.

We suggest that the construction of an individual's conception of relational competence is related to structural properties of their social networks. We will develop this notion by identifying dimensions of relational competence, third-party influence, and social structure that are meaningfully interconnected and illustrate as well as specify the hypothesized links between social structure and relational competence. Relational competence, third-party influence, and social structure can be thought of as varying along particular dimensions in such a way that variations along a dimension of social structure imply a concordant variation in third-party influence, which in turn implies a variation in the conceptions of relational competence. For example, conjugal networks that are highly overlapping may increase the turnout of "mediators" during a family dispute. Joint network members are apt to be highly invested in considering the positions of both spouses, finding potential common ground, and defining paths of reconciliation that maintain the integrity of conflicting parties. Whereas nonoverlapping network members are less apt to turn out to be mediators because the members of each network know only "their partner's" side.

Our first task, then, is to identify those dimensions of relational competence that can be meaningfully related to key dimensions of third-party influence. A second task is to identify dimensions of network structure that can be meaningfully related to the dimensions of third-party influence.

Dimensions of Relational Competence

A prominent task that requires some degree of relational competence is the management of interpersonal conflict. Conflicts are often viewed as if partners typically agree on the issues being contested and on whether a resolution has been achieved. In fact, laboratory research often proceeds from this assumption when couples are asked to construct a list of issues over which they experience conflict. This selection procedure then becomes the source of material about which couples are asked to chat under the gaze of video equipment and the later scrutiny of an army of dedicated coders (Weiss & Heyman, 1990). Although great insights into the sequence of behavioral, physiological, and cognitive events surrounding discrete episodes of conflict have been achieved, such procedures do not represent the phenomenology of conflict or the social and historical context in which it routinely occurs (Duck, 1990b).

In contrast, recent research on conflict in close, heterosexual relationships suggests that conflicts are often fuzzy events that are open to very different interpretations by partners and their close associates. In a study of 98 dating couples (Klein, 1992), partners gave independent accounts of their own, as well as their partner's, position regarding a recent conflict. Prior to reconstructing their separate accounts, partners first jointly selected a conflict they had recently experienced. Each then gave a written account of their own position as well as their partner's position regarding the conflict. Partners constructed these accounts separately and privately.

In many cases, partners' interpretations of the conflict were so divergent that they seemed to reflect two entirely different realities. Only 50% of the couples agreed on whether the conflict was resolved or still being contested. For example,

Ang: We really haven't resolved the issue.
Nick: Basically, it's the same but maybe a little less serious.
[Couple 101]

Other accounts were widely discrepant. For example,

Daggy: It's still kind of disruptive; it's always in the back of my mind.

Seb: The situation is cleared up and things are fine.

[Couple 105]

A majority of conflicts in this sample seemed to linger on indefinitely, being brought up occasionally and then pushed back again, still unsolved.

Although beyond the scope of this chapter, it is illustrative to consider how partners' discrepant views emerge. No doubt, each partner brings different feelings, needs, and expectations into the relationship and interprets relational events in light of these personal conditions. Klein's (1992) research suggests that the successful resolution of conflicts is related to the partners' ability to integrate their divergent perspectives. Consequently, relational competence is likely to vary along a dimension that represents whether only one or both sides in a conflict are taken into consideration (see Figure 3.2). This dimension captures the notions of "perceived common ground" and "dual concern" that play an important role in the analysis of organizational conflict (Carnevale & Pruitt, 1992; Pruitt, 1981; Pruitt & Rubin, 1986). One pole reflects solutions that consider only one partner and turn the conflict into a zero-sum, win-lose situation. The opposite pole reflects solutions that consider both partners, where conflict is viewed as a non-zero-sum situation in which both partners can benefit.

Our social constructionist approach is of course meant to draw attention to the role the social environment plays in the definition of relational competence, often reflecting the perceived appropriateness of relationship behavior, which is largely determined by social consensus. We do not think that relational competence is exclusively derived from conventional prescriptions, however. That would mean underestimating the effects of highly personal needs, goals, and preferences as they arise from the interaction history of a specific relationship. To a certain extent, relational competence will be defined in the partners' own idiosyncratic terms, will change as the relationship develops, and will need to be negotiated by the partners.

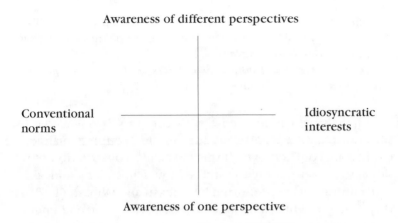

Awareness of different perspectives

Conventional
norms

Idiosyncratic
interests

Awareness of one perspective

Figure 3.2. Dimensions of Relational Competence

A second dimension of relational competence should then reflect that the interpretation of relationship tasks, the selection of instrumental behaviors, and the evaluation of relationship success depends on a degree of either highly personalized and idiosyncratic interests or conventional norms. The following examples illustrate idiosyncratic and conventional approaches. The first is taken from Cuber and Harroff's (1966) now classic study of affluent American families in which a physician of 50, married 25 years, describes his marriage:

> You know, it's funny; we have fought from the time we were in high school together. As I look back at it, I can't remember specific quarrels; it's more like a running guerrilla fight with intermediate periods, sometimes quite long, of pretty good fun and some damn good sex. In fact, if it hadn't been for the sex, we wouldn't have been married so quickly. Well, anyway, this has been going on ever since. . . . It's hard to know what it is we fight about most of the time. You name it and we'll fight about it. It's sometimes something I've said that she remembers differently, sometimes a decision—like what kind of car to buy or what to give the kids for Christmas. . . .
>
> Now these fights get pretty damned colorful. You called them arguments a little while ago—I have to correct you—they're brawls. There's never a bit of physical violence—at least not directed to

each other—but the verbal gunfire gets pretty thick. Why, we've said things to each other that neither of us would think of saying in the hearing of anybody else. . . .
Of course we don't settle any of the issues. It's sort of a matter of principle not to. (italics added; p. 45)

Although we cannot know with certainty if normative prescriptions play a significant role in this couple's manner of expressing conflict, overall this husband's construction of relational success is hardly the stuff of a widely endorsed ideal.

In contrast, a case reported by Dobash and Dobash (1979), in their study of abused Scottish wives, reveals a strong endorsement of normative beliefs that underlie this couple's management of conflict.

He's hit me in front of his friends. One night we were out—it was our wedding anniversary—and I was really angry that night. I think it was our fourth or fifth wedding anniversary and he says he was going to take me out, you know, he was going to take me for a night out. . . .

It ended up we were on a pub crawl. We went from place to place. By this time it was after eight—it was too late to really go anywhere to eat, to get in. So we went home and his friend says to me, "Can I go in to the kitchen and make some tea and toast?" I says, "Make yourself at home." [Joe, her husband, reentered the room and said:] "Where's Bruce?" I says, "He's making tea and toast. . . . " He says: "You make it. It's your house. You make it. . . . " Well, he started bawling and shouting and he came over and he punched me in front of them, and Susan and Bruce were there, you know. So I was mad. I mean he's hit me—I don't mind so much when I'm by myself but I hate him doing it in front of his friends and that. But I had witnesses, but right enough it was usually his side he did it in front of when he knew they wouldn't go witness for me. . . .

I don't think they [Bruce and his wife] wanted to get involved at all. I mean most of Joe's friends anyway was doing the same things to their wives. I mean Bruce used to give his wife knockings as well. (pp. 113-114)

In this case, violence is not unexpected by wives as a means husbands employ to resolve conflict, and to a certain extent it is implicitly endorsed by Joe's network members, who are also abusive. The use of violence in the domination of wives is based on "conventional" norms endorsed by a community of husbands and fully anticipated by their wives (Milardo & Klein, 1992; Straus, Gelles, & Steinmetz, 1980).

The two dimensions of relational competence are depicted in Figure 3.2. The first dimension refers to the extent to which relational competence is conceived in terms of conventional prescriptions versus idiosyncratic definitions. The conventional pole represents definitions of relational competence that are based on norms and tradition, whereas the idiosyncratic pole emphasizes conceptions based on the identification of individual needs and interests. For example, a normative solution to conflict over household chores in a marriage would be to split them up according to traditional norms concerning the sexual division of labor or along some equality rule such as taking turns, whereas an idiosyncratic solution would consist of determining each partner's preferences and talents and assigning chores accordingly. Personal relationships are likely to be influenced by both normative prescriptions that apply to many relationships and idiosyncratic definitions that apply only to one specific relationship.

Implementing social rules has the advantage that existing concepts can be adopted and that the adoption of these rules is likely to be approved by others. The downside is that they might not fit the needs of a specific relationship. The development of idiosyncratic definitions of relational competence may be an indicator of satisfying social relationships, as, for example, in the greater use of idiosyncratic codes by well-adjusted as opposed to unhappy couples (e.g., Baxter, 1987; Hopper, Knapp, & Scott, 1981; Locke, Sabagh, & Thomes, 1957; Maynard & Zimmermann, 1984; Navran, 1967).

We would like to emphasize that the two dimensions are, at least conceptually, independent. For instance, the development of idiosyncratic behaviors can serve the needs of both partners but does not necessarily do so. Depending on the relationship history and the power balance in the relationship, idiosyncratic patterns may evolve that benefit one partner more than the other. Similarly, normative prescriptions can take into account predominantly one partner's concerns or both partners' concerns. In the next section, we turn to those types of third-party influences that are likely to affect the two dimensions of relational competence. That is, which responses by third parties focus attention on one person's point of view and which focus attention on both partners' point of view, as well as which demonstrate a focus on conventional versus idiosyncratic solutions?

Dimensions of Third-Party Influence

We will concentrate on two dimensions of third-party influence and their association with the two dimensions of relational competence. In the preceding section, we suggested that the competent management of personal relationships differs in the extent to which each partner is aware of only one or both sides of a conflict. We suggest here that a partner's attempts to manage conflict differ to the extent that his or her network members point out the existence of different evaluations of the conflict as opposed to when the network emphasizes only one side in the conflict.

With regard to our second dimension of relational competence, partners may differ in the extent to which they focus on idiosyncratic solutions as opposed to conventional solutions. Third parties can influence the relative focus on this dimension by identifying and emphasizing underlying individual needs or identifying and emphasizing appropriate rules in response to the conflict.

We think of the two dimensions of third-party influence, eliciting input from one or both sides and emphasizing needs versus rules, as being conceptually independent. They are depicted in Figure 3.3 along with examples of third-party roles that would result from various combinations of both dimensions.

When describing the four different approaches below, we do not mean to imply that they are discrete categories. We would rather point out that they will vary along the two dimensions. They may reflect more or less normative influence, and the

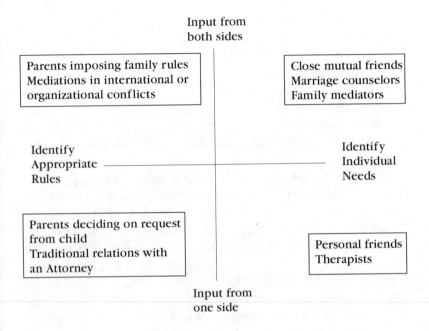

Figure 3.3. Dimensions of Third-Party Influence and Examples of Informal and Formal Third Party Rules

relative reliance on normative versus idiosyncratic approaches may change over time. For example, parents may begin to process a conflict between their children by applying previously established family rules but switch to an analysis of the underlying interests of each child when they realize that the normative approach is not successful. Conversely, overemphasis on the analysis of underlying needs may be too cumbersome and time-consuming in some situations and lead to an endless regression in the identification of ever more basic needs but no viable solution. In such situations, the application of previously agreed upon rules would lead to a faster, and fairer, agreement.

Research in the context of formal mediation suggests that mediators' preferred modes of dealing with a conflict are affected by underlying dimensions such as the mediator's interest in finding a solution and perceived feasibility of an agreement (Carnevale, Conlon, Hanisch, & Harris, 1989). Moreover, there is evidence that informal third parties approach conflicts with a priori conceptualizations or "frames" that serve to define the nature of the conflict and influence their preferred intervention strategy (Sheppard, Blumenfeld-Jones, & Roth, 1989). We see the influence of third parties extending even further into "teaching" partners their notions of the nature of conflict. The interventions third parties choose send a message to the conflicting partners of how to interpret and how to handle their conflict. For instance, is it important to attend to each partner's needs or is a conflict a matter of determining who is right and who is wrong? In this way, partners "learn" what conflict is and how to respond.

The upper-right quadrant of Figure 3.3 represents responses by third parties based on the identification of both partners' needs and interests. Consequently, managing conflicts involves input from both sides, disclosure by each partner, each partner's trust in the third party, identification of underlying needs and interests, tolerance of conflicting positions, problem solving, and the search for new, unconventional solutions. Interventions of this type are exemplified by the work of a marriage counselor or a family mediator (Blades, 1985). Another example would be interference in a pair conflict by an individual who is a close friend to both partners. Morton Deutsch (1973) comments on this type of third party influence by highlighting the importance of acknowledging the interpretation and evaluation of relationship events and moving beyond a singular concern with affecting the actual conflict tactics employed: "The third party, by recognizing the legitimacy of both sides, by treating each side with respect, by encouraging directness of communication, . . . can do much to promote a social framework that is conducive to cooperative negotiations rather than mere fair combat" (Deutsch, 1973, pp. 385-386).

The lower-right quadrant in Figure 3.3 represents solutions based on the identification of the individual needs and interests of only one partner. It may entail tailoring solutions that suit one partner's needs or demands. This approach may be taken by a therapist or lawyer and client facing a custody dispute or by any constituent who is primarily interested in the outcomes for one side, such as a close, personal friend of one partner. It may also be taken when the needs of one side seem to demand special attention or care (e.g., a sick child).

The lower-left quadrant of Figure 3.3 represents solutions based on the identification and application of appropriate rules that serve only one partner. This approach is based largely on a comparison of the conflict situation with other similar conflicts. In these cases, social comparison and normative prescriptions are more important than the identification of individual needs. This approach is related to establishing who is right and who is wrong, such as in an adversarial judicial system. It is aimed at maintaining social order and conventions but it may also maintain existing social inequalities. Mediation in nonindustrial societies, for example, is aimed not only at keeping social peace but also at maintaining the given social order. Without power, mediators can only mediate mutually acceptable solutions, which often translates into solutions in which the less powerful party makes more concessions. The settlements usually take into account the community norms and customs and reflect differences in social status between the disputants (e.g., high-status individuals are entitled to higher damage payments; Merry, 1989). Examples of informal third-party influence in this domain include parents who, in deciding whether they will allow their teenage child to go on a trip, compare their own decision with the decisions by parents of the child's friends, or parents who interfere with their child's dating relationships because they feel their children should not date before a certain age or should only consider partners of a certain age or ethnic background.

The upper-left quadrant in Figure 3.3 represents solutions based on the identification and application of rules that serve both protagonists in the conflict. An example of this approach would be the application of compensation procedures in the mediation of international conflict (e.g., J. C. Campbell, 1976) or a family that prides itself on egalitarian decision making with input from all members.

Dimensions of
Social Network Structure

The differential influence of third parties is illustrated in research concerning the impact of third parties on bargaining processes. Third parties can evoke very different concepts of what constitutes acceptable negotiator behavior. For example, constituencies (e.g., pressure groups, lobbies) often exert a strong influence on the negotiator to be firm and apply contentious tactics (Kogan, Lamm, & Trommsdorff, 1972). They thereby evoke "strong culturally defined pressures on individuals in our society toward projecting an image of competency, strength, and effectiveness to others" (J. Z. Rubin & Brown, 1975, p. 46). On the other hand, concern about loss of face decreases when concessions are made at the suggestion of a mediator (Pruitt & Johnson, 1970). This suggests that constituencies and mediators represent two types of third parties that differ in their evaluation and interpretation of concession making. The constituency signals to the negotiator that concession making is weak and a sign of incompetence, whereas the mediator signals to the negotiator that concession making is smart and an indicator of competence. Thus different criteria of relational competence, in this case competent bargaining, are evoked by different third parties with different implications for the development of the negotiations.

The type, availability, and coordination of influence attempts by informal third parties are affected by structural characteristics of networks. The significance of the social environment for the development and maintenance of personal relationships is widely recognized (Surra & Milardo, 1991) and has been investigated, for example, with regard to the support partners can derive from their social networks (Carpenter, in press; Duck, 1990a). Structural factors that affect the availability of third-party influence include the overall composition, density, and overlap of partners' networks.

Structural factors such as network composition, for example, the percentage of close friends or kin, affect the vested interests those third parties have in the solution of a conflict in the target relationship. In short, network members have personal interests in the actions of one another and they are motivated to act according to their self-interests, interests that result from their perception that their own outcomes are affected by the conduct of others. When members know one another (high density) and share interests, they may elect to coordinate their influence. For example, children or elderly persons might depend on a couple for emotional, social, and financial support and try to prevent a breakup of their marriage. Observers of a relationship breakdown might feel their own relationships threatened by this event. The interests and intentions of third parties affect their evaluations of a target relationship as in, for example, parents monitoring and evaluating their children's peer relations, mothers monitoring and evaluating their daughters' child-rearing practices, and friends, colleagues, and coworkers observing the development and maintenance of close relationships in their environment.

Analysis of constituencies and pressure groups reminds us that partners can have different networks, which affect the ability of partners to recruit support. McCall (1988) argues that, within dyads, coalitions cannot be formed but partners can try to "recruit" network members to build coalitions and buttress their positions. The ability and ease in forming these "extradyadic" coalitions depends on the availability of network members as much as on their values and beliefs, so that partners can get very different messages from their respective network members. In a close relationship, for example, a woman may get advice from *her* friends on how to improve the relationship, whereas men might get advice on how to improve their personal outcomes (Oliker, 1989). These different inputs from network members could be related to different experiences and life situations, which affect what is considered acceptable to express. For instance, women might shy away from overemphasizing their own concerns while centering instead on the needs of others. Whereas among men it might be more appropriate to talk about individual interests, such as careers and hobbies, while talking about relationships might be rare and only legitimate under extreme circumstances (e.g., sick wife). Therefore men's and women's networks can have different effects on what is acceptable in terms of self-disclosure (e.g., complaining, worrying, planning) and in terms of personal goals (e.g., relationships versus individual interests).

To illustrate the connection between social structure and third-party influence, we have chosen the two structural dimensions displayed in Figure 3.4. The dimensions are the overlap of each partner's network and the network's composition. Our aim is not to force every conceivable type of formal or informal third-party influence into a two-dimensional framework. We have chosen this conceptualization for two reasons. For one, it allows us to specify two dimensions that seem to be essential in the analysis of competent conflict resolution in personal relationships. More important, this framework allows us to illustrate how structural constraints (see Figure 3.4) are linked to relational factors (see Figure 3.3), both eventually influencing how individuals deal with conflicts in their relationships (see Figure 3.2).

Figure 3.4 may be illustrated with the following examples. An approach to conflict resolution that is based on an analysis of the needs of both partners should be more likely to the extent that the network members are concerned about both partners and have a fairly intimate knowledge of each partner. This should be more likely to the extent that the independent networks of each partner overlap (i.e., they have many mutual friends) and to the extent that the networks are composed of close associates in which partners would confide.

Third-party influence that is tailored around the needs of just one partner might prevail to the extent that only one partner has a network of close friends and the other partner is socially isolated or has access only to the partner's network.

A predominantly rule-based intervention may be more likely when network members, such as casual acquaintances, have no intimate knowledge about the target relationship. Again, the extent to which network members would be concerned about either one or both partners should depend on the amount of overlap of their respective networks.

Analysis of mediation in horticultural and pastoral societies sheds some light on how social structure and intervention in conflicting personal relationships can be intertwined because the political institutions in these societies are related to their

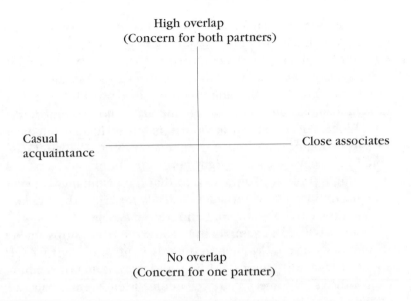

Figure 3.4. Dimensions of Social Network Structure

kinship systems (Merry, 1989). Mediation seems more likely the closer the conflicting parties are, both socially and geographically, for example, because they are close kin, or related by marriage, or live in the same village. That is, mediation occurs primarily in communities characterized by cohesion and mutual interdependence of its members, who are likely to interact in the future and have little or no opportunity to avoid the conflict by leaving the community.

With regard to the interrelation of social structure and third-party intervention in social conflicts, this evidence can be summarized as follows. Dense social environments characterized by high interdependence among members and a high probability of future interactions will display an interest in mediation that secures peace and social stability. To the extent that the mediation is confined to the community and its norms and values, this stability is reflected in mediated settlements that corroborate social inequality. Disputants of higher social status are likely to make fewer concessions than disputants of low social status.

Similar patterns may be observed in families and other forms of close relationships. Family systems are typically characterized by interdependence and the expectation of future interaction. Conflict avoidance via exit is difficult, when possible, and costly. Due to the sanctity of the family, conflict resolution is less institutionalized and disputants are often unequal in power. Individuals with higher social status disproportionately influence outcomes by suggesting or imposing settlements outright. The latter case could be exemplified by a fight between siblings and a parent imposing a solution. To the extent that the disputants are very unequal in power, any settlement is likely to reflect this inequality, as is the case in many contemporary marriages.

Oliker (1989), for example, in her study of friendships among women, details how women frequently confide in their friends about marital difficulties. Although deeply concerned about each other's happiness and well-being, friends encourage accommodation to husbands rather than encouraging each other's grievances or supporting strategies that advance their personal interests over those of their spouse. Oliker argues that "influence-oriented marriage work" is based upon power to yield its effects. Strategies range from direct bargaining to contentious tactics like coercion, manipulation, and verbal or physical combat. On the other hand, accommodative strategies promote commitment and "aim to adjust oneself to a situation or capitulate to the demands of another" (p. 123).

In Oliker's study, friends encouraged accommodation in a variety of forms. Sometimes they encouraged empathy for the position of husbands:

> So much of the time I only see my side—I've got blinders on. And June will say, "You know, he's probably feeling real insecure and angry." And for the first time I'll realize there's another human being mixed up in this, instead of just me and my own passions. (p. 125)

Sometimes friends encouraged strategies that "ennobled the adversary":

> A lot of the time I just looked at the negative. I'd compare Gary to the other husbands. And when you look at someone else's husband, you just see the good side, not the bad one. Jan will point out to me, "You know Gary helps with the dishes"—or does this or that—"and Eddie never does." I'd start to think, "Gee, I really am lucky he does that. He's not all bad." (p. 126)

And at other times friends encouraged humor or the direct expression and diffusion of negative feelings, especially anger, although usually with accommodation as the end result:

> Once after a big one, I left and went to stay with my sister. Lily called and said: "Janine, come on home. Your husband loves you. Don't do him that way." (p. 129)

Although Oliker found accommodation to be characteristic of the influence attempts of friends, occasionally wives reported that their friends and family encouraged confrontation.

> I'd packed up and moved out and gone to their house a lot of times. . . . I wouldn't say they tried to talk me into feeling worse about him, because nobody could have felt worse about him than I did. But I knew they were in favor of getting rid of him.
>
> One night he was ticked off about something and he went to bed. I went out for a bit, but when I got back he wasn't as asleep as I thought he was. He proceeded to go, Pow, pow, pow. I got my family; and my mother stuck a gun in him and told him to hit the road and he did. I was ready for him to go. (p. 130)

In this case, close friends and family represented a coordinated, direct, and eventually successful influence (at least in terms of their goals as they defined them). Such dramatic confrontations are probably all the more successful when wives maintain separate friends and alliances with kin, all of whom know one another, and perhaps when husbands have few alliances. Such alliances are important in the social construction of relational competence because they readily define problems, appropriate actions, and evaluative criteria. In this case, exit was the preferred action. In other cases, maintaining a marriage in the face of adversity is preferred.

For instance, family members who feel responsible for the breakup of a marriage in their kin group may try to pressure spouses, especially the wife, to save the marriage. These feelings of responsibility may originate in strong convictions about what constitutes a successful marriage, in concerns that the breakup might negatively reflect on their own social respectability, or in fears that their own marriages might be affected by a negative example (Spanier & Thompson, 1984).

Network members may be inclined to emphasize idiosyncratic needs of those they know well. To the extent that partners have nonoverlapping networks of close associates, this may lead to support of each partner by his or her respective network. The separate networks might function as two constituencies, each of them concerned primarily with the outcomes for "their" partner. More overlap between those networks, on the other hand, may increase the likelihood that network members are concerned about both partners. These effects should be stronger in dense as compared with loosely interconnected networks because in high-density networks members exchange more information and can more easily coordinate their activities.

Conclusions

We have throughout this chapter emphasized the social construction of relational competence. Our perspective is distinct from those of others, which treat competence as a selection of skills, like assertiveness, or as models of competence that center on relatively stable personal attributes, like shyness or extraversion. The paradox inherent in such perspectives is that competence is context specific; it is a relational, social, and gendered phenomenon in the sense that each element of competence— problem identification, behavioral selection, and evaluative criteria—occurs among partners who may have a long history of interaction, who routinely imbue one another's actions with unique meaning, who regularly take counsel from their close associates, and who exist in a gendered society.

Our social constructionist view avoids the problem of defining implicitly or explicitly what constitutes "competent actions" while still acknowledging that such evaluations are both powerful and inevitable in a social world. We do so by emphasizing the phenomenology of competence—that is, by emphasizing the elements of relational competence and how partners act in accord with idiosyncratic as well as conventional wisdom.

Our approach uses the notion of third-party influence to tie the process of the social construction of relational competence to the structural characteristics of society as they play out in the type and availability of an individual's social network. This approach emphasizes the relativity of competence and places it squarely within the realm of human relationships.

4

Felt Obligation in
Adult Family Relationships

Catherine H. Stein

Adult relationships with kin exist within a unique context of previous history and future involvement. Unlike most other social relationships, ties with family are not selected and relationships are assumed to be lifelong. Studies suggest that adults are generally in frequent contact with relatives, live in close geographic proximity, and engage in extensive exchange of goods and services (Adams, 1968; Griffith, 1985). For many people, family ties represent the most central and enduring type of social connections.

Despite this special nature of family relations, little attention has been given to the impact of mutual obligations that accompany kin membership. Obligation has been described as the

AUTHOR'S NOTE: I extend my appreciation to Marcia Ward, Jennifer Vaccaro, William Russner, Rebecca Rouiller, Michelle Gaines, and Lee Ann Bass for their interest and assistance in studying felt obligation. Gratitude is expressed to Mark Baron and Steve Duck for their helpful feedback on an initial version of the chapter and to Matthew Carlos Baron for his patience and impeccable sense of timing. I acknowledge that kinship definitions are cultural constructions and comments in this chapter are circumscribed to American culture.

"glue" that connects generations as well as the "oughts" and "shoulds" that surround individual relationships with family members. Family obligation represents a strong social force that shapes the conduct of individual personal relationships. This chapter focuses on the role of obligation toward family in adult relationships.

The concept of felt obligation presented in this chapter emphasizes rights and duties that are negotiated by family members in the context of their personal relationships across the life cycle. A working model of felt obligation is presented that considers both structural aspects of kin roles and qualities of family interactions. Initial empirical support for elements of the model is presented and general considerations for future research on felt obligation are discussed. Special attention is given to strategies for researching the nature and expression of felt obligation and the larger social context in which it is embedded.

Historical Views of the American Family

According to Schorr (1980), family relations in preindustrial America were largely based on mutual obligations and family solidarity. In a primarily agricultural America, the family was an economic unit, where parents typically owned the farm and children shared in the responsibility for production. Income was viewed as family income, and rights of inheritance and dowry were often explicit. Attached to blood ties and the family name were a host of societal privileges and responsibilities. Kinship rules were relatively structured and formalized as all members had a role in contributing to the survival of the family.

American expansion and the industrial revolution brought opportunities that were said to alter conceptions of the family. The availability of free land meant that parents' property did not have to be divided among children, which served to decrease parental control (Schorr, 1980). Where property was not freely available, an adult male child could purchase property from his father, or a father could formally turn over his property, specifying in legally binding documents what duties were owed to him and his wife while they lived (Demos, 1978). Individually earned cash income that resulted from work in factories supported the egalitarian notion that individuals have the right to exercise independent choice. Such new economic circumstances allowed children greater autonomy from kin and emphasized the emancipation from family in an atmosphere of social approval (Stone, 1977).

By the late nineteenth century, a shift had occurred in the view of the family from a set of relations governed by rights and duties to a set of social ties based on personal choice and affection (Hareven, 1986). Kin relations were seen as being motivated by warmth and intimacy, and family associations were thought to reflect a high degree of personal discretion (Gelfand, 1989). In this view, adults maintain relationships with family because they "want to," not because they "have to" do so. Compatibility, emotional closeness, and individual selection became qualities that characterized family ties.

It is not surprising that issues of autonomy, individuation, and affection in family relations should also be emphasized by modern theorists and researchers. For example, in the past four decades, sociological research on adult child-parent relations has been largely concerned with consequences of individuation in adulthood such as isolation of the nuclear family, lack of consensus and social values transmitted across generations, and problems of caregiving to adults in an aging society (Hagestad, 1987). Psychologists studying parent-child relations have been primarily interested in affectional family ties such as attachment of the mother-child dyad (Bowlby, 1980). Traditional theories of personality and adult development stress the importance of successful emancipation of children from their parents in adulthood (Erikson, 1963). Parent-child research has focused predominantly on the earliest and latest phases of the life course, with little information about family ties during the middle stages of adulthood (Hagestad, 1984). Moreover, few researchers have considered ways that ongoing family ties are maintained in the context of an individual's larger network of social relationships (Shulman, 1975; Stein, Bush, Ross, & Ward, 1992).

Although the rules of kin membership may be less formal and structured than in the past, the nonvoluntary and lifelong nature of family relationships continue to make them unique social ties. Yet, the importance of both individuation and connectedness issues in family relationships has been largely neglected by theorists and researchers. Relatively little is known about how forces such as kin obligation shape the nature of ongoing family ties and affect opportunities to engage in other types of social relationships over the life course.

Empirical Research on Obligation: Social Norm or Social Burden?

Early empirical studies of family obligation documented its presence as a social norm in contemporary society. When asked about duties that "people in general" hold toward relatives, studies found that adults consistently endorse contact and assistance as strong social expectations of kinship (Adams, 1968; Reiss, 1962). The strength of obligation norms was found to differ as a function of kinship role (e.g., greater obligation toward parents than toward siblings) and adults reported strong negative sanctions for nonperformance of kinship obligations (Adams, 1968; Bahr, 1976). Both men and women viewed adults as obligated to perform activities consistent with traditional sex roles (Adams, 1968; Bahr, 1976), although the relationship between the endorsement of obligation norms and the actual enactment of family duties was not investigated. Some studies have suggested that the endorsement of obligation norms is greater among the working class (Bahr, 1976), but overall findings regarding obligation norms and socioeconomic status have been mixed (Leichter & Mitchell, 1967; Muir & Weinstein, 1962).

More recent research on obligation has focused on adults' duties as caregivers to elderly parents. Researchers have investigated the concept of "filial responsibility," defined as obligations of adult children to meet the needs of their aged parents (Hanson, Sauer, & Seelbach, 1983; Seelbach, 1978). Research has shown that both parents and children have expectations regarding filial responsibility (Gelfand, 1989) and that filial responsibility differs as a function of geographic distance from parents (Finley, Roberts, & Banahan, 1988), race, and residential (rural versus urban) location (Hanson et al., 1983). Although some studies suggest that filial responsibility is positively related to feelings of affection toward elderly parents (Quinn, 1983), most authors view the construct as consisting of relatively unenjoyable responsibilities that adult children are required to perform for elderly parents (Schorr, 1980).

Findings regarding gender differences in filial responsibility have been mixed (Finley et al., 1988; Roff & Klemmack, 1986), although there is ample evidence that women are more likely to assume caregiving responsibilities to elderly parents than are men (Shanas, 1979). Research on gender differences often investigates "competing responsibilities" that women face in having to care for their own families and elderly parents. Studies suggest that women expect daughters rather than sons to adjust their work schedules to help their elderly parents (Brody, 1978, in Brody, 1986). Retrospective accounts show that women between the ages of 30 and 54 have more responsibilities caring for both their parents and their own children than did their elderly mothers during those ages (Brody, 1986). Authors agree that women are typically the ones to be "saddled" with the extra social burden of caring for elderly parents (Brody, 1986; Cantor, 1983).

In summary, researchers interested in family obligation have conceptualized it as a general attitude that people hold regarding responsibilities to kin and have demonstrated its continued existence. Most of the research focus on obligation has been limited to elderly parents and their adult children, with an emphasis on the difficulties of assuming caregiving duties that may follow from norms about filial responsibility. Implicit in such research is the assumption that norms regarding kin duties are salient when parents are elderly, infirm, and in need of assistance.

Although such research provides an important foundation for the study of family obligation, it is limited in several respects. The existing literature says little about factors that may give rise to kin obligation norms or the development of obligation attitudes across the life cycle. For example, there are few, if any, conceptual models that specify factors that might influence the endorsement of obligation attitudes or consider levels of kin obligation as a function of the life cycle stage of adults and their families. Also, little is known about the degree to which attitudes about obligation are transformed into personal expectations for conduct with kin. In other words, how much does subscribing to general social norms about kin duties increase the likelihood of actually fulfilling kin responsibilities such as regular contact and assistance? Are there societal and familial factors that affect the degree to which obligation attitudes are used by family members to guide behavior? Does family obligation serve to constrain other types of personal relationships?

The potential positive aspects of kin obligation also have not been well explored. Negative aspects of obligation are emphasized by researchers when obligation is contrasted with affection or discretionary motives for family interaction (Walker et al., 1990) or discussed in the context of added family responsibilities for women (Brody, 1986). There has been little acknowledgment in the literature of aspects of solidarity and connectedness that may also be associated with kin responsibilities (Blieszner & Mancini, 1987).

Structural Features
of American Kinship

Much is revealed about connectedness and solidarity by the denotation of "who is a relative," the terms used to distinguish types of relatives, and the scheme for their classification. Structural features of kinship implicit in the language used to distinguish family from other social ties reflect salient aspects of American family life. Kinship definitions are not absolutes but are cultural constructions that influence interpersonal transactions among family members and between family and other types of social ties.

In his study of American kinship, Schneider (1980) found that people typically define a "relative" as a person who is related by blood or marriage. Schneider divides kinship terms into two groups: basic terms that identify kin categories such as *father, mother, brother, sister, aunt, uncle,* or *cousin* and derivative terms that distinguish genealogical distance (e.g., *second cousin, great uncle*) or associations by marriage (e.g., *father-in-law, step-brother*). From his analysis of this kinship classification system, Schneider concludes that American kinship is constructed of two major cultural orders: the order of nature and the order of law.

The blood relationship in American culture is defined in genetic terms. Relatives "in nature" share heredity. For example, it is believed that both mother and father give substantially the same amounts of genetic material to their child and thus both parents are responsible for the child's "makeup." When a person is related to a blood relative, the individuals share a common genetic heredity and thus are connected to one another through a common ancestry. The degree to which individuals share these genes is assessed and identified by their degree of genealogical distance.

In contrast, relatives "in law" are bound only by law, traditions, or custom. The order of law is imposed by society and consists of rules and regulations. When a person is related to another "by law," the individuals are associated by virtue of their relationship, defined as a code or pattern of conduct, and not by their genetic attributes. The termination of "in-law" relationships is typically easier than the severing of blood ties and has fewer negative social sanctions. The focus of family ties obtained by marriage is not on a shared heritage or intergenerational continuity but on the circumstances that created the current, temporal kinship tie.

How do these structural features of American kinship relate to issues of family connectedness? The language used to identify kin membership in American culture suggests the importance of connectedness and continuity of family relations. Embedded in the language of kinship is an explicit structural distinction between family ties acquired by marriage and through blood and the differential rules for conduct that follow from these two types of relationships. The degree of family connectedness is measured in genetic terms and explicitly identified in the names given to kin relations.

Obligation in the Context
of Personal Relationships

Previous operational definitions of kin obligation as a general
social attitude about adults' responsibility toward kin provide
little insight into the unfolding of obligation within the context
of ongoing family relationships over the life course. Although
structural features of kinship suggest the importance of connectedness and solidarity in family relations, the mere existence
of blood ties is not sufficient to explain the nature of kin
obligation in ongoing relations with family. For example, full
siblings share as much common genetic heredity as parent and
child, yet adults report stronger feelings of obligation toward
parents than toward siblings (Bahr, 1976). Consideration of both
the features of kin structure *and* the qualities of personal relationships provide a more complete framework in which to
examine family obligation.

Relationships can be viewed as processes that occur within
social structures such as social roles (Hendrick, 1988). Social roles
carry with them general normative expectations about appropriate
behavior, but individuals must negotiate their personal relationships within the context of their own roles (Hendrick, 1988;
Mutran & Reitzes, 1984). The rules and norms that accompany
social roles must be applied in the process of relating and are
adapted, reproduced, and transformed in that process (Argyle &
Henderson, 1985; Hendrick, 1988). Thus duties and rights inherent in kin roles both shape the nature of social transactions and
are shaped by them as relationships flow through time. Given
this conception, *felt obligation* is viewed as expectations for
appropriate behavior as perceived within the context of specific, personal relationships with kin across the life cycle.

When viewed within the context of ongoing family relationships, it is likely that obligation is not limited to a single expectation but is multidimensional in nature. That is, expectations
for appropriate behavior are likely to be negotiated with family
across a number of relevant relationship domains. The fundamental importance of both separation and connectedness issues

throughout the life cycle provides a framework in which to identify basic dimensions of felt obligation.

Operational definitions of obligation typically have been limited to primary aspects of family connectedness such as maintaining regular contact with family and providing assistance in times of need (Hanson, Sauer, & Seelbach, 1983). Yet, the need to avoid conflict in family interactions may also be quite strong, given the ideal of positiveness in adult communication (Montgomery, 1988) and the negative sanctions against severing family ties (Allan, 1979). Moreover, expectations about appropriate levels of communication and personal sharing become salient when a lifetime of personal involvement is assumed. For example, there is evidence to suggest that elderly parents expect their adult children to maintain open and honest lines of communication with them (Blieszner & Mancini, 1987), and expectations about sharing important matters are reported by both elderly parents and their adult children (Hamon & Blieszner, 1990). In other words, it may not be sufficient that family members should simply maintain contact; family might well have other expectations about the kinds of personal information that they should share and should avoid in interactions with one another.

Obligation in family relationships is likely to involve issues surrounding individuation as well as closeness. There is substantial evidence that the need for autonomy and independence is a key aspect of adult family relationships (Nydegger, 1983). Strong social norms encouraging independence from family in adulthood are likely to enhance expectations about appropriate levels of self-sufficiency and place limits on personal sharing and communication in specific kin interactions (Cohler & Geyer, 1982). Expectations about appropriate levels of personal sharing can facilitate a sense of independence as well as a feeling of connectedness. Thus dimensions of felt obligation may include a duty to maintain appropriate levels of self-sufficiency, personal sharing, and the avoidance of interpersonal conflict as well as expectations about contact and assistance.

A number of authors suggest that obligation should be particularly strong in the parent-child dyad (Adams, 1968; C. L. Johnson, 1988b). Obligation of children to parents assumes that personal sacrifices made by parents in child rearing should be acknowledged in adulthood. The nonreciprocal flow of resources from parent to child during childhood is thought to be associated with a personal sense of indebtedness to parents in adulthood. Duties performed by adult children over the life course serve as "repayment" that helps to alleviate personal indebtedness and increase a sense of reciprocity as adult relationships continue over time.

The structure of kin roles also suggests that feelings of obligation would typically not be as strong for relations obtained through marriage as for blood ties. Although the structure of both parent and parent-in-law ties are intergenerational and asymmetrical (Fischer, 1983), relationships with parents-in-law have some distinct structural features. Ties with in-laws develop in adulthood and originate solely as a product of marriage. By definition, individuals are structurally linked to their in-laws through their spouses, and thus aspects of marital relationships are likely to affect felt obligation toward in-laws. In fact, it may be that felt obligation toward in-laws lies within the marital relationship as well as within the context of personal relationships with in-laws per se. In other words, felt obligation toward in-laws may be motivated by a sense of duty toward one's spouse and a desire to maintain a satisfactory marital relationship as well as a sense of responsibility toward parents-in-law themselves.

The structural link between marital partners and in-laws might also affect the termination of in-law relationships. For example, ending ties with in-laws as a result of the death of a spouse may have different implications for felt obligation than terminating in-law relations as a result of marital separation or divorce. Conflict may serve to mitigate a partner's sense of duty toward his or her spouse and in-laws in the case of separation and divorce, whereas feelings of loss that typically accompany the death of a marital partner might heighten a sense of responsibility toward one's former spouse and his or her family. The unique structural features of parent and parent-in-law relationships are likely to contribute to differences in negotiation of obligation for the two types of kin relations and in maintenance of family ties.

It is also important to make a distinction between felt obligation and its enactment in family relationships. Performance of kin activities may or may not result from felt obligation. In some cases, individuals may choose not to act on feelings of obligation as a way of renegotiating family relationships. For example, after marriage, a man might decide not to participate in holiday activities with his parents or may suggest an alteration in holiday tradition. Both enactment and nonperformance of felt obligation can be powerful elements in negotiating adult relationships with family.

A Working Model of Felt Obligation

Aspects of the current discussion of kinship can be used to form a working model for the study of felt obligation in ongoing family relationships across the adult life cycle. Elements of the model are presented in Figure 4.1. Dyadic relationship and individual factors, family of origin influences, and cultural and social influences are thought to affect the nature and expression of felt obligation.

The working model assumes the importance of particular life tasks at various periods throughout the adult life cycle. The concept of felt obligation assumes that relationships with family members are negotiated across the life course within a larger cultural and social context (see the chapter by Allan in this volume). Felt obligation is seen as dynamic in nature as relationships flow through time and is assumed to reflect issues of both separation and connectedness in family relationships. The model is constructed in the general case so as to be applicable to various kinds of relations with kin.

Relationship Influences
and Individual Factors

At the heart of the felt obligation construct is the negotiation of rights and duties in the context of ongoing relationships with family. Yet, the expression of felt obligation in dyadic relationships is likely to be relatively subtle, often implicit, and psychologically complex. The process of communication about obligation is thought to be similar to the development of "relational communication

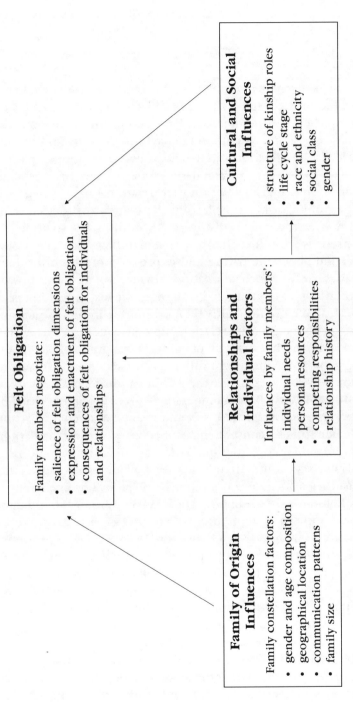

Figure 4.1. Elements of a Working Model of Felt Obligation

Felt Obligation

Family members negotiate:

- salience of felt obligation dimensions
- expression and enactment of felt obligation
- consequences of felt obligation for individuals and relationships

Cultural and Social Influences

- structure of kinship roles
- life cycle stage
- race and ethnicity
- social class
- gender

Relationships and Individual Factors

Influences by family members':

- individual needs
- personal resources
- competing responsibilities
- relationship history

Family of Origin Influences

Family constellation factors:

- gender and age composition
- geographical location
- communication patterns
- family size

89

standards" in close relationships as articulated by Montgomery (1988).

Just as partners in close, personal relationships come to establish their own system of beliefs and actions for "relating well to each other" (Montgomery, 1988), so do kin members develop their own belief systems and behavioral patterns for the expression of felt obligation and its enactment in relationship transactions. Over time, kin members come to "identify" aspects of obligation that are salient for their relationship. The negotiation of felt obligation takes place in the context of routine interactions over the course of the relationship, until some levels of consensus are achieved for a particular life cycle stage. Communication about the nature and expression of obligation for the dyad is likely to occur at relationship levels of meaning, however, rather than at content levels. In other words, obligation is communicated more implicitly than explicitly through the actions of kin members and their relationship consequences. For example, a mother and her married daughter are more likely to "get into the habit" of calling each other on the telephone every Sunday than they are to discuss their "obligation to maintain regular family contact." Both members may give the calling ritual little thought unless the routine should change or become disrupted. At such times, consequences for the perceived violation of relationship rules about obligation are likely to become salient.

Theorists posit that guilt may be a major psychological mechanism used to ensure that family obligations are generally met (C. L. Johnson, 1988b; Nydegger, 1983). Mothers are thought to invoke guilt in their children as a means to ensure that they will be cared for in old age (Nydegger, 1983). Yet, the relationship between felt obligation and psychological well-being is likely to be complex, as obligation offers relationship opportunities (e.g., chances to increase reciprocity, feelings of connectedness) as well as relationship responsibilities (e.g., duty to maintain contact and to provide assistance).

Individual factors, such as the emotional and tangible needs and available resources of family members, are likely to affect the expression and enactment of felt obligation. Life circumstances and historical aspects of the kin relationship can serve to create unique expressions of felt obligation that are functional for the perpetuation of family ties. For example, some college-age adults from divorced families report the need to provide tangible assistance to that parent who most requires their help, regardless of who has had primary responsibility for their upbringing (Stein, Gaines, Ward, Bass, & Russner, in preparation). The nature and expression of felt obligation reflect the life circumstances of the individual actors as well as the relational history and behavior patterns of the dyad.

Family of Origin Influences

Family constellation factors are likely to offer a different set of opportunities and constraints for the nature and expression of felt obligation. Structural features such as number, gender composition, and geographic location of an individual's family of origin are likely to affect the distribution of obligation among family members. Birth order, gender and ages of siblings, marital status of parents, and prevalence of extended family are indices of family structure that set parameters for more dynamic aspects of family life.

The influence of family constellation factors can be seen in research on family caregiving. For example, Horowitz (1985) found that sons of elderly infirm parents tended to become caregivers only in the absence of an available female sibling. Tonti (1988) reported that, in families with several adult daughters, the daughter living closest to elderly parents was most likely to be chosen as the primary caregiver. In terms of caregiving and birth order of adult siblings, Wake and Sporakowski (1972) found that the youngest daughter was most likely to provide assistance to aged parents. Such findings suggest important structural elements associated with the enactment of family activities and provide direction for the study of felt obligation and its expression in family relationships.

Cultural and Social Influences

As previously outlined, inherent in the structure of kinship roles are basic normative expectations for conduct with family

(Schneider, 1980). The emphasis on blood ties, shared genetic makeup, and common personal attributes in American kinship perpetuates norms for connectedness and solidarity among family. Expectations inherent in kinship roles reflect the most general guidelines for family relationships.

Life cycle stage, however, is also seen as an important factor that affects kinship norms. Each phase of the life course is associated with a host of societal expectations about appropriate life tasks, level of available resources, and reciprocity of family relationships (Wortley & Amatea, 1982). For example, young adulthood is typically a time when children are expected to emancipate themselves from parents. Parents often provide assistance and resources to their children to help facilitate their independence from the family. With limited material resources, children in young adulthood are typically not expected to provide tangible assistance to parents. Yet, dependence on parents for support and assistance in young adulthood may help maintain a state of "indebtedness" to parents from childhood. Thus some aspects of felt obligation toward parents may be strong for young adults with continued dependency and little opportunity to "repay" parents for sacrifices that continue to be made on their behalf.

Life cycle stage also suggests developmental tasks or circumstances that might mediate expectations regarding kinship duties. For example, "competing responsibilities" of adulthood such as marriage, family, or a demanding career may serve to mitigate expectations about the nature of adult children's responsibilities to parents. There is evidence to suggest that daughters who are married or employed outside of the home provide fewer caregiving activities to elderly parents than their unmarried or nonemployed counterparts (Lang & Brody, 1983).

Social and cultural expectations of kinship may also be influenced by factors such as gender, social class, and ethnicity of family members. In relationships with family, women are most frequently expected to be the "kinkeepers," in charge of maintaining contact with both parents and in-laws, coordinating family events, and keeping track of special occasions (Hagemann-White, 1984). Assistance is more likely to flow between families related through females than males (Lee, 1979), and bonds between mothers and adult daughters are typically among the strongest intergenerational ties (Cohler & Geyer, 1982). Research also suggests that issues of family solidarity and connectedness may be more strongly emphasized among the working class (Adams, 1968; Troll, 1971). Working-class people have greater contact with kin, and adult ties between mothers and daughters are stronger than those of the middle class (Adams, 1968; Troll, 1971).

There is also evidence that kinship structure and social expectations for family roles differ as a function of ethnicity (McGoldrick, 1982). Although there is considerable heterogeneity within ethnic groups (Ho, 1987), the unique characteristics of a cultural group help determine kinship definitions and acceptable family attitudes, values, and forms of behavior. For example, while the primary focus for the dominant, white Anglo-Saxon Protestant (WASP) culture is generally the intact nuclear family extending back over generations, African Americans often expand their definition of family to include a wide informal network of kin and community. Italian Americans often tend to think of family in terms of tightly knit, multigenerational families with hierarchical structures for family decision making. Chinese Americans may include all of their ancestors and descendants in their definition of family membership (McGoldrick, 1988). Although elements of felt obligation have been outlined in relation to general kinship definitions of the majority culture in America, the impact of ethnicity on family structure and obligation must also be understood.

Researching Felt Obligation

Assessment Issues

The current working model of felt obligation suggests a number of relevant domains for empirical investigation. Yet, development of methods to assess the construct of felt obligation is a necessary first step to conducting systematic research. Previous qualitative research on kin obligation (Stein & Rappaport, 1986) and theoretical discussions of obligation (Adams, 1968; Bahr, 1976; Karpel & Strauss, 1983) led to the development of the Felt Obligation Measure (FOM), a 34-item self-report instrument designed to tap adults' expectations regarding appropriate interactions in relationships with kin. Items for the measure were generated to reflect issues of separation and connectedness in adult relations.

Using a 5-point Likert scale format, the FOM asks respondents to rate how often they feel they "need to" or "should" do or say particular things in their relationships with specific family members such as their parents or their parents-in-law. Felt obligation is operationalized as the frequency with which respondents report particular expectations (defined as a "need" or a "should") in their ongoing relationship with a specified (target) family member. In addition to an overall score of felt obligation, the FOM yields scores on five empirically derived subscales that assess expectations regarding contact and family ritual, conflict avoidance, assistance, self-sufficiency, and personal sharing. Reliability and construct validity data suggest that the FOM has good psychometric properties (see Stein, 1992, for further description of the instrument).

Empirical Studies of Felt Obligation

To examine some basic features of felt obligation using the FOM, a series of three studies were undertaken with samples at two different life cycle stages (Stein, 1992). The studies investigated differences in respondents' self-reports of felt obligation as a function of gender, kin role (parent, parent-in-law, mother, father), and life cycle stage (first-time married couples and single, college-age adults from intact families). Psychological well-being correlates of felt obligation were explored for the sample of young married couples.

Findings across all three studies indicated that, on average, women reported higher overall levels of obligation and scored significantly higher on most dimensions of felt obligation than did men. These gender differences were found for adults at both life cycle stages. For married couples, wives reported higher overall levels of obligation on average toward both parents and parents-in-law than did their husbands.

Results also highlighted the importance of kin role relationship in the experience of felt obligation. For married couples, expectations surrounding conflict avoidance, assistance, and personal sharing were significantly greater toward their own parents than their parents-in-law. Obligation to maintain contact and family rituals and to be self-sufficient were equally important in both types of family relationships. When parental role relationships were investigated in more detail in a college-age sample, adults reported higher levels of obligation on average toward their mothers than their fathers across four of the five obligation dimensions. Women were significantly more likely than men to report that they should engage in personal sharing with their mothers.

Findings comparing levels of obligation toward parents at two stages of early adulthood indicated that single, college-age adults experienced significantly higher levels of felt obligation than married couples. In the sample of married couples, felt obligation toward parents was also associated with significantly higher levels of self-reported depression, neuroticism, and global severity of psychological symptoms for husbands. Obligation toward parents was not, however, significantly related to mental health measures for wives.

Results of these initial studies provide empirical support for some fundamental aspects of felt obligation. Gender differences in felt obligation are consistent with a variety of studies that emphasize the importance of gender in family relationships (Cohler & Geyer, 1982). Life cycle differences in felt obligation highlight the dynamic nature of kin relations in adulthood and expand previous notions that limit filial responsibility to adults' interactions with elderly parents.

Although men's relationships are often characterized as being principally in the world outside of the family (Cohler & Geyer, 1982), study results suggest that felt obligation toward parents may be more strongly related to psychological distress for men than for women. It may be that women are accorded more opportunities than men to discharge feelings of obligation by enacting family responsibilities. Enactment of felt obligation may serve to "repay" family for sacrifices made in child rearing, thereby alleviating a woman's sense of personal indebtedness and increasing reciprocity as adult family relationships continue over time. These initial findings are provocative and underscore the need to study intergenerational ties for both men and women at various stages of the life course.

Felt Obligation in a Social Network Context

Findings from these initial studies have established some of the basic elements of felt obligation and offer encouraging directions for future research. Yet, critical to a systematic understanding of felt obligation in ongoing family relationships is a careful consideration of the social context in which felt obligation is embedded.

Given that adults typically have a finite amount of energy available for social relationships (Shulman, 1975), obligations to family may often be in competition with other aspects of daily life. Marital and nuclear family relationships, friendships, and social ties from work, school, church, or other organizations together with kinship ties typically constitute an individual's network of social relations. Relationships with family in adulthood exist in a larger social context.

Viewing felt obligation with kin in the context of individuals' *networks* of personal relationships offers some important options for research. A network approach can provide information about the structure of an individual's social world such as network size, role composition (number of family, friends, work associates, neighbors, and so on), and interconnectedness among members (Milardo, 1988). Applied to the study of felt obligation, such network data can be used to identify the matrix of personal relationships in which family obligations must be juggled and maintained.

By considering family ties in a personal network context, researchers can describe distinct and overlapping functions that kin and kith ties may serve. For example, in their study of young

married women, Stein and Rappaport (1986) found that supportive nonkin ties sometimes substituted for strained relations with
family for a number of participants. Women who expressed
conflictual kin relations and negative feelings of family obligation often reported instances where a neighbor or a friend was
"like a mother to me" or where nonfamily network members
were "adopted" into family roles as sisters, brothers, aunts, or
uncles. Allan (1979) has noted similar kinds of "boundary span-
ning" relationships, where nonfamily members serve family
functions, particularly among working-class families.

A network perspective can also be used to identify various
subsystems or network sectors relevant to the expression and
enactment of felt obligation. For example, the structural properties of a family subsystem consisting of nuclear family, family
of origin, and in-law ties may be identified for married adults and
used to study couples' strategies for the management of felt
obligation and its enactment. Such an investigation might focus
on how couples with different network structures perceive
obligation to their own and their spouses' families and how
couples divide their time and energies between these sets of
family relations.

Studies of kinship subsystems may also explore mechanisms
for the dissemination of kin rights and responsibilities among
particular sets of family members such as adult siblings. Such
research could take the form of quantitative studies of felt
obligation obtained from various individual family members or
more qualitative, hypothesis generating case studies with sets of
kin members representing particular family circumstances. For
example, qualitative studies could focus on the activation of kin
subsystems in times of family crisis, such as with the illness of
parent or other family member, or examine more routine dimensions of felt obligation, such as how siblings ensure that both
regular contact and participation in family ritual are maintained.

Another direction for research involving kin subsystems is the
examination of felt obligation for family members in different
kin roles. For example, Victoria Bedford (personal communication, October 1991) included a modified version of the Felt
Obligation Measure in her study of adult sibling relationships.

The research was not interested in siblings' perceptions of felt obligation toward parents but in siblings' feeling of obligation toward one another and its impact on their personal relationships. Research that examines levels of felt obligation as a function of kin role may have implication for the study of social support and help seeking in family relationships.

At the dyadic level, there is much to learn about the process of negotiation, communication, and enactment of felt obligation expectations among specific pairs of family members. It is hypothesized that family members not only negotiate salient aspects of felt obligation for their relationship but come to develop interpersonal cues for its expression and activities related to its enactment. Self-report data from quantitative measures such as the FOM obtained from both members of the dyad could assess the degree to which expectations about felt obligation are shared by family pairs. Other types of assessment methods could be used to identify ways both members of the family experience obligation and its expression in their relationship.

A network approach underscores a view of felt obligation as a set of rights and duties negotiated within the social context of relationships rather than obligation as a purely societal prescription or individual personality trait. Research on felt obligation can be organized around the number and types of network relationships that are the focus of investigation, ranging from the study of dyadic ties to research on larger network sectors or subsystems.

A network perspective also allows the possible influence of felt obligation on nonfamilial ties to be examined. Given finite social resources, enacting family obligation may restrict opportunities for interactions with friends, limit contacts with work associates, or constrain involvement in other social settings. For example, women who are employed outside of the home and who take primary responsibility for both their own nuclear family and extended kin ties may have little time or energy for friends or other social commitments. A highly interconnected network consisting mostly of family may offer a woman a sense of stability and consistent identity but may also leave her particularly vulnerable in times of family conflict and crisis (Hirsch,

1985). It is possible for a highly interconnected family-dominated network to become a "closed system" with little access to nonfamilial resources or points of view.

Potential positive effects of felt obligation toward family on friendships and other types of social relationships can also be explored with a network approach. Although possibly restricting the number of friendships that can be maintained, felt obligation toward family may positively affect the quality of adult friendships. It may be that only a few of the most satisfying friendships can endure over time for individuals with a strong sense of family obligation. Moreover, it may be that expectations regarding regular contact, assistance, conflict avoidance, sense of autonomy, and personal sharing negotiated within the context of family relationships become salient for those friendships that are sustained over time. In other words, friends may become "more like family" as obligation rules for interacting with kin are applied to select adult friendships.

Summary

Although the special nature of family relationships has long been recognized, surprisingly little research has focused on the impact of mutual obligations that accompany kin membership. This chapter has attempted to highlight the potential importance of felt obligation in family relations across the life cycle and to sketch elements relevant to its systematic study.

Felt obligation is seen as a set of expectations for appropriate behavior negotiated within the context of specific, personal relationships with kin across the life cycle. It is viewed as a strong social force that shapes the conduct of individual personal relationships. The conceptual picture of felt obligation is currently painted in very broad strokes and this chapter raises many more issues than it attempts to answer. Yet, there is great potential for family obligation research to provide rich descriptive information about issues of continuity, support, and interdependence of family relationships across the life course.

5 Daily Life in Relationships

Niall Bolger

Shannon Kelleher

Most people's daily lives are played out in a range of social institutions, such as the home, workplace, church, and school. These institutions are interconnected, moreover, such that people's relationships in one institution can be affected by events in another. For example, many theorists have pointed to the strong connections between events in the workplace and those in the home (Bronfenbrenner, 1979; Crouter, 1984; Kanter, 1977; Piotrkowski, 1979). A focus on daily life in relationships therefore inevitably highlights the links between relationships and their broader social context.

In this chapter, we will illustrate the social context of relationships by describing a program of research that uses intensive daily diary methods to study relationships, stress, and psychological well-being. We hope to demonstrate that research that relies on more conventional survey research methods may miss important relationship processes such as the key role of conflict

AUTHORS' NOTE: We thank Geraldine Downey and Adam Zuckerman for comments on an earlier draft of this chapter.

100

in daily life and the precise mechanisms whereby problems in the workplace have repercussions on relationships at home, and vice versa. More generally, we will show that focusing on the daily level of analysis enriches the study of relationships by allowing investigators to translate key relationship concepts such as relationship quality into their referents in recurrent patterns of daily interaction.

Interest in the psychology of daily life has increased greatly over the past decade, and relationships researchers have been at the forefront of this work (Tennen, Suls, & Affleck, 1991; Wheeler & Reis, 1991). In fact, daily experience research on relationships was pioneered more than 15 years ago, in diary studies of everyday social interactions using the Rochester Interaction Record (Reis, Nezlek, & Wheeler, 1980; Wheeler & Nezlek, 1977). Adaptations of the basic approach have been used to study, among other things, initial relationship development (Duck & Miell, 1986), the role of conversation in everyday relationships (Duck, Rutt, Hurst, & Strejc, 1991), and the interactional characteristics of growing, stable, and disengaging relationships (Baxter & Wilmot, 1986).

Studies of daily life have also become more prominent in the literature on stress (Coyne & Downey, 1991). Daily stressors have been shown to have potent effects on psychological and physical well-being (Bolger, DeLongis, Kessler, & Schilling, 1989; DeLongis, Coyne, Dakof, Folkman, & Lazarus, 1982; DeLongis, Folkman, & Lazarus, 1988; Eckenrode, 1984; Kanner, Coyne, Schaefer, & Lazarus, 1981), and these findings have propelled the field to examine the daily manifestations of other stress-related variables. These include stress appraisals, coping, and, of central interest in this chapter, relationship variables such as social support and social conflict (Coyne & Downey, 1991).

Relationships, Stress, and Well-Being

It is a well-accepted finding that relationships matter for health and psychological well-being. Results of many studies, from large-scale epidemiological investigations to in-depth research on particular subgroups, show that deficiencies in social relationships such as social isolation and lack of support are associated with increases in physical and mental health problems (Cohen, 1988; House, Umberson, & Landis, 1988). Given that this basic phenomenon is well established, the focus of research has now shifted to understanding the processes whereby relationships influence physical and mental health.

A working assumption in the field is that the importance of relationships for health is due, in part, to their role in stressful experiences (Cohen & Wills, 1985). Stressful experiences are usually classified into three types: chronic, acute, and daily. Chronic stressors are those that are a constant feature of people's lives for long periods of time. Examples include living in poverty, being in an overly demanding job, being in a conflicted marriage. Acute stressors, also known as major life events, are more time-limited events such as becoming divorced or unemployed, failing an exam, and relocating. Clearly, the boundary between chronic and acute stressors is relative: Depending on their duration, certain "acute" problems such as unemployment could also be classified as chronic.

Although acute stressors received almost exclusive research attention in the early years of stress research, there is now an increasing awareness that chronic stressors, because of their unrelenting nature, may be even more important for health and psychological well-being (Coyne & Downey, 1991; Kessler, Price, & Wortman, 1985). Moreover, it appears that the effects of both acute and chronic stressors on mental health are mediated, in part, by daily stressors (Eckenrode, 1984; Kanner et al., 1981; Pearlin, 1983). Thus the stress of unemployment is likely to emerge in the day-by-day experience of being unable to pay bills and of receiving rejection letters from prospective employers. In the same way, the stress of being in a bad marriage is likely to emerge in recurrent daily tensions and conflicts over housework, child care, and spending.

Relationships and Stress in Daily Life

What is the role of personal relationships in these daily stress processes? It is reasonable to think that personal relationships may act as sources of both daily stress and protection against stress. We already know from conventional survey research that conflicts in relationships can have a more potent effect on well-being than support in relationships (Fiore, Becker, & Coppel, 1983; Rook, 1984, 1987). Our recent research complements this work by showing that relationship conflicts are indeed potent sources of stress in daily life.

In a large-scale daily diary study of married couples, we found strong evidence that relationships are the major source of daily stress (Bolger, DeLongis, Kessler, & Schilling, 1989). Subjects in the study were 166 married couples, and both husbands and wives in each couple kept a structured daily diary each day for 6 weeks. Each diary was in fact a short questionnaire that subjects completed at bedtime, a task that took no more than several minutes to complete. In the diary, subjects reported their negative moods and the occurrence of 21 categories of daily stressors such as conflicts at home and at work, transportation problems, financial problems, and work overload. As expected, these daily stressors were strongly associated with concurrent daily mood: On high-stress days, subjects tended to be more angry, anxious, and depressed than they were on low-stress days. The surprising finding was that interpersonal conflicts at home and at work uniquely accounted for over 80% of the explained variance in these daily negative affects. All the remaining events (such as work overloads, transportation problems) uniquely accounted for less than 5% of the explained variance in mood. This suggests that the main sources of stress in daily life are interpersonal conflicts.

We noted above that relationships, in addition to acting as a source of stress, may also help protect against the effects of stress. We will discuss the process separately for chronic, acute, and daily stressors. A major source of chronic stress for many people is managing the joint demands of work and family life (Eckenrode & Gore, 1989; Piotrkowski, 1979). One important way in which this is manifested is through a process that family researchers call "crossover" (Crouter, 1984), whereby stressors in the work domain spill over to affect the spouse at home.

Crossover is usually represented as the deleterious effect of stress experienced by an individual in the workplace on the individual's spouse at home. Examples of such effects include cases where work stressors lead to increases in avoidable domestic conflicts. We found, for example, that on days when men had an argument at work, they were more likely to argue with their spouse at home later that day (Bolger, DeLongis, Kessler, & Wethington, 1989). Crossover effects, however, can also represent instances of how one partner selflessly protects the other from the daily manifestation of chronic stress. For example, we found evidence that on days when husbands experienced work overload, their wives reported an increase in housework overload that day (Bolger, DeLongis, Kessler, & Wethington, 1989). This process was mediated in the following way: After a difficult day at work, husbands would withdraw from home activities that evening (a process also identified by Repetti, 1989, 1992). In response, wives "took up the slack" and reported more home stressors. In constrast, no equivalent compensation process occurred when wives had a stressful day at work. This process is a concrete example of how relationships help protect against the effects of chronic stress in daily life. It may also provide insight into why men derive more benefits from marriage than women do (Mirowsky & Ross, 1986).

If relationships protect against the daily manifestation of chronic stress, do they also protect against the daily manifestation of acute stress? To examine this question, we used a diary design to study premedical students' coping with the MCAT, a daylong examination taken by most medical school applicants (Bolger & Eckenrode, 1991). For 35 days surrounding the examination, students reported their daily experiences and their emotional distress. The specific focus of the study was whether a lack of social involvement would predict increases in anxiety as the examination approached. Although everyone's anxiety increased substantially as the examination approached, socially isolated persons showed the largest increases.

The daily reports revealed that this increase in anxiety occurred much sooner for the socially isolated people, such that they were not only more anxious under stress, but they were anxious for a longer period of time. For example, socially isolated persons showed substantial increases in anxiety by 6 days before the examination, whereas socially integrated persons showed marked increases only 2 days before the examination. Thus this study not only replicates the finding that social relationships can protect against the deleterious effects of stress, but it also prompts more focused questions about temporal issues such as why the effects emerge earlier in socially isolated persons than in socially integrated ones.

The finding that relationships affected the dynamics of adaptation to a major event is echoed in the results of a diary study of everyday stressful events (Caspi, Bolger, & Eckenrode, 1987). One goal of this study was to assess the effect of social support on adaptation to daily stressors in a population of low-income mothers. In doing so, Caspi et al. separated the effects of support on the initial impact of daily stressors from the effects of support on the speed of recovery from stressors. They found that support did not buffer the initial (same-day) effects of stressful events on mood but it buffered the later-day effects such that only the low-support group showed enduring effects of stressors on mood.

From this brief survey, it should be clear that relationship processes are heavily involved in the experience of stress in daily life. Next we will argue that relationship processes may be key mediators of the effect of other variables on adaptation in daily life. We will use, for illustrative purposes, the case of personality.

Relationship Processes Mediate
the Effects of Personality
in Daily Life

Earlier we reviewed evidence suggesting that the stressful aspects of daily life are, overwhelmingly, interpersonal conflicts in work and family relationships. If relationship conflicts are the proximal sources of daily distress, then it seems plausible that they are *mediators* of the effects of other, more distal variables such as personality and living conditions. Support for this notion was found in a recent study of the effects of personality in daily life by Bolger and Schilling (1991).

Bolger and Schilling examined the mechanisms through which a major personality disposition, neuroticism, was expressed in day-to-day distress. They examined three potential mechanisms: Neuroticism might lead people to (a) become more exposed to daily stressors, (b) become more upset by the stressors to which they were exposed, or (c) become more distressed for reasons that have nothing to do with exposure or reactivity to daily stressors.

The authors found that exposure and reactivity to daily stressors did, in fact, account for a substantial amount of the effect of neuroticism on daily distress. What was particularly interesting about their results was that two of their nine categories of stressors, interpersonal conflicts with spouse and with other adults, accounted for 50% of what could be explained about the effect of neuroticism on daily distress.

It seems very likely that relationship conflicts mediate the effects of other variables in daily life. For example, environmental conditions such as neighborhood quality and degree of overcrowding affect psychological and physical well-being. In the study described earlier, Caspi et al. (1987) showed that these factors affected the initial impact and speed of recovery from daily stressors. Although the authors did not distinguish between different types of stressors, we suspect that interpersonal conflicts played a key role in mediating the effects of these environmental conditions.

Summary and Implications

The research reviewed above clearly shows that the effects of relationships on psychological well-being are mediated, in part, through recurrent patterns of support and conflict in daily life. This is true of the beneficial effects of relationships, which we illustrated with the example of wives' responses to husbands' work stress. It is also true of the powerful negative effects of relationships, which we illustrated with the example of daily conflicts at home and at work. The research also shows that these daily conflicts are, in addition, channels for the expression of other factors such as personality traits. Finally, the research demonstrates that relationship effects cannot be understood without reference to larger social structures and contexts such as the workplace.

There are at least three implications of this work for future research. First and most obvious, relationships researchers should pay serious attention to the findings in the stress literature showing that daily stressors have deleterious psychological and physical effects. These findings imply that everyday life in relationships is at least as worthy of research attention as major events in relationships. For example, although divorce can be a major trauma for the partners involved (Hetherington, Cox, & Cox, 1978), it is important to contrast this trauma with the cumulative effect of spending days, months, and years in a failed relationship.

The second implication of the work reviewed above is that traditional relationship concepts become meaningful when translated into the language of daily experience research, that is, when they are defined as recurrent patterns of daily interaction. For example, the term *relationship quality* becomes more vivid, and perhaps more useful, when it is specified as a recurrent pattern of reciprocal support in a relationship. We believe that the clarity and precision of other concepts in the literature, such as commitment and loneliness, would be increased by their being specified in this way.

The third implication is that daily experience methods can be used to assess the external validity of relationship processes studied in the laboratory. For example, Levenson and Gottman have demonstrated that distressed couples are more likely than nondistressed couples to exhibit affective linkage—where the negative emotions of one partner predict those of the other—when discussing a relationship problem in the laboratory (Levenson & Gottman, 1983, 1985). This is a fascinating discovery, but as yet we do not know whether such effects exist in the interactions of couples outside the laboratory. By tracking the negative emotions of spouses using daily diaries, it would be possible to ascertain whether couples in poor relationships exhibit greater emotional linkage and, if so, establish the contexts in which this occurs. It may well be that a contagion of stress between work and home is an important way in which some couples show greater affective linkage than others. Such concrete knowledge would facilitate interventions to limit distress in relationships.

Daily experience research is an orientation that continues to grow in both the stress and the relationships literatures. Clearly, we and others (Duck, 1986, 1991) see this as a good thing. The ultimate fruitfulness of the approach, however, will depend on investigations carried out in the years ahead. For now, we hope we have provided the reader with a flavor of work at this level of analysis, a level that we view as critical for understanding relationship processes, stress processes, and the interaction between the two.

6

Celebrations in Personal Relationships: A Transactional/Dialectical Perspective

Carol M. Werner

Irwin Altman

Barbara B. Brown

Joseph Ginat

B y focusing on contexts, the chapters in this volume address a neglected aspect of research on relationships. Our perspective is somewhat different than the others, in that we examine how both the physical environment and the social contexts are integral to relationship processes. For example, relationships take place in physical environments, and people use objects and settings as communicative symbols. Also, people are involved in myriad relationships that can both support and conflict with their roles in other relationships. In this chapter, we explore how celebrations (a) involve the physical and social environments and (b) help participants manage their roles in multiple relationships. Celebrations are an important aspect of relationships; they occur across societies, are pervasive over time, and can include frequent or infrequent events and major or minor activities. All, nevertheless, are an integral part of relationship development and all serve as important symbols of the relationship. They can contribute to relationship viability by highlighting the relationship itself, marking significant events in the history of the relationship, reflecting the degree of cultural influences on the relationship, and also recognizing unique aspects of the individuals in the relationship.

Our approach to relationships is guided by a dialectical and transactional worldview (Altman & Rogoff, 1987; Altman, Vinsel, & Brown, 1981; Brown, Altman, & Werner, 1992; Werner, Altman, Oxley, & Haggard, 1987) in which phenomena are treated as holistic unities involving people, psychological processes, physical and social contexts, and temporal qualities. One emphasis of this approach is that contexts are neither an inert background against which relationships develop nor the sole cause of relationship processes. Instead, contexts are *integral parts* of relationships. These features of our transactional perspective will be used to illustrate how celebrations enable dyads and families to highlight simultaneously their multiple and often conflicting identities as individuals, dyads, families, neighbors, and so on.

We begin with a discussion of a transactional worldview, then provide two case studies that explore celebration processes in greater depth, and end with suggestions for future theory and research.

A Transactional Worldview

Definitions and Assumptions

(1) Phenomena are composed of mutually defining aspects. Individuals define and are defined by their social and physical worlds. An individual's many roles as husband, friend, father, and so on require counterparts (wife, friend, offspring, and so on), and the individual gains meaning and identity in interac-

tions with that counterpart just as the counterpart gains and gives meaning to the individual. At a broader level of scale, families and groups gain and give meaning through interactions with larger collectives, such as the family that simultaneously strengthens familial bonds and contributes to neighborhood identity as it participates in a local street festival (or, alternatively, the family that strengthens its internal ties but contributes to a fractionated neighborhood identity by refusing to participate in the festival). As discussed below, the physical environment is not a passive background for these interactions but also contributes to and gains meaning from events. In this chapter, we focus on dyads and families and how celebrations highlight the relationship, individuals in the relationship, and broader social contexts.

(2) Social units and their embeddedness. Relationship participants can be viewed at many levels of analysis, and each of these levels is or can be embedded in myriad larger social contexts (see, in this volume, the chapters by Klein and Milardo and by Stein). At one level is the individual—a complex, psychological entity who may be linked to another person in a dyad, with both participants seeking to maintain separate identities while simultaneously becoming a couple. At another level is the dyad as a unity, also embedded in myriad social contexts, such as each partner's social network, their joint social network, each partner's kin group, their neighbors, institutional groups, and the larger society. Many of these social groups themselves encompass smaller subgroups and are simultaneously nested in and parts of larger groups.

What is crucial about our perspective on these participants and their physical contexts is that they form *coherent social units* (Altman, 1977); they are not treated as separate "interacting" parts. Individuals give meaning to and are defined by their membership in dyads and larger collectives; dyads give meaning to and are defined by families; and so on. These various social units (along with temporal qualities) are best viewed as being embedded in and as *aspects* of one another, not as separate entities. For example, Baxter (1991) argued persuasively that individuals do not come fully formed to relationships but, instead, are created in the process of bonding and developing the relationship. While endorsing this dynamic, transactional view of relationships, we would expand it in two respects. First, individuals gain meaning in other transactions as well (e.g., school, work, play), and the selves created in these other domains are part of what each individual brings to the relationship. Second, we would expand the unit of analysis beyond individuals bonding dyadically and would include relationships involving all of the social units, such as couple/kin group bonding, family/neighbor bonding, and so on. Thus these "social units" do not come fully formed to a relationship but are also molded and continually shaped in the process of building relationship ties. In this chapter, we examine how celebrations and other rituals reflect and support developing dyad/family and family/neighborhood relationships.

(3) Time and temporal qualities. In other contexts, we have examined temporal qualities of phenomena (Werner, Altman, & Oxley, 1985; Werner & Haggard, 1985; Werner, Haggard, Altman, & Oxley, 1988), distinguishing between unique and recurrent events (linear and cyclical temporal qualities) and their relative emphasis on continuity and change. We have noted that time and temporal qualities are integral to relationship phenomena (e.g., a transition from acquaintances to friends does not occur on a predetermined, outside-of-the-relationship schedule). In the current analysis, we focus primarily on commonly celebrated, recurrent events, such as annual birthdays, anniversaries, and holidays, exploring how dialectical processes between individuals and social groups are reflected in these activities. Although our case studies focus on established dyads and families, celebrations are important to relationships of all types and stages.

(4) The physical environment. Physical environments range in size from micro to macro environments and can be natural or built forms. Social relationships involve objects and things, take place in homes, yards, neighborhoods, and outdoors, and—as we shall illustrate in this chapter—can be symbolized and supported by their environments in many ways (Altman, Brown, Staples, &

Werner, 1992). In the transactional view, these objects and places are not outside of relationships but are an integral part of them: They gain from and give meaning to the relationship. The time and place for events, the objects that are involved, and the person(s) who provide(s) them are all significant aspects of individual and relationship definition. In analyses of courtship and weddings (Altman et al., 1992; Brown, Werner, & Altman, in press), we found that physical places and objects played central roles in these celebrations and were also important indicators of which kin and in-laws would play important roles in the couple's future life. For example, some societies prescribe that particular household items or parts of the home be given as wedding gifts by particular relatives; this connects that relative and kin group to the newlyweds in both concrete and symbolic ways. This chapter examines relationship-environment unities in the exploration of where events occur and what objects are involved as central aspects of celebrations.

(5) Dialectical and psychological processes are dynamic and unifying aspects of relationships. Elsewhere, we have described how people and physical environments are connected into ho-listic, transactional unities by myriad psychological processes such as self-disclosure, territorial regulation, dominance and control processes, and so on (Werner et al., 1985). This chapter complements that work by adding a dialectical "motor" to those processes; we explore how activities and environments ebb and flow between those that highlight the focal relationship (e.g., the dyad, the family) and those that highlight competing identities or relationships (e.g., partners' uniqueness or kin-group ties).

We focus on the general dialectical opposition involving people and society and its subordinate dialectic of individual/community identity. The person-society dialectic includes the idea that people need and desire to be unique, distinctive, and autonomous while at the same time, but to varying degrees, need and desire to be part of a larger group (e.g., individual/dyad, dyad/kin group; Altman, in press; Altman et al., 1981). This person/society dialectic can be seen in a variety of more specific opposites such as individual/col-lective identity, physical accessibility/inaccessibility, psychological openness/closedness, connection/autonomy, and the like, all reflecting a fundamental interplay among social units. Each of these dialectics can be manifested at the micro level in specific relationship events. For example, the individual/collective identity dialectic can be expressed in wedding gifts that reflect the giver's and recipient's unique identities as well as their union in marriage (monogrammed gifts). We assume that the two opposing sides are always present and that their relative salience varies. As we will illustrate in the case studies below, sometimes individual or couple identity is salient and sometimes family or collective identity is salient, and their relative salience varies with time and circumstances. In this chapter, we explore how dyads and families use celebrations to manage the often competing identities in their relationships.

Rituals in Interpersonal Relationships

The current analysis focuses on how rituals provide opportunities and obligations for social units—individual/dyad, dyad/nuclear family, nuclear family/kin group, and so on—to explore, develop, and celebrate their unique and their collective identities *simultaneously*. Thus, as our case studies will suggest, a dyad may celebrate a birthday that highlights the celebrant, the partner, and the couple; they may celebrate a wedding anniversary in a way that highlights their unity as a dyad but also signals each partner's uniqueness and autonomy; and they may celebrate a holiday that declares their uniqueness as a dyad but also emphasizes and strengthens their membership in each one's family of origin. Families may celebrate holidays in ways that emphasize their unique bonds as a family but simultaneously reflect their membership in larger collectives such as religious or neighborhood organizations or the society at large. In each of these events, although one pole of the identity dialectic may be salient, the other is present and lends an additional level of meaning to the activities. Sometimes the participants achieve a harmonious and satisfactory blend of these various identities, and sometimes one identity is achieved at the expense of the other, potentially resulting in disharmony and dissatisfaction.

An array of terms have been used to refer to special occasions: *rituals, festivals, celebrations, holidays.* The trend among family and relationship scholars has been to follow Wolin and Bennett (1984) and use the word *ritual* as a broad category, with other terms used for more specific events. Many relationships researchers draw extensively on anthropological literature, such as the work of Turner (1967), Van Gennep (1909/1960), and Moore and Myerhoff (1977); however, a detailed explication of those writings is beyond the scope of this chapter. Wolin and Bennett (1984) described three types of family rituals: *Celebrations* are holidays and rites of passage prescribed by the larger society such as Christmas, birthdays, and Mother's Day. *Family traditions* are activities not prescribed by the larger society but done recurrently, such as particular ways of celebrating Christmas and other societal holidays, regular trips to favorite vacation spots, eating or preparing favorite foods, and so on. *Patterned routines* are smaller scale but recurrent events, such as greeting and leave-taking styles among friends and family members, regular or recurrent routines and get-togethers, and so on.

Although Wolin and Bennett limited their analyses to family rituals, we have adopted a perspective that includes social units at many levels of scale—individuals, dyads, nuclear families, extended families, networks, neighborhoods, and so on. Furthermore, whereas Wolin and Bennett suggested that each type of tradition enhanced a particular identity (cultural, familial, or individual), in accord with a dialectical approach, our thesis is that all three kinds of rituals can support an *array* of identities. For example, Christmas can be celebrated in ways that emphasize membership in the broader society (decorating a home's exterior), with innovations that emphasize family or group bonds and the group's unique identity (photo greeting cards of the family), as well as with features that emphasize individual uniqueness (gifts that emphasize the personalities of both giver, recipient, and/or the relationship between them). Our dialectical perspective allows us to explore the relative emphases on and interplay among these sometimes conflicting identities. We next turn to two case studies that illustrate these processes. Our focus is on "celebrations"; however, the analysis could easily be extended to other kinds of rituals.

Case Studies

Celebrations Among Mormon Polygynists

This case study examines how modern-day polygynous families maintain multiple, unique, dyadic relationships between a husband and each wife, while simultaneously attempting to establish harmonious communal relationships between wives and across the family as a whole. This analysis is based on Altman and Ginat's (1989, 1990) research on fundamentalist Mormon polygynists who currently reside in the western United States. The group practices polygyny because of religious convictions even though these beliefs conflict with edicts of the larger Church of Jesus Christ of Latter-Day Saints (Mormons) and state laws that outlaw polygyny. There are several sects of modern Mormon polygynists; Altman and Ginat's work is with two main groups, each numbering between 6,000 and 10,000 people, one in a rural and the other in an urban area. More than 100 interviews and observations were conducted with husbands and wives from two dozen polygynous families. Information was collected on a range of topics pertaining to family management of the ongoing opposition between dyadic and familial bonds, such as decisions to add a wife to a family, husband/wife relationships, wife/wife relationships, family structure, living arrangements, rotation of husbands among households, privacy regulation, management of husband's belongings, and others.

The Research Focus

The research program examines dialectical oppositions associated with husband/wife and wife/wife relationships in plural families. Modern-day Mormon polygynists hold to Western culture's monogamous values regarding the uniqueness and special character of the dyadic relationship between a husband and a wife. They believe in romantic love, the ideal of a special bond that prevails in marital relationships, and the importance of building a close relationship with a marital partner. At the same time, they are guided by religious beliefs holding that the plural family should ideally function as a harmonious and unified communal system, with wives supporting, loving, sharing, and cooperating with one another and with the family functioning in a constructive and unified fashion. The generic question addressed is how the fundamentalist culture as a whole, and individual families and family members in particular, deal with and develop mechanisms for simultaneously meeting *dyadic* and *communal family* goals. Altman and Ginat are pursuing this general question in several aspects of couple and family life, including celebrations, holidays, and special events. Their analyses tap into a variety of social and psychological processes, such as interpersonal relationships, family dynamics, and use of the physical environment.

Polygynist families participate in and develop celebration practices that sometimes are primarily dyadic, sometimes are primarily communal, and sometimes involve both communal and dyadic features. In fact, in accord with a dialectical perspective, many seemingly purely dyadic or purely communal celebrations often contain aspects of the other. Furthermore, stresses and strains in marriages or family relations can be reflected in celebratory practices that go awry with respect to dyadic and communal processes.

Individual and Dyadic Celebrations

A wife's birthday. A polygynous wife's birthday usually involves the husband and wife doing something special in her honor. Over and over, family members reported that the husband usually paid special attention to the wife and/or planned special activities for just the two of them. In addition, a wife's birthday celebration usually took place in special environmental settings—usually away from home.

- Family 5 (husband and 4 wives): A wife's birthday was celebrated separately with the husband. The husband and wife would go out to a movie or to dinner, with the wife choosing the activity. On occasion, they might also visit a temple, relatives, or friends.
- Family 18 (husband and 4 wives): The husband always spent an extra day with a wife on her birthday. They went to a movie and dinner and sometimes spent the night at a hotel.

Thus a wife's birthday honors both her individuality and the unique dyadic relationship with the husband, and it does so in a distinctive environmental setting. Similar to the event in monogamous relationships, birthdays permit each member of a couple to acknowledge the other and simultaneously emphasize their special relationship. It is important to realize that celebrating a wife's birthday in the manner described above is a very special event, because most of these families are in difficult financial straits and have time-consuming responsibilities in large families and in church that leave little time for out-of-the-ordinary activities. Thus celebrating a wife's birthday and doing so in an environmental context away from home is a special event that couple members anticipate and remember.

Although strongly individualistic and dyadic, wives' birthday celebrations can have communal aspects, such as when a cowife participates in the event:

- Family 2 (husband and 4 wives): Although the husband and each wife usually celebrated a wife's birthday by themselves, there were occasions when another wife baked a birthday cake for her cowife. On some occasions, a wife's birthday was celebrated by everyone in the family. Furthermore, one of the wives would sometimes remind the husband about another wife's birthday.
- Family 12 (husband and 2 wives): Although a wife's birthday was typically celebrated by the husband and wife going out to dinner and a movie alone, on some occasions a wife cared for the celebrating wife's children. On one birthday, another wife cooked and served dinner to the celebrating wife and husband.

Thus wives' birthday celebrations sometimes involved other wives, symbolizing the communal aspect of family life while simultaneously acknowledging the individuality of a sister wife and the validity of her dyadic bond with the husband. A wife reminding the husband of the birthday of another wife, or hosting a dinner for the husband and another wife, may reinforce the importance of that wife and her birthday, the special character of that husband/wife dyad, and the communal unity of the family.

In summary, the birthday of a plural wife is an occasion that highlights the individuality of the wife and the unique dyadic relationship of that wife and her husband. At the same time, there often are communal elements to birthday celebrations in which other wives sometimes participate, therefore yielding a blend of dyadic and communal aspects to wives' birthday celebrations. Furthermore, there is a tendency for birthday celebrations to take place away from home when they are treated as a dyadic event and to take place at home when they involve a communal feature.

Communal Family Celebrations

Communal celebrations bring together all or many members of a plural family in a common activity, thereby displaying their unity as a family. Such celebrations include a husband/father's birthday, Sunday dinner, a family vacation, Thanksgiving, and Christmas.

Husband's/father's birthdays. The husband/father is a significant individual and patriarchal symbol to his family. Is his birthday celebrated in a communal fashion by all wives and children? Or are there separate celebrations with each of his families? Our information indicates that it is customary to celebrate a husband's birthday as a family communal event. In some respects, the husband/father's birthday serves several purposes: It honors him as an individual; it symbolizes the communal unity and organization of the family; it highlights his role as family leader.

- Family 1 (husband and 4 wives): The husband/father's birthday is celebrated in a variety of ways but usually involves all of the wives and/or the whole family. For example, one year the wives and children gave him a surprise party, and the wives and his mother took him out to dinner. Although children are often involved, more typically the wives celebrate collectively with him.

- Family 4 (husband and 5 wives): "Father's birthday" is celebrated as a major family event in the family—actually as an alternative to Christmas. Several hundred relatives also attend. All the children and grandchildren are given a small gift from him, and the children give him gifts. The celebration also involves children and grandchildren performing as well as a family meal prepared by the wives and daughters. This is an important celebration that emphasizes family unity and the man's role as family patriarch.

- Family 5 (husband and 4 wives): This family celebrates the husband's birthday intermittently, usually with the whole family having dinner together. Because the husband was born on his own father's fiftieth birthday, the celebration also links the family to the husband's patriarchal line. On his most recent birthday, the wives presented him with an album of pictures of all the wives and their children, thereby reflecting family communality.

In a few cases, there are dyadic aspects to a husband's birthday celebration in which each wife and her children celebrate separately with the husband/father. Or, occasionally, subsets of wives living in the same dwelling might have special celebrations:

- Family 10 (husband and 8 wives): On some occasions, the whole family celebrates the husband/father's birthday together; at other times, separate celebrations occur with each wife and her children—resulting in eight birthday parties! On another occasion, four families who live in one dwelling held a joint birthday for him, as did three other families in the other dwelling.

In summary, most families celebrate the husband/father's birthday as a family communal event, simultaneously honoring him as an individual but also symbolizing his patriarchal leadership of a unified family. Because wives often jointly celebrate a husband/father's birthday, they can provide an event that reinforces the idea of a plural family as a harmonious group of sister-wives and children.

Family celebrations and traditions. Several families participated in weekly, monthly, and other periodic communal gatherings. Often, Sunday church and mealtime activities brought whole families together

• Family 12 (husband and 2 wives): On Sunday the entire family would have dinner and go to church together, with the husband sitting between his two wives. On Sunday evening they would often invite guests to their home for tea.

Some families also celebrated in special places and at certain times:

• Family 6 (husband and 8 wives): This family holds a large party every couple of years. One wife noted that her own parental family had a large get-together every other year, usually on the birthday of her father or grandfather.
• Family 4 (husband and 5 wives): One major event that signals the communal and patriarchal spirit of this family is a monthly meeting of all members of the family. The 37 sons and 28 daughters and their families return to the family home for a weekend every month for religious and family meetings and activities. This monthly meeting was organized by the husband/father more than 20 years ago to foster and sustain a sense of family unity, especially among sons. At their religious meetings and in collective meals and recreational events, the unity of the family is emphasized. The husband/father conducts events and continually emphasizes the role of each male and female member of the family in sustaining the family as a communal and unified group.

In summary, plural families often develop unique family celebrations in which everyone participates in a communal fashion, in specified physical environments, thereby enhancing and making visible the idealized unity and communality of the whole plural family.

Cultural Holidays

Plural families often celebrate traditional American holidays in a communal fashion, with the physical setting an intrinsic aspect of the event:

- Family 5 (husband and 4 wives): The family celebrates Thanksgiv
ing, Memorial Day, and Mother's Day communally. Thanksgiving is
held at the home of the wife with the largest living room, with the
wives coordinating and sharing the preparation of the meal. Other
holidays are also celebrated communally in different homes. The
family celebrates the 4th of July and a Mormon pioneer holiday with
family picnics.

Christmas. The celebration of Christmas often highlights the
communal quality of each family. At the same time, observances
in some families also involve dyadic subgroups within the communal whole. This blend of communal and dyadic aspects of Christmas
is reflected in the location of celebrations, gift giving practices,
and other unique family modes of observing the holiday.

(1) Physical settings. Some families celebrate all or part of the
holiday in a single home—sometimes to exchange gifts in the
family, sleep over together, have a family dinner, or the like.

- Family 1 (husband and 4 wives): The whole family slept in one home
on Christmas Eve. The adults slept in the living room near the
Christmas tree and presents, and the children slept elsewhere in the
home—in beds, on sofas, and in sleeping bags.
- Family 10 (husband and 8 wives): The entire family gathered in one
of their homes to exchange gifts and have a meal together. It is the
only occasion during the year when all of the married sons and their
families come to the family home.

Spending Christmas Eve or Christmas Day together is a complicated affair in plural families. Imagine family members sleeping everywhere, activity and noise ever present as children
anticipate the festivities and play with one another, parents and
older children preparing massive amounts of food and undertak-
ing the organization and logistics necessary to keep things on an
even keel. Amidst the expected stresses of such an experience,
one might expect such a celebrations to be arousing and mem-
orable for family members, adding to their sense of being part
of a unified and communal family. It is likely that the physical
setting adds to the meaning and memory of such events.

Although most families celebrate Christmas as a communal event, some wives also observe Christmas in their own homes with their children. For example, in one family, each wife has her own Christmas tree that she decorates with her children while also celebrating part of the holiday communally with one another, the husband, and all the children.

(2) Gift giving. The exchange of gifts at Christmas time—environmental symbols of the holiday—can be a real challenge in plural families, given the fact that there are often large numbers of children. Do all wives give gifts to all of the children in the family, including those of other wives, thereby reflecting a communal practice? Or are gifts given only by mothers to their own children, reflecting a strong dyadic orientation? Information suggests that some families are highly communal in their orientation to gift giving, whereas others combine communal and dyadic practices. Strong communal orientations are reflected in several families:

- Family 2 (husband and 4 wives): Most gifts in this family are made by the wives, although a few are purchased. Each wife makes a gift for each child in the family, not just her own children, and the adults all exchange gifts with one another.
- Family 5 (husband and 4 wives): Family members draw a name out of a hat at Thanksgiving and give gifts at Christmas to the person whose name they select. Selection of gift recipients is not based on subfamilies but is done across the whole plural family.

Gift giving practices reflect a strong communal orientation when all children receive gifts from all wives or when gift giving transcends a mother and her children. At the same time, there are cases reflecting both communal and dyadic orientations.

- Family 1 (husband and 4 wives): Members of the family draw lots to give each other gifts without regard to their natal family. Each mother also gives gifts to her own children, yielding a blend of dyadic and communal practices.

(3) Special Christmas celebrations. Some families engaged in unique and occasional celebrations that reflected blends of communal and dyadic activities.

- Family 1 (husband and 4 wives): One year when the husband's father was ill, the wives and their children organized activities over the "twelve days of Christmas." Each wife and her children were responsible for giving gifts to the ill grandfather on a rotating basis. On alternating nights, they anonymously left a present on the doorstep of the grandfather's home. On the twelfth and final night, the husband, wives, and children assembled outside the grandfather's home, presented him with a gift from all of them, and sang Christmas carols.

The organization of the celebration, the collective gift, and the caroling by the whole family on the twelfth night of Christmas reflect nicely the communal aspect of this family's celebration. Yet, the responsibility of each wife and her children to provide individual gifts symbolizes their distinctiveness as a set of dyadic families. Furthermore, these communal and dyadic features of polygynous families are displayed in active use of the physical environment, such as gift giving and the locations of special events.

Breakdowns in Family Celebrations

Celebrations do not always go smoothly in polygynous families—just as they are not always perfect in monogamous families. In many cases, stresses and conflicts about celebrations mirror fundamental tensions in other aspects of family life. Problems associated with celebrations often reflect underlying conflicts concerning the family's failure to manage a successful blend of dyadic and communal family dynamics. In the following examples, the sole informants are wives who had left their husbands and the polygynous community.

- Family 12 (husband and 2 wives): The two wives in this family had conflicts in a variety of aspects of life. The second wife (the informant) felt that the husband favored the first wife. For example, for a while the whole family went to church and had dinner together every Sunday. They eventually stopped this communal family practice, however, because there was too much tension between the two wives and with the husband.

- In addition, although the family celebrated Thanksgiving together fairly regularly at either wife's home, the second wife indicated that decisions about how, when, and where Thanksgiving would be celebrated were made by the husband and first wife. The second wife felt left out of the decision making and never even had very much advance notice about the details of the event.

- As another example, they had a tradition of opening Christmas presents as a whole family, spending the evening with guests, and having a large family Christmas dinner. At the same time, there was conflict around the celebration of Christmas because on some occasions the husband and the first wife went to visit that wife's parents, leaving the second wife alone or visiting with her own parents without the husband.

- Family 14 (husband and 2 wives): In another family, there was serious tension between the two wives, some of which focused around Christmas gift giving practices. The first wife, who eventually left the family, described how the second wife saved money from the family budget for Christmas presents for her own children while living off the budget and income of the first wife. The result was that the first wife's children did not have very many Christmas gifts, resulting in considerable tension between the wives and families. On occasion, the first wife spent Christmas with her parents because she knew that they would treat her children better than would the husband and second wife.

These two families could not resolve the competing goals of building strong dyadic ties and strong family bonds. The dialectical opposition between dyad/family identities was not handled successfully, and the systems deteriorated.

Summary

The case studies of contemporary Mormon polygynous families highlight several key themes of this chapter. First, social relationships exist and function in social contexts that are part and parcel of the very definition of relationships. Thus husband/wife dyads in polygynous families are embedded in one another as well as being embedded in relationships among wives. Dyadic relationships cannot be understood separately from multiple husband/wife and cowife relationships. Nor can monogamous relationships be fully understood without taking into account family and kin relationships, work and social relationships, and other social contexts within which they are embedded.

Second, the physical environment is a crucial context within which polygynous and monogamous relationships are played out. Social and psychological processes occur in, make use of, and are reflected in settings, places, and objects. Thus it is essential to see how celebrations and other activities in contemporary Mormon polygynous families involve the physical environment as a salient context.

Family and Neighborhood Celebrations

Research by Werner and Brown and their colleagues illustrates how many Salt Lake families use holiday celebrations simultaneously to strengthen bonds within families and between families and the neighborhood, thereby focusing on the interplay between a family's unique identity and their membership in a larger social group. Data come from several different neighborhoods. One analysis is based on a sample of almost 150 students in the university's student housing village to learn how they celebrate Halloween (Werner, 1989). A second analysis drew participants from a suburban as well as a downtown neighborhood. The suburban data set includes interview and observational data from over 130 residents at Halloween and Christmas (Brown & Werner, 1985), with a follow-up at Halloween 5 years later (Werner, 1989). These data were supplemented with data from a downtown neighborhood in which Christmas decorating data were opportunistically collected as part of another study. Third is an examination of a single block and their activities as "Christmas Street," a 40-year tradition of extensive decorating and planned Christmas activities (Oxley, Haggard, Werner, & Altman, 1986; Werner et al., 1987).

Celebrating Halloween

Halloween is a community event in many Salt Lake neighborhoods. It is a time when children (often accompanied by their parents) traverse the whole neighborhood, seeking treats and making threats of tricks. Children of all ages plan their costumes well in advance, wear them around the neighborhood and to school as well as for trick-or-treating, and in general become very involved in the anticipation and actual experience of Halloween. Household decorations range from a few school projects displayed in windows to porches arranged with carefully carved pumpkins or elaborate displays of scarecrows, enormous spider webs, and the like. During the 1980s Halloween was a major event in Salt Lake City, and newcomers to the area remarked on the vigor of celebration here compared with their cities of origin. The research suggests that Halloween provides opportunities for intrafamily bonding, both family and community bonding, and predominantly community bonding. Different neighborhoods offer these opportunities to different degrees and different families participate at different levels of involvement and enthusiasm.

University student housing. This study provided a rich description of how residents celebrated Halloween, their attitudes toward the holiday and its activities, and its relationship to their identities as family and community members. Data came from questionnaires with open- and closed-format items and from raters' observations of residents' Halloween decorations. Responses to the questionnaire indicated that many student families used this holiday as an opportunity to bond as a family as well as to link themselves to and express their identities as part of the larger neighborhood and society. Some activities tended to emphasize the family side of a family/neighborhood identity dialectic, others emphasized neighborhood identity, and others appeared to give equal weight to family and neighborhood identities.

For many participants, family identity and bonding were evident in an array of activities and attitudes toward Halloween. First, although having a child in the home was not a prerequisite for enjoying and participating in Halloween, children were a central feature of the holiday. In open-ended comments, parents reported that their own involvement and pleasure in Halloween were strongly linked to their children's enthusiasm. Residents with children were more likely to participate in a variety of Halloween-related activities, such as buying and carving pumpkins as a family, decorating the home together, buying, making, and showing off costumes to each other, trick-or-treating as a family, and so on. Furthermore, high rates of participation in these family-initiated activities were associated with reports of strong personal and family Halloween spirit and statements that Halloween strengthened their identities as individuals, partners, and parents (the sample contained very few single-parent families). So, for many, Halloween provides an assortment of opportunities for expressing and enhancing selected individual and family bonds and identities.

Halloween also served as the interface between family and community, simultaneously supporting individual, family, and neighborhood identities. One opportunity for connecting to neighbors is by encouraging trick-or-treaters, and respondents used a variety of techniques for accomplishing this. The most frequently cited mechanism was to display a cutout figure provided by housing management (it had been devised in response to noncelebrants' complaints that trick-or-treaters disturbed their studying). Other cues ranged from the traditional illuminated porch light to more dynamic mechanisms such as playing Halloween music or dressing in costumes and standing in the doorway to welcome the trick-or-treaters. A number of respondents wrote how much they enjoyed meeting neighborhood children in this way as well as the trick-or-treaters' pleasure at the spooky, scary music or costume, suggesting that their individual as well as family and neighbor identities were enhanced with these practices. Connections between families and their neighbors were also supported through participation in a variety of other holiday-related events (parties, costume and decorating competitions, and so on). Many activities had been specifically designed by the housing management to increase recognition, interaction, and a sense of community among residents, and, indeed, residents who participated in these activities reported that the holiday strengthened their identity as a neighbor. So this holiday provides opportunities for residents to strengthen their friendships with neighbors and neighborhood children, but these same activities can contribute to individual and family identities as well.

Finally, there was also evidence that Halloween provided opportunities for community bonding independent of family-related activities. A set of questionnaire items tapped how much respondents liked their neighbors; this scale was not associated with house decorating, or Halloween spirit, or family Halloween activities. It was, however, associated with neighborhood holiday activities; the more respondents knew and liked their neighbors, the more likely they were to participate in community-sponsored Halloween activities and to feel as though Halloween strengthened their identity as a neighbor. So, in some ways or for some people, Halloween provides opportunities to express neighborhood cohesiveness, and these can be independent of other activities and feelings.

Although Halloween was greeted enthusiastically by most residents and was the source of family and community bonding, many people—especially those without children—did not enjoy or participate in any Halloween events (especially the interruptions by trick-or-treaters). Some families with children even refused to participate or to allow their children to trick or treat. This small minority cited the ancient pagan meaning of Halloween or the witchcraft aspect and said that this was contrary to their values. Often, these parents arranged alternative activities more in accord with their particular beliefs, such as a family trip to the library or family gatherings without Halloween themes as a way to keep the evening special for their children without invoking any Halloween spirit. The activities were variable, some involving only the nuclear family, some involving broader kin ties, and others linking family to community groups such as religious subgroups. By choosing particular activities and social contexts, these families still used the holiday as an opportunity for family bonding while systematically connecting themselves to particular groups and traditions and avoiding connecting themselves with others.

Suburban neighborhood. A similar profile of Halloween as an opportunity to express and build both family and community identities was observed in the large suburban neighborhood (Brown & Werner, 1985; Werner, 1989). For example, with respect to Halloween decorations, residents differentiated between the interior and exterior of their homes, decorating their home's interior to show off homemade decorations and to enhance their family's holiday spirit and decorating their home's exteriors to please neighbors and enhance the neighborhood's holiday spirit.

Summary. Thus participation in Halloween activities gives many respondents a great deal of pleasure and provides opportunities for families to bond together as families to strengthen their personal identities and their identities as family members as well as to strengthen their ties to and identification with the neighborhood. At the same time, people selectively participated in events; many families did not participate in any community activities except for trick-or-treating; many without children did not participate at all; and a few with children rejected the holiday for its sinister meaning. So, in accord with a dialectical perspective, this holiday allows people to express individual, family, and community identities in varying ways and to varying degrees. Furthermore, the holistic analysis indicated that the physical environment was an integral part of these events, as revealed in how and where people decorated, how they made trick-or-treaters feel welcome or unwelcome, and where they went for parties and trick-or-treating activities.

Celebrating Christmas

Many analyses of Christmas activities focus on its role in family bonding (Caplow, 1982; Caplow, Bahr, Chadwick, Hill, & Williamson, 1982), emphasizing that it is a time of family reunions, family reminiscence, family food rituals, and family gift giving. Indeed, Caplow (1982) mostly found evidence of contact among immediate family and other relatives, even those living far apart; his respondents reported very few get-togethers with neighbors during the Christmas season. Research in Salt Lake has focused on Christmas as an opportunity for community bonding and the expression of community identity, although some evidence emerged in these studies that Christmas can serve individual and family identity functions.

Christmas Street. Christmas Street is a cul-de-sac of approximately 30 homes in a modest Salt Lake neighborhood. The neighbors—many original residents on the block—have a more than 40-year history of collective decorating: Every year, almost every home is decorated; decorations are put up and taken down on the same dates by all residents; they turn the lights on and off in unison every evening; they have collective decorations such as a neon sign declaring the block to be "Christmas Street" and a large communal tree; they share expenses for the celebration; and they hold an annual block party and children's parade (Oxley et al., 1986; Werner et al., 1987). We reasoned that a group of neighbors who could mount a celebration of this scale would provide a unique opportunity to study celebration and community bonding as a holistic phenomenon. Indeed, the data emerged in clear patterns such that people who were most committed to the annual activities expressed the strongest Christmas spirit, reported the most social contact with neighbors during this time of year, and had more elaborate Christmas decorations. This convergence of attitudes, friendships, and exterior decorating did not occur in the summer. So the analysis revealed that community identity was stronger at Christmas than in summertime and that this community identity was expressed in a coherent pattern of attitudes, neighboring relationships, involvement in Christmas Street activities, and decoration of the homes' exteriors.

This analysis was not designed to examine how family bonds were strengthened during Christmas; however, the theme did emerge in interviews with the residents of Christmas Street in two ways. First, parents often participated in the monthlong series of events because their children enjoyed the activities so much. In fact, one new resident on the street reported that the person who had sold him his home had deliberately concealed the fact that this was "Christmas Street" for fear the resident would not want to participate in the obligatory events. Although he disliked the deception, the resident became quite enthusiastic about living on this block because his child took so much pleasure in the activities; he saw it as a special opportunity that he, as a father, could provide his family. The second family-related theme that emerged involved the annual children's parade and party. Many older residents reported using it as a family event by inviting their children and grandchildren to attend and paying the nominal fee so that the grandchildren could also receive the traditional stocking gift. So, although the annual celebration has many aspects that emphasize neighborhood bonds (e.g., former residents are invited to the children's parade), many families treat it as an opportunity for intrafamily bonding as well.

Suburban and downtown neighborhoods. Aside from Christmas Street, Christmas is not so clearly a communal celebration in Salt Lake City (although it may provide opportunities for bonding and expressing identity with other groups that were not studied, such as religious, friendship, or professional entities). For example, data from the large suburban sample indicated no association between psychological bonding to the block and decorating the home's exterior for Christmas and no association between bonding to the block and the creativity or attractiveness of exterior decorations. In the downtown neighborhood (Werner, 1992), there was a weak association between a sense of neighborhood bonding and the presence of Christmas decorations. So the evidence that Christmas decorations reflect bonding with proximal neighbors may vary from neighborhood to neighborhood.

On the other hand, closer analysis indicates that Christmas decorations may be part of a total process whereby Salt Lake residents can integrate themselves into a neighborhood. So, for example, in the suburban neighborhood, the *locations* where people placed decorations were associated with a sense of neighborhood cohesiveness and identification with the neighborhood. Residents who liked their neighbors and were attached to the block were more likely to decorate their home's entryway, as though welcoming visitors and neighbors into their home. In addition, undergraduate students *expected* people who decorated their homes' exteriors to be more accessible and friendly. That is, when examining photographs taken during the Christmas season, students rated the residents of holiday-decorated homes as being more gregarious and open, and more likely to be friendly and accessible neighbors, than the residents of homes not decorated for the Christmas season (Werner, Peterson-Lewis, & Brown, 1989). So Christmas decorations may be part of a total system whereby residents can signal their unity with neighbors, and others can read those cues and respond by initiating contacts and building communal ties.

Summary. These analyses support the view that Christmas can provide opportunities for community bonding and that different residents and neighborhoods participate in these opportunities at different levels. The strongest evidence for community bonding comes from Christmas Street, where the entire neighborhood is involved in communal decorating and celebrating. People do experience stronger ties with neighbors and a stronger "Christmas spirit" the more actively they participate in the block's activities, so these events do support identification and bonding with neighbors. Data from other neighborhoods are variable, but some analyses suggest that residents may use Christmas as a time to express their cohesiveness or to initiate contacts with neighbors. Although not a focus of our studies, but consistent with a dialectical approach, other research (Caplow, 1982) indicates that Christmas is a time in which family bonding is a central focus.

Summary of Christmas and Halloween

These qualitative and quantitative analyses show the myriad ways in which people celebrate family and community holidays and indicate that people can use these celebrations to emphasize and strengthen social bonds at different levels of scale. Some activities and events primarily involve family bonding; some involve community bonding; and some reflect both family and community bonding. Although these particular studies were not done to allow comparisons across neighborhoods, the variety of activities and the different patterns of correlations/absence of correlations among attitudes, behaviors, and social ties fit with the view that different families and neighborhoods celebrate in different ways and ascribe different meanings to events.

Discussion

Implications for Relationship Research

Holistic Analyses

We have used a dialectical/transactional perspective to analyze how celebrations permit people to develop and express their identities as individuals and as members of dyads, families, and neighborhoods. The analysis supports the views that individuals and dyads are embedded in, and define and are defined by, myriad social relationships. Thus it is impossible to understand relationship processes outside of their social and physical contexts. We illustrated how celebrations can be used to make salient one or the other side of an "individual/community identity" dialectic and suggested that in making decisions about people, place, and time—how, when, and where to celebrate, what objects to use, who to involve, how long to spend, and so on—people implicitly and explicitly use celebrations to manage the often competing identities in their relationships.

The examples on which we drew tended to emphasize that celebrations can reflect the dialectical "unity of opposites," or the idea that practices can support various identities *simultaneously,* such as when a single act reflects both the individual and the dyad or when competing identities are supported by different features of the same celebration. Other scholars have also argued that both sides of an identity dialectic benefit from the other, such as when the individual's separate identity is strengthened through intimate interactions while the dyad simultaneously grows and becomes stronger with intimacy (see, for example, Askham, 1976; Goldsmith, 1990), when the family bond grows stronger as adolescents are allowed greater autonomy from the family (Davis, 1988), or when a daughter and mother find new bases of relating as the mother guides her newlywed daughter in her unaccustomed roles as wife and homemaker (Leonard, 1980). Other research, however, has found more evidence of dialectical "opposition," or work indicating that building one set of bonds can make it difficult or impossible to develop others. Nydegger (1986) reported a common pattern wherein fathers who remarried late in life became distant from their adult children, and Milardo, Johnson, and Huston (1983) found that increasing intimacy between a man and woman often resulted in the loss of connection to each one's separate social network. So it is important to examine both constructive and destructive processes in social units and to consider how actions and changes in one aspect may reverberate into other areas of this and other relationships.

Continuity and Change

One consequence of adopting a dialectical approach is that relationships are not viewed as static but as containing both continuity and change. Indeed, although we did not focus on this dynamic in our current case studies, we assume that relationships need both continuity and change to remain viable and that too much of either can destroy the relationship (Altman et al.,

1981; Baxter, 1988, 1990; Montgomery, 1992). Future analyses of relationships might examine how the relative emphasis on one identity or another might change over time, especially as people grow and mature and as new members join the family and others leave or move away. So future research may look at degrees of stability/change in various aspects of relationships: where events occur, what objects are used, who participates, what kinds of bonds are encouraged or discouraged during the events, who decides the locations, people, and activities, and so on.

In addition to providing opportunities for needed innovation and novelty, rituals can help people cope with changes in their lives. As C. L. Johnson (1988a) said, "Rituals become particularly prominent during times of tension, change, and uncertainty . . . [operating] as system-maintaining mechanisms" (p. 685). She showed how rituals help divorcing and divorced couples maintain civility when circumstances (e.g., children's weddings) required that they fulfill aspects of their changing or changed roles as husband/wife, father/mother, and in-law. In therapeutic contexts, there has been a great deal of work on how rituals can best be used to help families adjust to changing circumstances and how rituals can actually help effect change in dysfunctional families (Imber-Black, Roberts, & Whiting, 1988). Families have been encouraged to develop rituals to help them cope with death and divorce (e.g., Imber-Black, 1988), the integration of blended families into a more coherent and effectively functioning "new" family (Whiteside, 1988), and immigration to the United States (Imber-Black, 1988), among other problems. Other authors showed how community-level rituals allow people to express conflicting values, especially when those values reflect conflicts between traditional and modern practices (Caplow et al., 1982; Manning, 1983; O'Connor, 1989). So celebrations can both reflect and support change and continuity in relationships.

Implications for
Transactional/Dialectical Analyses

Several theoretical/philosophical issues could be the subjects of future theorizing and research.

Temporal Qualities

Our case studies did not probe deeply into temporal qualities of rituals—their rhythms and pace, the scale (duration) and sequencing of events, or continuity and change in the celebrations themselves—yet these concepts provide fertile research questions. Several authors emphasize that rituals occur on particular dates and flow through particular stages and sequences of events that enhance their special and distinctive character (Manning, 1983; Roberts, 1988; Van Gennep, 1909/1960). Other work might examine temporal flow and rhythm on mundane as well as special occasions (Warner, 1991; see Bolger and Kelleher in this volume).

Varieties of Dialectical Dimensions

There are many dialectical dimensions that might be applied to relationships, and other analyses have focused on and used them effectively, such as autonomy/connection (Baxter, 1988, this volume; Goldsmith, 1990; Montgomery, 1992), public/private (Rawlins, 1989), novelty/predictability (Baxter, 1988), openness/closedness (Altman, 1975/1981), to name just a few. On the surface, some of them seem quite similar or at least seem to have a great deal of overlap. Even when oppositional pairs can be defined and observed as distinct processes, in fact several may be interrelated. For example, Baxter (1990) stated that the predictability/novelty dialectic supported dyadic bonding (namely, individual/society identity) by keeping the relationship fresh without it becoming chaotic. Given the increasing interest in dialectical analyses, it may be important to consider carefully whether all are needed, whether they can be organized into a coherent framework (e.g., a "table" of dialectical opposites), or if they can be compared and contrasted in some systematic way (see, i.e., Baxter, this volume). In addition, we drew from both dialectical and transactional perspectives in our analyses and found this to be a fruitful approach. Although we perceive a great deal of overlap between the two, each perspective is complex and contains some explicit assumptions and values, so a worthwhile task for the future is a careful and systematic comparison and possible integration of the two.

Conclusion

Research on couple and family rituals has burgeoned in the past decade, with studies of rituals in the therapy process, the transmission of family rituals across generations, how rituals facilitate the establishment of new families, and so on. We have approached rituals from a dialectical/transactional perspective, with an emphasis on how rituals are holistic events that can support both sides of the person/society identity dialectic. Our case studies illustrated how rituals can be an integral part of how dyads and families manage dialectical oppositions involving unique and collective identities.

Other studies of relationship processes may also benefit from a transactional/dialectical approach that emphasizes a holistic analysis involving people, place, and temporal qualities and that assumes that continuity and change are natural and integral parts of phenomena. This chapter focused on celebrations as reflecting cultural, familial, and interpersonal dynamics; however, there are many other aspects of family and close relationships that are worthy of attention such as place attachment, privacy regulation, conflict resolution, resource management, and so on. As illustrated nicely by the other chapters in this volume, understanding close and family relationships requires tapping into a variety of life domains as well as viewing phenomena holistically and in context. Work that explores social and physical contexts of relationships, temporal processes, and multiple domains of life can provide a first step toward a holistic and transactional perspective on relationships.

7

The Social Side
of Personal Relationships:
A Dialectical Perspective

Leslie A. Baxter

The starting assumption of this volume, and my starting assumption in this chapter, is that the personal relationship is embedded in a web of sociality that extends beyond the boundaries of the dyad. Although several scholars (e.g., Blumstein & Kollack, 1988; Hinde, 1979, 1987; Lannamann, 1991; Parks & Eggert, 1991) have noted the social side of personal relationships, researchers generally have been slow to recognize this fact. Researchers who subscribe to a dialectical view share with their nondialectical colleagues an undersocialized vision of personal relationships, focusing largely on contradictions that are situated within the boundaries of the dyad. The current chapter takes a dialectical perspective in examining contradictions that are situated at the interface of the personal relationship with the larger social order composed of the networks of the two parties.

The chapter is organized into three sections. The first section discusses the particular variant of dialectical thinking to which

I subscribe and introduces a typology of dialectical contradictions that capture central themes in the counterpoint of personal relationships. This typology is based on a fundamental conceptual distinction in dialectical theory between internal contradictions and external contradictions. The second section discusses at length the three contradictions that are situated at the nexus of the relationship and the social order, that is, the external contradictions. The third and final section considers the possible linkages among internal contradictions and external contradictions in personal relationships. I privilege the relationship parties' experiences of the external contradictions to the relative neglect of how members of the social network manage the dialectical dilemmas posed by personal relationships in their midst (for a more macro-oriented dialectical perspective, see Montgomery, 1992).

A Typology of Internal and External Contradictions in Personal Relationships

Dialectical theory is not unitary and more accurately could be referred to as a cluster of theoretical perspectives that share in common a commitment to contradiction as the central organizing feature of social life (e.g., Altman, Vinsel, & Brown, 1981; Baxter, 1988; Billig, 1987, 1991; Montgomery, 1992; Rawlins, 1989). The particular variant of dialectical thinking to which I subscribe is Bakhtin's dialogism. The dialogue, in both metaphorical and literal senses, is the core concept in dialogism. To Bakhtin (1929/1984, 1981), the essential quality of the dialogue is its simultaneous fusion or unity of multiple voices at the same time that each voice retains its distinctiveness. All of social life is a dialogue to Bakhtin in that sociality is organized around the central contradiction of unity and separation. In addition to its role as the central metaphor of sociality, the dialogue in its literal sense also occupies a central role in dialogism. To Bakhtin (1981), social experience is constituted at the level of communicative exchange, or dialogue, between persons.

The particular appeal of Bakhtin's dialogism should be apparent even from this brief discussion of the theory's core concept. The personal relationship constitutes a paradigm case of Bakhtin's dialogic opposition; it is a part of the social order at the same time that it is separated from the social order through the parties' construction of a "culture of two" (Betcher, 1981). In addition, Bakhtin's emphasis on the centrality of communicative exchange holds appeal for someone of my disciplinary background who seeks to understand the social experience through examination of people's communication practices.

Bakhtin's dialogism is a theory of the contradicting process as realized in the ongoing tension between centripetal (i.e., unifying) and centrifugal (i.e., differentiating) dialectical poles. Each pole of the centripetal-centrifugal contradiction is constituted in the particulars of the situation at a given point in time. The centripetal pole consists of whatever phenomenon or quality occupies the dominant or normative position, whereas the centrifugal pole consists of whatever phenomena are subordinate, peripheral, or secondary. Substantial fluidity characterizes centripetal and centrifugal poles, in that a phenomenon that is dominant at one point in time can be subordinate or secondary at another point in time, and vice versa.

Because dialogism is a general theory of sociality, rather than a context-specific theory, Bakhtin did not pursue the particular phenomena that constitute centripetal and centrifugal forces for any specific context, including the context of personal relationships. Thus a first step in extending dialogism to personal relationships is to particularize Bakhtin's abstract centripetal-centrifugal contradiction. In the context of personal relationships, the centripetal-centrifugal contradiction is manifested in six basic contradictions, which in turn can be organized into a typology that draws extensively on a distinction made by many dialectical theorists (e.g., Ball, 1979; Riegel, 1976) between internal contradictions and external contradictions.

As the term *internal* suggests, contradictions of this type are constituted within the social unit under study; by contrast, external contradictions involve a dialectical tension between the social unit and the suprasystem in which the social unit is embedded. To date, personal relationships researchers who have taken a dialectical perspective, including myself, have been concerned almost exclusively with internal contradictions, that is, those oppositions situated within the boundary of the dyadic relationship. For example, several researchers have focused on the internal contradiction between connection and autonomy, that is, the need for parties to sustain both interdependence and independence in their relationship (e.g., Askham, 1976; Baxter, 1988, 1990; Baxter & Simon, 1993; Goldsmith, 1990; Masheter & Harris, 1986; Rawlins, 1983a). Researchers have also devoted attention to the internal contradiction of predictability-novelty, that is, the need for parties to sustain both certainty and uncertainty in their relationship (e.g., Altman et al., 1981; Baxter, 1988, 1990; Baxter & Simon, 1993). The internal contradiction of openness-closedness, that is, the need for parties to sustain both candor and discretion in their relationship, has also been the subject of scholarly attention (Altman et al., 1981; Baxter, 1988, 1990; Baxter & Simon, 1993; Petronio, 1991; Rawlins, 1983b). The exigence for all of these contradictions is situated in the internal fabric of the relationship between the two parties, not in the interface of the relationship with the broader social order.

The connection-autonomy, predictability-novelty, and openness-closedness contradictions are the internal manifestations of more fundamental dialectics: integration-separation, stability-change, and expression-privacy, respectively (Baxter, 1989). These three fundamental dialectics have external manifestations, as well. Figure 7.1 summarizes the typology of internal contradictions and external contradictions for the three fundamental dialectics.

The *dialectic of integration-separation* refers to the fundamental tension between social solidarity or unity on the one hand and social division or separation on the other hand. In its internal manifestation, this fundamental dialectic represents the tension between integration and separation of the two individuals. In its external manifestation, the *inclusion-seclusion* contradiction, this fundamental dialectic captures the tension between the pair's involvement as a couple with others versus the pair's

	Dialectic of Integration-Separation	Dialectic of Stability-Change	Dialectic of Expression-Privacy
Internal	Connection-Autonomy	Predictability-Novelty	Openness-Closedness
External	Inclusion-Seclusion	Conventionality-Uniqueness	Revelation-Concealment

Figure 7.1. A Typology of Internal and External Contradictions in Personal Relationships

isolation from others. On the one hand, a relational pair needs isolation from others for dyadically focused interaction (McCall, 1970). On the other hand, the couple needs identity as a social unit, which comes through joint presentation of coupleness in interactions with family and friends (see Montgomery, 1992).

The *dialectic of stability-change* refers to the fundamental opposition between stability and flux. In its internal manifestation, this dialectic captures predictability and uncertainty in the perceptions and behaviors of the relationship parties as they interact with each other. In its external manifestation, the contradiction of *conventionality-uniqueness*, the tension is that of perpetuating the social order by reproducing conventionalized ways of relating as opposed to deviating from social conventions through the construction of unique ways of relating. On the one hand, compliance with social conventions provides the relationship with a public identity that is familiar and known to outsiders, thereby easing the couple's interactions with others and making it possible for the relationship to fit in easily with the broader social order. On the other hand, carbon-copy relationships do not provide couples with the sense of uniqueness so central to their intimacy (McCall, 1970; Owen, 1984).

The *dialectic of expression-privacy* centers on what is expressed versus what is not expressed. The internal manifestation of this fundamental dialectic captures the extent to which the relationship parties display candor or discretion in their interactions with one another. The external manifestation of this dialectic, the *revelation-concealment* contradiction, captures the extent to which parties reveal or fail to reveal information about the nature and status of their relationship to outsiders. On the one hand, parties potentially benefit from making the existence and character of their relationship known to others; others cannot support and legitimate a relationship unless they have knowledge of it. On the other hand, others may interfere with a relationship if they have knowledge of it (e.g., M. P. Johnson & Milardo, 1984). Further, public disclosure of relational details may jeopardize the relationship's norms of privacy and confidentiality (McCall, 1970).

The six internal and external contradictions can be experienced both intrapersonally and interpersonally by relationship parties. When a given contradiction is experienced intrapersonally, a relationship party recognizes the need to fulfill both polarities and experiences an internal struggle between the two poles. Given the centripetal-centrifugal dynamic that characterizes the contradicting process, one polarity is likely to be perceived as unfulfilled, or subordinate, at a given point in time because of the dominance of the opposite polarity. For example, a relationship party might want both to spend time alone with his or her partner and to spend time as a couple with family and friends. At a given point in the relationship's history, however, the person might feel as if time alone is insufficient because of excessive time spent as a couple with others, that is, the person would feel the dominance of inclusion and the subordination of seclusion. When a given contradiction is experienced interpersonally, the two relationship parties align their respective interests and needs with opposing polarities. For example, at a particular point in their relationship's history, one partner might want to spend time as a couple with family and friends, but the other partner might want to spend time alone as a couple. Contradictions that are experienced interpersonally are referred to as "antagonistic" (Mao, 1965) or conflictual (Giddens, 1979) contradictions because they typically involve conflict between the two parties. By contrast, contradictions that are experienced intrapersonally do not involve a conflict of interests between the parties; instead, both parties experience internally the dilemma of how to fulfill two oppositional needs.

In an attempt to complement existing research on internal contradictions, I recently examined romantic and marital partners' intrapersonal perceptions of the three external contradictions (Baxter, 1993). Multiple Likert-type items were developed for each A-B contradiction to capture the two kinds of domination-subordination relations that can emerge in the contradicting process: pole A dominant over pole B, and pole B dominant over pole A. Items relevant to the inclusion-seclusion contradiction, for example, included those designed to tap the perception that inclusion was dominant over seclusion (e.g., "our commitments to others as a couple prevent us from having enough time for just the two of us") as well as those designed to tap the perception that seclusion was dominant over inclusion (e.g., "as a couple, we're too isolated from others"). The domination-subordination relations for the conventionality-uniqueness contradiction included items that captured a perception of excessive constraint imposed by social conventions (e.g., "we feel 'boxed in' by the perceptions that people have of a relationship such as ours") as well as items that captured a perception of excessive couple uniqueness (e.g., "because our relationship is so unique, we don't fit in very well as a couple with others"). Finally, the domination-subordination relations for the revelation-concealment contradiction included items that represented excessive public revelation of the relationship to others (e.g., "we're too open in disclosing to others information about our relationship") and items that represented excessive concealment of the relationship from others (e.g., "our relationship is too much of a secret from others").

Results of this study indicated that the external contradictions do not function independently of one another but constitute a total system in which certain domination-subordination relations co-occur among contradictions. Such interdependence among the external contradictions is not surprising, illustrating what dialectical theorists refer to more generally as the principle of totality (Rawlins, 1989). For both males and females, a complaint of excessive isolation from others as a couple was significantly correlated with a complaint of insufficient public revelation about the relationship (and, reciprocally, a complaint of excessive inclusion was significantly correlated with a complaint of excessive public revelation). This particular co-occurrence is unsurprising; if a couple is socially isolated from others, the parties have more limited opportunities to reveal the nature of their relationship to others. The perception of excessive isolation from others was also significantly correlated with a reported excess in uniqueness for both males and females (and, reciprocally, excessive inclusion was correlated significantly with excessive constraint from social conventions). The fact that a couple experiences difficulty in fitting in with others might lead them to withdraw into seclusion. Alternatively, a couple's isolation might uniquely distinguish them as a pair, thereby making it difficult for them to fit in with other couples. Finally, for both males and females, a report of excessive privacy about the relationship significantly co-occurred with a perception of excessive uniqueness (and, reciprocally, excessive public revelation was correlated with excessive constraint from others' conventions). In having relationship information withheld from them, third parties might experience uncertainty about the relationship and find themselves unsure about how to categorize it.

In this section, I have argued that three fundamental dialectics organize personal relationships: integration-separation, stability-change, and expression-privacy. Each of these dialectics is manifested in both internal and external contradictions with which relationship parties must cope. The contradictions that are relevant to the interface of the relationship with the broader social order, that is, the external contradictions, are discussed at length in the next section of this chapter. I begin with the revelation-concealment contradiction because I regard it as the most significant of the external contradictions. Others' knowledge of a relationship's existence is central to its status as a social entity; in the absence of others' awareness of a relationship's existence, the other external contradictions are rendered moot.

The External Contradictions
of Personal Relationships

Revelation-Concealment

Although substantial research has addressed the effects of the social network on relationship development and maintenance, researchers have tended to take for granted that relationships exist as established social fact to friends and family members. The prior question, as Ginsburg (1986) has noted, is that of determining how network members know that a relationship exists and what it is like. As Goffman (1971) so insightfully observed over 20 years ago, outsiders can gain information about a relationship in two basic ways: (a) unintentional tie-signs given off or leaked by relationship parties while they are in public that signal their status as a couple and (b) strategic tie-signs that relationship parties intentionally employ to control what outsiders know about their relationship. Despite the limited quantity of research activity that is framed explicitly in terms of Goffman's work (e.g., Fine, Stitt, & Finch, 1984; Mandelbaum, 1987), our understanding of unintentional tie-signs is already informed by substantial research on the nonverbal and verbal cues that persons display under conditions of increased attraction, liking, and intimacy. Because reviews of this body of work exist elsewhere (e.g., Knapp & Hall, 1992), I will focus my attention on the more limited body of work that addresses the strategic information management efforts of parties to affect what network members know about their relationship.

Four studies (Baxter & Widenmann, in press; Goldsmith, 1988; Goldsmith & Parks, 1990; Holland & Eisenhart, 1990) have addressed, through different methods, the reasons people identify for revealing or concealing relationship-related information to members of their social network. The results of these studies consistently suggest that the revelation-concealment dialectic is phenomenologically real to relationship parties. Parties identify a complex set of reasons in favor of revealing and in favor of concealing information from others.

First, parties are motivated to inform others about their relationship to obtain recognition, legitimation, and emotional or material support for it. This motive appears well founded; social network research suggests that relationships benefit from network support (for reviews, see Parks & Eggert, 1991; Surra, 1988). On the other hand, relationship parties report apprehension that others will react negatively to the relationship. This countermotive also appears well founded; M. P. Johnson and R. M. Milardo (1984) have found that network interference increases as relationship parties move from casual dating to serious involvement. The greatest negative reaction is perceived to come from parents (Baxter & Widenmann, in press; M. P. Johnson & Milardo, 1984), who employ a variety of negative actions, including refusal to interact with the partner, suggestion of alternative partners, and encouragement to delay involvement in the relationship (Leslie, Huston, & Johnson, 1986).

Second, relationship parties are also motivated to reveal relationship-related information out of the sheer joy or catharsis of expression. Yet, they fear loss of control over that information through others' gossiping behavior, a concern that appears well founded given the pervasiveness of relationship gossip among social network members. In their ethnographic study of female students at two college campuses, Holland and Eisenhart (1990, p. 86) observed that college women spent many hours "discussing who was attractive and why, who was 'going with' whom, who wanted to go out with whom, what couples were doing when they went out, how well-matched members of a couple were, what was needed to become more attractive, and so forth."

Third, people are motivated to reveal relational information because they think it is expected of or would enhance the relationship with the target recipient; indeed, to the extent that relationships with social network members are close, self-disclosure is a normative expectation (e.g., Davis & Todd, 1985). On the other hand, people are motivated to refrain from revelation of relationship-related information because they believe it would violate the expectations of or otherwise harm the relationship they have with the target recipient (e.g., Baxter & Wilmot, 1985).

Fourth, relationship parties are motivated to reveal their own relationship experiences as a way to provide support to the target recipient; in fact, research indicates that personal stories can be a useful form of social support (e.g., Glidewell, Tucker, Todt, & Cox, 1982). On the other hand, relationship parties are motivated to refrain from revelation of relationship information because of the perception that it would harm the target recipient in some way, such as hurt his or her feelings.

Fifth and finally, parties express a desire to reveal relational information to others out of the belief that such public revelation is an expectation of or would enhance the relationship with their partner; indeed, research supports the notion of "going public" as an important rite of passage for developing relationships (e.g., Baxter & Bullis, 1986; Baxter & Wilmot, 1984). On the other hand, parties report apprehension that "going public" would violate an expectation of or otherwise damage the relationship with their partner; this countermotive is supported by research that underscores the importance of couple privacy and confidentiality (e.g., Krain, 1977).

What do relationship parties reveal and conceal about their relationship, to whom, and how do they accomplish such information management? Two recent studies that colleagues and I have conducted provide insight into this question. In a quantitatively oriented study (Baxter, 1993), married and romantically involved parties were asked to fill out a questionnaire that elicited their perceptions of the current state of their relationship with respect to the three external contradictions and their self-reports of the relationship maintenance strategies they currently enacted. As expected, respondents who complained that others knew too much about their relationship reported less use of public disclosure and greater use of pair withdrawal from others when compared with respondents who complained of insufficient public knowledge about the relationship.

In a qualitatively oriented study, a colleague and I (Baxter & Widenmann, in press) interviewed over 100 young adults involved in romantic relationships to determine what they said or did to affect others' knowledge of the relationship. In analyzing over 1,900 reported acts of revelation and concealment, we identified six primary categories of relationship information that were revealed and/or concealed. *State-of-the-relationship* information, that is, explicit information about the relationship's existence or information concerning its progress or status, was the most frequent topic of both revelation and concealment. *Information about oneself* and *information about the partner* were the second and third most frequent topics, respectively. In disclosing to or concealing from others such information about themselves as buying a new outfit in preparation for going out with the partner, our informants thought that they were managing information about the seriousness or importance of the relationship. In disclosing to or concealing from others such information about the partner as his or her physical attractiveness, our informants similarly thought that they were managing information about the relationship's value or importance. Information about the partner was proportionately more likely to be revealed than concealed, suggesting that relationship parties regarded themselves less in the business of keeping the partner's negative qualities hidden and more in the business of advertising the partner's desirable features. Leslie et al. (1986) similarly found that revealing positive information about the partner was a foremost tactic employed by young adults to influence their parents' attitudes toward their dating partners. Our respondents also indicated that pair identity was revealed or concealed through information about the *public activities* of the couple, such as where the pair was going on a date. The couple's *sexual activities* were also subject to information management and were proportionately more likely to be concealed than revealed. Finally, a couple's identity was manipulated through strategic revelation or concealment of the *relationship's problems or complaints about the partner.*

A variety of communicative tactics were reported by our informants in managing the information about the relationship that was made available to others. Not a surprise, the most frequently reported tactic was *proactive verbal exchange* initiated by the informant with the target recipient. Although this communicative form was the most common for both revelation and concealment, proportionately more acts of concealment than revelation were conducted through this tactic, a finding that probably reflects the ease with which information omission can be enacted. The second most frequent information management tactic was *copresence manipulation.* Consistent with Goffman's (1971) description, this tactic involved jointly enacted "couple appearances," in which the pair arrived and left an event together and conducted themselves as a single unit during the event. This tactic was proportionately more likely in revelation than in concealment, perhaps suggesting the difficulty of using this tactic successfully in concealments. One male informant alluded to this difficulty in sharing with us the extraordinary coordination required by himself and his female boss when they became romantically involved. They carefully coordinated their arrivals in the morning to make certain that no one would see them walking in together from the parking lot and similarly made certain that they left work at different times. They never took lunch together and were never alone with one another in their respective offices. In fact, our informant indicated that what gave them away to office mates was their studied avoidance of copresence!

The first two strategies, proactive verbal exchange and copresence manipulation, are similar to those reported in the Baxter (1983) study, but our respondents identified additional strategies as well. In contrast to proactive verbal exchanges, *reactive verbal exchanges* were more likely to involve revelation than concealment. Because such a tactic was typically in response to a pointed inquiry from a network member, relationship parties may have been unable to enact concealment successfully. The next most frequent tactic, *labeling,* involved the strategic use or avoidance of conventionalized relationship terms, such as referring to the partner as one's boyfriend or girlfriend. Our informants often went out of their way to differentiate this tactic from proactive or reactive verbal exchange, indicating to us that it instantiated the relationship as a social unit more so than other information management tactics. One female informant illustrated the care and caution with which conventionalized labels are employed by sharing with us her shock and embarrassment when she heard herself describing her partner as her "boyfriend" and her immediate subsequent action to call her boyfriend and apologize, telling him that it had "just slipped out." *Affect displays* were also employed by relationship parties to manage strategically the revelation or concealment of relationship information. Through control of such nonverbal behaviors as touching the partner and such verbal behaviors as affection terms, parties managed the extent to which network members were aware of their closeness. This tactic is fully compatible with the finding by several researchers that romantic pairs in part use idiomatic behaviors in public to display to others their unique identity as a couple (Baxter, 1987; R. A. Bell, Buerkel-Rothfuss, & Gore, 1987). *Object markers,* such as wearing the partner's clothing, displaying a photograph of the partner, or wearing a ring or similar symbol of bonding, were also used strategically by parties to control others' knowledge of their relationship; a similar finding was reported by Baxter (1987). Finally, parties made use of what we called *situation manipulations* to control what others knew about their partner or the relationship. One form of this tactic involved telling a known gossip some relational information with the expectation that he or she would transmit that information to others. Another frequent form of this tactic was to set up a meeting between the partner and network members for the purpose of letting the network members discover for themselves the positive attributes of the partner. This second form of the situation manipulation tactic was also reported by Leslie et al. (1986) as a frequent tactic young adults use to affect their parents' attitudes toward their dating partners.

As predicted, we found that the closer the relationship, the greater the proportion of information management acts that were jointly enacted by both relationship parties. Parties from close relationships thus not only manage public knowledge of their relationship through these seven tactics but doubly signal their couple status by enacting those tactics jointly.

Our informants indicated that they strategically determined who would be a target of revelation and who would be a target of concealment. Because our respondents expected parents to react more negatively than other network members, it is not surprising that parental targets received disproportionately more acts of concealment than were received by other network members. By contrast, close friends were the recipients of proportionately fewer acts of concealment. Close friends are perceived to be supportive listeners (Goldsmith & Parks, 1990) who display limited interference with romantic relationships (Johnson & Milardo, 1984), qualities that account for their greater appeal as targets for revelation of relationship information.

Although M. P. Johnson and L. Leslie (1982) found that parties disclose less about their relationship to network members as their relationship development progresses, we did not find a significant difference in the proportion of concealment activity as a function of relationship closeness. This discrepancy in findings could represent a method artifact; our study excluded married couples, whereas the Johnson and Leslie (1982) study found the greatest decline in disclosure to friends and family among couples who had reached the developmental stage of marriage.

The data in these two studies were not elicited with reference to the overarching strategies of selection, separation, and integration that have been identified by Baxter (1988, 1990) as key ways in which relationship parties manage dialectical contradictions. Nonetheless, the findings tentatively point to a general pattern of segmented separation in the management of the revelation-concealment dialectic. That is, parties demarcate some target recipients and some types of relationship information as appropriate for revelation while other targets and relationship topics are regarded as inappropriate for revelation. Such a pattern would be consistent with how relationship parties manage the internal manifestation of the *expression-privacy* dialectic; separation through segmentation has been reported as the dominant coping strategy with respect to openness-closedness (Baxter, 1990).

In sum, the revelation-concealment dialectic appears to be salient in the everyday relational experiences of romantic pairs. Parties strategically seek to control who knows what about their relationship, enacting a variety of revelation and concealment tactics. Future research energies need to focus on the extent to which such efforts are successful in shaping what others know about the relationship. Network members form impressions about relationships not only from the strategic tie-signs of the pair, but, additionally, they have access to the couple's unintentional displays as well as information acquired from fellow network members. Longitudinal research is also needed to track patterns of revelation and concealment as relationships develop.

Inclusion-Seclusion

As Altman and his colleagues (Altman, Brown, Staples, & Werner, 1992) have noted, cultures differ enormously in the extent to which a couple's integration with the social order is obligated. Cultures in which mate selection, courtship, wedding, consummation, and domestic life are enacted in the presence of, if not controlled by, kin members and friends seem strange to members of contemporary Western societies, where couple separation or seclusion from others is valued. Reciprocally, it is probably safe to predict that members from more communally oriented cultures would find strange the claim that pair seclusion is the requisite act of crystallization that creates the couple as a social unit (Lewis, 1972). Nonetheless, even societies that value couple independence cannot ignore the fundamental embeddedness of personal relationships in a web of sociality. Thus the exigence is born for the inclusion-seclusion dialectic, or what Altman and Gauvain (1981) refer to as the dialectic of openness/closedness to interaction with outsiders. Couples need privacy away from others to form their dyadic culture, yet they need the recognition of others afforded through such efforts as inclusion of the couple as a pair in social activities and verbal reinforcement of the pair's coupleness (Lewis, 1973).

Network overlap, that is, the presence of people who are in the interaction network of both relationship parties, provides a couple with opportunities to participate jointly in activities with others and thereby establish and sustain social recognition. Substantial research, using a variety of methods, supports the correlation between network overlap and relationship development (e.g., Eggert & Parks, 1987; Kim & Stiff, 1991; Milardo, 1982; Parks & Adelman, 1983; Parks, Stan, & Eggert, 1983). The opportunity for joint integration with others, however, does not mean that the opportunity is always used by couples. Although noting differences among relationships, Surra (1985) reported a general decrease in the proportion of leisure activities enacted jointly by the pair with others as their relationship progressed from serious dating through marriage, whereas the proportion of leisure activities enacted with the partner alone increased. Such isolation from others may pose a problem for the couple as their relationship continues. In analyzing the data set on the perceived state of the relationship with respect to the three external contradictions (Baxter, 1993), I found that excessive seclusion of the couple from others was more likely to be a complaint among married persons than among romantically involved persons. Apparently, the threshold of tolerance that relationship parties have for isolation from others wears thin once parties are married. A perception of excessive isolation from others makes sense in light of Baxter and Simon's (1993) finding that a complaint of excessive predictability and boredom was more likely among married persons as opposed to romantically involved persons. Thus, for married couples, inclusion with others may be needed as much for its stimulation value as for its social recognition value. The problem that seclusion can pose for married couples is supported in Stafford and Canary's (1991) finding that married couples (more so than seriously dating couples) reported inclusion with the joint network as maintenance work on behalf of the relationship's well-being.

Although integration of the couple with others can benefit a personal relationship through social recognition and/or external stimulation, integration is a double-edged phenomenon. Cissna and his colleagues (Cissna, Cox, & Bochner, 1990) vividly illustrated this point with respect to the challenges that face remarried couples in their interactions with stepchildren. Stepfamily dynamics featured a dialectical theme of "the marriage versus the kids" (Cissna et al., 1990, p. 51), with stepchildren seeking to reject the authority of the stepparent and win the natural parent's loyalty against his or her spouse. The challenge to remarried couples was to sustain their couple solidarity in the presence of stepfamily dynamics that worked against the pair's unity. The initial reaction of stepchildren to a stepparent might represent an extreme case of how outsiders can strain a couple's unity, but even the most pleasant and benign of inclusion situations can focus a couple's energies away from intimate exchange between the parties' private selves.

Relationship parties are likely to cope with the inclusion-seclusion dilemma in a variety of ways. In the Baxter (1993) study discussed earlier, respondents who complained of excessive inclusion reported that they sought to maintain their relationship through romance-oriented and network-withdrawal strategies more so than respondents who complained of excessive seclusion. The finding with respect to network withdrawal is straightforward; the most direct way to restore equilibrium between inclusion and seclusion is to reduce the time spent with others as a couple if that is perceived to be excessive. Through such romantic gestures as candlelight and flowers or the celebration of special relational events, relationship parties not only increase the time they spend alone with their partners but do so in ways that might additionally offset possible problems of relationship boredom and predictability that can occur with seclusion. The use of romance-oriented and network-withdrawal strategies points to a more general coping strategy of separation through cyclic alternation, that is, a cycling between inclusion-enhancing efforts and seclusion-enhancing efforts on an as-needed basis (Baxter, 1988, 1990). Of interest, cyclic alternation is also the most frequently used strategy in managing the internal counterpart of inclusion-seclusion, that is, the connection-autonomy contradiction (Baxter, 1990).

I suspect that cyclic alternation between inclusion-enhancing and seclusion-enhancing efforts is used throughout a relationship's developmental history as the parties cope with fluctuations in the importance of couple integration to the well-being of their relationship. Until the two parties feel comfortable with having a relationship, such integration could be premature and thus could jeopardize the fragile bond between the parties; under such circumstances, relationship parties probably would be motivated to isolate themselves from others. As the parties increasingly perceive that they have a relationship, however, public integration probably becomes an important source of legitimation; the pair probably would be motivated to seek more public integration with others. For such well-established relationships as marriage and domestic partnerships, the everyday domestic isolation of the pair needs to be punctuated with public integration events to avoid the excessive isolation that long-term relationship parties appear to experience.

In addition, I suspect that separation through segmentation is also likely to be employed by relationship parties as a dialectical coping strategy. Regardless of developmental stage, certain relational domains are likely to be open to couple interaction with outsiders, whereas other areas are likely to be restricted to moments of seclusion. Birthdays, for example, might be regarded as celebratory occasions for public integration, whereas anniversaries might be strictly private between the two parties. Furthermore, couples are likely to differ with respect to which domains are public and which are private.

Relationship parties might also cope with the inclusion-seclusion dilemma through use of idiomatic communication codes, interacting with one another in ways that seem appropriate in the presence of outsiders yet carry hidden, private meanings known only to the relationship parties (e.g., Baxter, 1987; R. A. Bell et al., 1987). Such private meanings might give a couple the psychological sense of seclusion without sacrificing their pair integration with others. Idiomatic communication illustrates the broader dialectical coping strategy of integration, that is, fulfilling both poles of a contradiction at the same point in time (Baxter, 1988, 1990).

This section has focused on the external contradiction of inclusion-seclusion, that is, the dilemma of integrating with and separating from others as a couple. Longitudinal studies that give us a rich sense of the inclusion and seclusion practices of relationship parties over time should be a research priority. Research also needs to examine differences among couples in the salience of this external contradiction. For example, I would suspect that marital *Independents,* that is, pairs whose bond is constructed around substantial partner autonomy, would display limited tolerance for couple integration with others, in contrast to marital *Traditionals*, who would display greater acceptance of time spent as a couple with family and friends (Fitzpatrick, 1988).

Conventionality-Uniqueness

The third and final external contradiction addresses the issue of reproducing the social order through conformity to conventionalized forms and norms of relating versus the production of a unique, nonconventional relationship. Of the three external contradictions depicted in Figure 7.1, conventionality-uniqueness has probably been mentioned the most frequently among dialectical theorists of relationships, although with widely different vocabularies and with differences in emphasis: communality-identity (Altman & Gauvain, 1981), the contextual dialectics of public-private and ideal-real (Rawlins, 1989), and connection-autonomy (Montgomery, 1992). To avoid redundancy with other discussions of this external contradiction, I am adopting a fairly narrow conceptualization of the conventionality-uniqueness contradiction.

On the one hand, intimacy for a couple is based on their perception that their relationship is uniquely different than all other relationships (Baxter, 1987; McCall, 1970; Owen, 1984). But excessive uniqueness could make the relationship and its parties sources of social uncertainty to others, thereby jeopardizing the social legitimation and support that is also crucial for the well-being of an intimate bond. Relationship parties are thus caught in the dilemma of conforming to social conventions so as to be understood and accepted by others, thereby risking loss of uniqueness, or deviating from conventionality to construct a unique bond, thereby jeopardizing others' acceptance.

Of the three external contradictions depicted in Figure 7.1, conventionality-uniqueness is the most amenable to integrative reframing by relationship parties, that is, a transformation of the contradiction in such a way that the two poles are no longer regarded as oppositional (Baxter, 1988, 1990). The key to the transformation rests with the centrality of the parties' individual selves to the construction of relationship uniqueness. As several cultural analysts (e.g., Carbaugh, 1988; Katriel & Philipsen, 1981) have observed over the last decade, contemporary American conventions of relating celebrate individual selfhood. For example, in following such social conventions as self-disclosure, relationship parties accomplish not only conformity with social expectations of relating but simultaneously construct their relationship's uniqueness through the individual selves that are revealed.

The celebration of selfhood through relationships implicates a generic normative practice that de Certeau (1984) refers to as cultural "poaching." The "poaching" metaphor is a powerful one, invoking images of a crafty person who becomes empowered through creative appropriations from the social order; de Certeau (1984) argues that individuals recapture freedom from the constraints of society by appropriating or poaching cultural products (both symbolic and material) for their own uses and purposes. Poaching is more than passive consumption to de Certeau; rather, it is inventive construction of new identities. In the context of personal relationships, individuals poach from the society's templates of relating, transforming them creatively by invoking their individual selves. The product of such poaching is the construction of a relationship's unique identity.

The celebration of selfhood in personal relationships occurs not only from poaching such obvious cultural templates as "love," "commitment," and "intimacy." In addition, relationships are constructed as unique through more mundane poaching. A recent study I conducted on intimate play in personal relationships illustrates this point (Baxter, 1992a). Playful repartee is certainly mundane at one level, but as Oring (1984, p. 27) has observed, "It is the spirit of play that strongly imprints the culture of [the dyadic] relationship." Intimates are playful with one another by transforming some ordinary, nonplayful event, phenomenon, cultural form, or cultural artifact into a source of private humor for the pair. One form of intimate play that my informants described was role-playing, in which story lines or characters from the broader social order were acted out by the relationship parties, such as impersonations of mutual friends or reenactments of scenes from movies. Such enactments, appropriated from the parties' shared repository of social knowledge, are occasions for the relationship parties to display their own idiosyncratic interpretations and thus celebrate their unique selfhoods. To an outsider, such playful enactments by a relational pair appear trivial at best. To the relationship parties, however, intimate play is an important thread in their fabric of intimacy.

Because one of the commonly held conventions of personal relationships is that they are unique, relationship parties must somehow manage the paradox of demonstrating to others through their information management efforts that their relationship is conventional because it is unique. Because most of a relationship's uniqueness is likely to be realized in the privacy of the pair's dyadic culture, parties may experience a complex tension between revelation-concealment and conventionality-uniqueness dilemmas.

To this point in the discussion, I have assumed that *uniqueness* is a nonproblematic term that is commonly understood by all members of the culture. Owen's (1984) interpretive study of natural discourse about relationships suggests instead that *uniqueness* is a multivocal term that holds different meanings for different relationship parties. In particular, he noted that, when married persons referred to their relationship as "unique," they simply meant that their marriage was atypical in not breaking up in a society where divorce is prevalent. By contrast, opposite-sex friends referred to their relationship as "unique" if it lacked a behavioral practice common to male-female relationships, such as sexual intercourse. These are two quite different constructions of what it means to be "unique" and suggestive of possible systematic differences as a function of relationship development stage. To the extent that *uniqueness* holds different meanings for relationship parties, the conventionality-uniqueness contradiction may be experienced and managed differently, as well.

For so-called blended relationships (Bridge & Baxter, 1992), that is, relationships such as close friendships and romantic involvements in which the parties simultaneously have a role-based relationship, the network composed of work associates becomes a significant social order whose conventions are problematic. Although some researchers have examined romantic relationships among work associates, their focus of attention has not been on issues relevant to this chapter; instead, researchers have largely regarded romance at work as a variable whose presence is predicted from various organizational and individual factors or whose presence predicts the romantic partners' work performance (for a review, see Dillard & Miller, 1988).

In an effort to initiate study of the dialectically based problems experienced by blended relationship parties, a colleague and I (Bridge & Baxter, 1992) recently examined the contradictory tensions that close friends experience when they simultaneously are work associates. We asked over 160 adults to identify the ways in which their close friendship with their partner was facilitated and hindered by the fact that the relationship was embedded in a shared work environment.

Respondents confirmed that the *conventionality-uniqueness* contradiction is salient in the social order of the work setting, reporting several ways in which the conventions of the work setting constrained their unique friendship at the same time that the friendship was facilitated by the conventions of work. In particular, our respondents reported five dilemmas that were implicated in the tension between the conventions of work and their unique bond of friendship. The most frequent dilemma was one we labeled *impartiality-favoritism* to signal its similarity to Rawlins's (1989) work. On the one hand, respondents reported that their relationship as work associates positioned them to assist their friend, thereby fulfilling their expectation that friends provide unique support for one another. Friends were positioned through their roles to provide one another with a variety of kinds of material, informational, and psychological support. On the other hand, the normative expectations of the work environment favored impartiality in the conduct of professional relations; efforts to support one's friends were interpreted negatively as favoritism by one's fellow work associates.

The second most frequent dilemma identified in our sample was *judgment-acceptance* (Rawlins, 1989). Through working together, friends gained empathic understanding of the difficulties and challenges associated with each other's work, thereby positioning them to fulfill a friendship expectation of total acceptance of the other. Work often placed respondents in the position of judging or criticizing their friend's work performance, however, thereby straining this friendship norm of acceptance.

Third, respondents reported an autonomy-connection dilemma (Baxter, 1988; Rawlins, 1989). On the one hand, working together in a common setting facilitated the friendship by providing proximity, accessibility, and shared interests. Yet, friends reported that their work association gave them too little "space" and "distance" from one another, thereby imposing a strain on their friendship.

The fourth most frequently mentioned dilemma was *equality-inequality.* A variety of types of structural inequalities in the work environment, such as a superior-subordinate relationship, strained the friendship's norm of egalitarianism.

Finally, respondents reported to us a dilemma of openness-closedness (Baxter, 1988; Rawlins, 1989). On the one hand, the common work setting provided friends with valuable information that they were motivated to share with one another in the spirit of openness, yet work norms of confidentiality often precluded such disclosures among friends. Thus friends often found themselves in the awkward position of knowing more than they could say, displaying excessive closedness by the standards of close friendship. Furthermore, friends often felt divided loyalties between their friendship and the organization when information that their friend shared with them in confidence should have been reported to the organization.

Reported dialectical tension was not experienced universally among respondents in our sample. Friends whose work settings were characterized by high formalization of positions and practices reported more overall dialectical tension than did friends from less formalized work settings. This finding is not surprising; the more formalized the organization, the less flexibility and discretion available to employees with respect to such matters as impartiality and information management.

Parties whose friendships were closer reported less overall dialectical tension than was reported by less close friends. The lesser tension experienced by close friends is not a function of differences in how the associated dilemmas were managed. Closer friends were no more likely than less close friends to privilege either the work or the friendship component of their relationship, to confine the friendship and work association halves of the relationship to separate spheres off the job and on the job, or to compromise both the expectations of the job and the expectations of the friendship. Somehow, closer friends seem to have constructed a seamless bond in which their daily interaction in a work setting is part of the fabric of their friendship in fully complementary ways.

In this section, I have examined the last of three external contradictions that I posit as central to the conduct of personal relationships: conventionality-uniqueness. Whether the conventions originate in their shared work setting or in their networks of family and friends, relationship parties must construct a sense of their own pair uniqueness amidst others' expectations. A top research priority is the examination of how relationship parties manage the conventionality-uniqueness contradiction. I suspect that the general strategy of integrative reframing plays a significant role in parties' ability to cope with this dilemma, but empirical work is needed.

Possible Linkages Among Internal and External Contradictions

Thus far in this chapter, I have greatly oversimplified the dialectics of close relationships by ignoring linkages among internal and external contradictions. Although empirical research is lacking on this issue, I would like to suggest some possible linkages that could be pursued productively in future research. The internal and external manifestations of the dialectic of integration-separation could conceivably relate in one of two ways contingent on the type of integration experienced by a relational pair. For some couples, integration events could be experienced as autonomy oriented. For example, time that a pair spends with "his" friends and family might symbolically be interpreted by "her" as an autonomy-enhancing move on "his" part. By contrast, other couples might envision their integration experiences as ways to celebrate and sustain their connection, with neither party perceiving that individual priorities are being fulfilled. The distinction between autonomy-oriented and connection-oriented types of integration is an important issue in future social network research.

The internal and external manifestations of the stability-change dialectic are also likely to function interdependently. Highly conventionalized relationships will probably find internal predictability easier to achieve than internal novelty; by contrast, relationships characterized by limited conventionality will probably experience the reverse pattern, with internal novelty easier to achieve than internal predictability. If relationship parties adopt societal conventions of relating, they have ready-made templates that should afford certainty and predictability in their interactions with one another; for such conventionalized pairs, the challenge will be that of preventing the boredom and emotional deadening that can result from excessive predictability. Nonconventional couples, by contrast, will have to create de novo their own templates of relating; for such pairs, the challenge will be that of achieving predictability from their emergent interaction.

How a given pair manages the openness-closedness contradiction in their interactions with one another could relate in several possible ways to patterns of revelation and concealment with outsiders. Couples whose dyadic culture is characterized by high closedness could simply generalize this nondisclosive style in the parties' interactions with outsiders, just as highly open couples could generalize their disclosive style in the parties' revelations to outsiders. Alternatively, couples could display opposite styles in their internal and external manifestations of expression-privacy. Relationship partners who are closed in their interaction with one another could rely on outsider confidants, and partners who are open in their interaction with one another could establish a boundary of privacy in withholding relational information from others. Of course, relationship pairs might be characterized by all of these patterns, depending on the stage of relational development.

Certain co-occurrences are likely, as well, among internal and external manifestations of different underlying fundamental dialectics. I earlier noted the stimulation value of integration with outsiders, which suggests a probable linkage between external inclusion and internal novelty. Although the features that typify a conventional relationship will vary at different moments in a culture's history (see Montgomery, 1992), contemporary societal conventions of relating, typified by Fitzpatrick's (1988) *Traditional* marital type, suggest probable linkages between external conventionality and the internal poles of connection, predictability, and openness.

This section of the chapter, of necessity, has been highly conjectural in nature. My goal has been that of generalizing the dialectical principle of totality to encompass both internal and external manifestations of the fundamental dialectics of integration-separation, stability-change, and expression-privacy.

Conclusion

Although the dialectical thinker Bakhtin believed that dialogic opposition was central to all that was meaningful in the human experience, he concentrated his own scholarly energies on the study of language and the novel. I have made the argument here and elsewhere (Baxter, 1992b, in press-b) that the personal relationship is a paradigm case of the dialogic condition. Both unity with the social order (in the form of inclusion, conventionality, and revelation) and separation from the social order (in the form of seclusion, uniqueness, and concealment) are essential to relationship well-being. Given the focus of this volume, I have focused in detail on the three external contradictions that result from the unity-and-separation dynamic. In the interests of placing these three external contradictions in a larger theoretical framework, however, I have articulated a typology of contradictions that is organized around the fundamental dialectical themes of integration-separation, stability-change, and expression-privacy.

References

Adams, B. N. (1968). *Kinship in an urban setting.* Chicago: Markham.

Allan, G. A. (1979). *A sociology of friendship and kinship.* London: George Allen & Unwin.

Allan, G. A. (1982). Property and family solidarity. In P. Hollowell (Ed.), *Property and social relations.* London: Heinemann.

Allan, G. A. (1989). *Friendship: Developing a sociological perspective.* London: Harvester Wheatsheaf.

Allan, G. A., & Crow, G. P. (Eds.). (1989). *Home and family: Creating the domestic sphere.* London: Macmillan.

Allen, S., Waton, A., Purcell, K., & Wood, S. (Eds.). (1986). *The experience of unemployment.* Basingstoke: Macmillan.

Altman, I. (1975). *Environment and social behavior: Privacy, personal space, territory, and crowding.* Monterey, CA: Brooks/Cole. (Reprinted by Irvington, New York, 1981)

Altman, I. (1977). Research on environment and behavior: A personal statement of strategy. In D. Stokols (Ed.), *Psychological perspectives on environment and behavior: Conceptual and empirical trends* (pp. 303-323). New York: Plenum.

Altman, I. (in press). Dialectics, physical environments, and personal relationships. *Communication Monographs.*

Altman, I., Brown, B. B., Staples, B., & Werner, C. M. (1992). A transactional approach to close relationships: Courtship, weddings, and placemaking. In B. Walsh, K. Craik, & R. Price (Eds.), *Person-environment psychology: Contemporary models and perspectives* (pp. 193-241). Hillsdale, NJ: Lawrence Erlbaum.

Altman, I., & Gauvain, M. (1981). A cross-cultural and dialectic analysis of homes. In L. Liben, A. Patterson, & N. Newcombe (Eds.), *Spatial representation and behavior across the life span* (pp. 283-320). New York: Academic Press.

166

Altman, I., & Ginat, J. (1989, Spring). *Social relationships in polygamous families.* Invited address presented at the Second Conference of the International Network on Personal Relationships, University of Iowa, Iowa City.

Altman, I., & Ginat, J. (1990, August). *Ecology of polygamous families.* Invited address presented at the annual meeting of the American Psychological Association, Boston.

Altman, I., & Rogoff, B. (1987). World views in psychology: Trait, interactional, organismic, and transactional perspectives. In D. Stokols & I. Altman (Eds.), *Handbook of environmental psychology* (Vol. 1, pp. 1-40). New York: Academic Press.

Altman, I., Vinsel, A., & Brown, B. B. (1981). Dialectic conceptions in social psychology: An application to social penetration and privacy regulation. In L. Berkowitz (Ed.), *Advances in experimental social psychology* (Vol. 14, pp. 107-160). New York: Academic Press.

Argyle, M., & Henderson, M. (1984). The rules of friendship. *Journal of Social and Personal Relationships, 1,* 211-237.

Argyle, M., & Henderson, M. (1985). The rules of relationships. In S. W. Duck & D. Perlman (Eds.), *Understanding personal relationships* (pp. 63-84). Beverly Hills, CA: Sage.

Askham, J. (1976). Identity and stability within the marriage relationship. *Journal of Marriage and the Family, 38,* 535-547.

Aukett, R., Ritchie, J., & Mill, K. (1988). Gender differences in friendship patterns. *Sex Roles, 19,* 57-66.

Bahr, H. M. (1976). The kinship role. In F. I. Nye (Ed.), *Role structure and analysis of the family* (pp. 61-80). Beverly Hills, CA: Sage.

Bakan, D. (1966). *The duality of human existence.* Boston: Beacon.

Bakhtin, M. (1981). *The dialogic imagination: Four essays by M. M. Bakhtin* (M. Holquist, Ed., C. Emerson & M. Holquist, Trans.). Austin: University of Texas Press.

Bakhtin, M. (1984). *Problems of Dostoevsky's poetics* (C. Emerson, Ed. and Trans.). Minneapolis: University of Minnesota Press. (Original work published 1929)

Ball, R. (1979). The dialectical method: Its application to social theory. *Social Forces, 57,* 785-798.

Balswick, J., & Peek, C. W. (1976). The inexpressive male: A tragedy of American society. In D. David & R. Brannon (Eds.), *The forty-nine percent majority* (pp. 55-67). Reading, MA: Addison-Wesley.

Bankoff, E. A. (1981). Effects of friendship support on the psychological well-being of widows. In H. Z. Lopata & D. Maines (Eds.), *Research in the interweave of social roles: Friendship.* Greenwich, CT: JAI.

Bauman, Z. (1990). *Thinking sociologically.* Oxford: Blackwell.

Baxter, L. A. (1987). Symbols of relationship identity in relationship cultures. *Journal of Social and Personal Relationships, 4,* 261-280.

Baxter, L. A. (1988). A dialectical perspective on communication strategies in relationship development. In S. Duck (Ed.), *A handbook of personal relationships* (pp. 257-273). New York: John Wiley.

Baxter, L. A. (1989). *On structure and its deconstruction in relationship "texts": Toward a dialectical approach to the study of personal relationships.* Paper presented at the annual convention of the International Communication Association, San Francisco.

Baxter, L. A. (1990). Dialectical contradictions in relationship development. *Journal of Social and Personal Relationships, 7,* 69-88.

Baxter, L. A. (1991, November). *Bakhtin's ghost: Dialectical communication in relationships.* Paper presented at the meeting of the SCA, Atlanta, GA.

Baxter, L. A. (1992a). Forms and functions of intimate play in personal relationships. *Human Communication Research, 18,* 336-363.

Baxter, L. A. (1992b). Interpersonal communication as dialogue: A response to the "Social Approaches" forum. *Communication Theory.*

Baxter, L. A. (1993). *Self-reported relationship maintenance strategies and three external contradictions of relating.* Unpublished manuscript.

Baxter, L. A. (in press-a). A dialogic approach to relationship maintenance. In D. J. Canary & L. Stafford (Eds.), *Communication and relational maintenance.* New York: Academic Press.

Baxter, L. A. (in press-b). Thinking dialogically about communication in personal relationships. In R. Conville (Ed.), *Structure in communication study.* New York: Praeger.

Baxter, L. A., & Bullis, C. (1986). Turning points in developing romantic relationships. *Human Communication Research, 12,* 469-493.

Baxter, L. A., & Simon, E. P. (1993). Relationship maintenance strategies and dialectical contradictions in personal relationships. *Journal of Social and Personal Relationships, 10,* 225-242.

Baxter, L. A., & Widenmann, S. (in press). Revealing and not revealing the status of romantic relationships to social networks. *Journal of Social and Personal Relationships.*

Baxter, L. A., & Wilmot, W. W. (1984). "Secret tests": Social strategies for acquiring information about the state of the relationship. *Human Communication Research, 11,* 171-202.

Baxter, L. A., & Wilmot, W. W. (1985). Taboo topics in close relationships. *Journal of Social and Personal Relationships, 2,* 253-269.

Baxter, L. A., & Wilmot, W. (1986). Interaction characteristics of disengaging, stable and growing relationships. In R. Gilmour & S. W. Duck (Eds.), *Emerging field of personal relationships* (pp. 145-159). Hillsdale, NJ: Lawrence Erlbaum.

Beechey, V., & Perkins, T. (1987). *A matter of hours.* Cambridge, UK: Polity.

Belk, S. S., & Snell, W. E., Jr. (1988). Avoidance strategy use in intimate relationships. *Journal of Social and Clinical Psychology, 7,* 80-96.

Bell, R. A., Buerkel-Rothfuss, N. L., & Gore, R. E. (1987). "Did you bring the yarmulke for the cabbage patch kid?" The idiomatic communication of young lovers. *Human Communication Research, 14,* 47-67.

Bell, R. R. (1981). Friendships of women and men. *Psychology of Women Quarterly, 5,* 402-417.

Bellah, R. N., Madsen, R., Sullivan, W., Swidler, A., & Tipton, S. M. (1985). *Habits of the heart.* Berkeley: University of California Press.

Bergner, R. M., & Bergner, L. L. (1990). Sexual misunderstanding: A descriptive and pragmatic formulation. *Psychotherapy, 27,* 464-467.

Bernard, J. (1972). *The future of marriage.* New York: World.

Betcher, R. W. (1981). Intimate play and marital adaptation. *Psychiatry, 44,* 13-33.

Billig, M. (1987). *Arguing and thinking: A rhetorical approach to social psychology.* New York: Cambridge University Press.

Billig, M. (1991). *Ideology and opinions: Studies in rhetorical psychology.* Newbury Park, CA: Sage.

Binns, D., & Mars, G. (1984). Family, community and unemployment: A study in change. *Sociological Review, 32,* 662-695.

Blades, J. (1985). *Family mediation.* Englewood Cliffs, NJ: Prentice Hall.

Blieszner, R., & Adams, R. (1992). *Adult friendships.* Newbury Park, CA: Sage.

Blieszner, R., & Mancini, J. (1987). Enduring ties: Older adults' parental role and responsibilities. *Family Relations, 36,* 176-180.

Blumstein, P., & Kollack, P. (1988). Personal relationships. *Annual Review of Sociology, 14,* 467-490.

Bolger, N., DeLongis, A., Kessler, R. C., & Schilling, E. A. (1989). Effects of daily stress on negative mood. *Journal of Personality and Social Psychology, 57,* 808-818.

Bolger, N., DeLongis, A., Kessler, R. C., & Wethington, E. (1989). The contagion of stress across multiple roles. *Journal of Marriage and the Family, 51,* 175-183.

Bolger, N., & Eckenrode, J. (1991). Social relationships, personality, and anxiety during a major stressful event. *Journal of Personality and Social Psychology, 61,* 440-449.

Bolger, N., & Schilling, E. A. (1991). Personality and the problems of everyday life: The role of neuroticism in exposure and reactivity to daily stressors. *Journal of Personality, 59,* 355-386.

Bowlby, J. (1980). *Attachment and loss: Loss, stress and depression.* New York: Basic Books.

Brannen, J., & Moss, P. (1991). *Managing mothers: Dual earner households after maternity leave.* London: Unwin Hyman.

Brannen, J., & Wilson, G. (Eds.). (1987). *Give and take in families.* London: Allen & Unwin.

Bridge, K., & Baxter, L. A. (1992). Blended friendships: Friends as work associates. *Western Journal of Communication, 56,* 200-225.

Brody, E. M. (1986). Filial care of the elderly and changing roles of women (and men). *Journal of Geriatric Psychiatry, 19,* 175-201.

Bronfenbrenner, U. (1979). *The ecology of human development.* New York: Harvard University Press.

Bronstein, P. (1988). Father-child interaction: Implications for gender role socialization. In P. Bronstein & C. P. Cowen (Eds.), *Fatherhood today: Men's changing roles in the family* (pp. 107-124). New York: John Wiley.

Brown, B. B., Altman, I., & Werner, C. M. (1992). Close relationships in the physical and social world: Dialectical and transactional analyses. In S. A. Deetz (Ed.), *Communication yearbook* (Vol. 15, pp. 508-521). Newbury Park, CA: Sage.

Brown, B. B., & Werner, C. M. (1985). Social cohesiveness, territoriality, and holiday decorations: The influence of cul-de-sacs. *Environment and Behavior, 17,* 539-565.

Brown, B. B., Werner, C. M., & Altman, I. (in press). Close relationships in environmental contexts. In A. Weber & J. Harvey (Eds.), *Perspectives on close relationships.*

Buhrke, R. A., & Fuqua, D. R. (1987). Sex differences in same- and cross-sex supportive relationships. *Sex Roles, 17,* 339-352.

Burnett, R., McGhee, P., & Clarke, D. (Eds.). (1987). *Accounting for relationships.* London: Methuen.

Caldwell, M. A., & Peplau, L. A. (1982). Sex differences in same-sex friendship. *Sex Roles, 8,* 721-732.

Campbell, A., Converse, P. E., & Rogers, W. L. (1976). *The quality of American life.* New York: Russell Sage.

Campbell, J. C. (1976). *Successful negotiation: Trieste 1954.* Princeton, NJ: Princeton University Press.

Cancian, F. (1986). The feminization of love. *Signs, 11,* 692-708.

Cancian, F. (1987). *Love in America: Gender and self development.* Cambridge: Cambridge University Press.

Cancian, F. (1989). Love and the rise of capitalism. In B. Risman & P. Schwartz (Eds.), *Gender in intimate relationships* (pp. 12-25). Belmont, CA: Wadsworth.

Cancian, F., & Gordon, S. L. (1988). Changing emotion norms in marriage: Love and anger in U.S. women's magazines since 1900. *Gender and Society, 2,* 308-342.

Cantor, M. H. (1983). Strain among caregivers: A study of experience in the United States. *The Gerontologist, 15,* 23-34.

Caplow, T. (1982). Christmas gifts and kin networks. *American Sociological Review, 47,* 383-392.

Caplow, T., Bahr, H., Chadwick, B. A., Hill, R., & Williamson, M. H. (1982). *Middletown families: Fifty years of continuity and change.* Minneapolis: University of Minnesota Press.

Carbaugh, D. (1988). *Talking American: Cultural discourses on "Donahue."* Norwood, NJ: Ablex.

Carnevale, P. J. D., Conlon, D. E., Hanisch, K. A., & Harris, K. (1989). Experimental research on the strategic-choice model of mediation. In K. Kressel, D. G. Pruitt, and associates (Eds.), *Mediation research* (pp. 344-367). San Francisco: Jossey-Bass.

Carnevale, P. J. D., & Pruitt, D. G. (1992). Negotiation and mediation. *Annual Review of Psychology, 43,* 531-582.

Carpenter, B. N. (in press). Relational competence. In W. H. Jones & D. Perlman (Eds.), *Advances in personal relationships* (Vol. 4, pp. 1-28). London: Jessica Kingsley.

Caspi, A., Bolger, N., & Eckenrode, J. (1987). Linking person and context in the daily stress process. *Journal of Personality and Social Psychology, 52,* 184-195.

Chodorow, N. (1978). *The reproduction of mothering: Psychoanalysis and the sociology of gender.* Berkeley: University of California Press.

Chodorow, N. (1989). *Feminism and psychoanalytic theory.* New Haven, CT: Yale University Press.

Christensen, A., & Heavey, C. (1990). Gender and social structure in the demand/withdraw pattern in marital conflict. *Journal of Personality and Social Psychology, 59*(1), 73-81.

Cissna, K. N., Cox, D. E., & Bochner, A. P. (1990). The dialectic of marital and parental relationships within the stepfamily. *Communication Monographs, 57,* 44-61.

Cohen, S. (1988). Psychosocial models of the role of social support in the etiology of physical disease. *Health Psychology, 7,* 269-297.

Cohen, S., & Wills, T. A. (1985). Stress, social support, and the buffering hypothesis. *Psychological Bulletin, 98,* 310-357.

Cohler, B. J., & Geyer, S. (1982). Psychological autonomy and interdependence within the family. In F. Walsh (Ed.), *Normal family processes* (pp. 196-228). New York: Guilford.

Collins, P. H. (1989). The social construction of black feminist thought. *Signs, 14,* 745-773.

Coyne, J. C., & Downey, G. (1991). Social factors and psychopathology: Stress, social support, and coping processes. *Annual Review of Psychology, 42,* 401-425.

Crouter, A. C. (1984). Spillover from family to work: The neglected side of the work-family interface. *Human Relations, 37,* 425-442.

Crow, G. P., & Allan, G. A. (1990). Constructing the domestic sphere: The emergence of the modern home in post-war Britain. In H. Corr & L. Jamieson (Eds.), *Politics of everyday life.* London: Macmillan.

Cuber, J. F., & Harroff, P. B. (1966). *Sex and the significant Americans.* Baltimore: Penguin.

Daunton, M. J. (1983). Public place and private space: The Victorian city and the working-class household. In D. Frazer & A. Sutcliffe (Eds.), *The pursuit of urban history.* London: Edward Arnold.

Davidoff, L., & Hall, C. (1987). *Family fortunes: Men and women of the English middle class 1780-1850.* London: Hutchinson.

Davis, J. (1988). Mazel tov: The bar mitzvah as a multigenerational ritual of change and continuity. In E. Imber-Black, J. Roberts, & R. A. Whiting (Eds.), *Rituals in families and family therapy* (pp. 177-208). New York: Norton.

Davis, K. E., & Todd, M. J. (1985). Assessing friendship: Prototypes, paradigm cases and relationship description. In S. W. Duck & D. Perlman (Eds.), *Understanding personal relationships* (pp. 17-38). Beverly Hills, CA: Sage.

de Certeau, M. (1984). *The practice of everyday life.* Berkeley: University of California Press.

Degler, C. N. (1980). *At odds: Women and the family in America from the revolution to the present.* New York: Oxford University Press.

Delia, J. (1980). Some tentative thoughts concerning the study of interpersonal relationships and their development. *Western Journal of Speech Communication, 44,* 97-103.

DeLongis, A., Coyne, J. C., Dakof, G., Folkman, S., & Lazarus, R. S. (1982). The relationship of hassles, uplifts, and major life events to health status. *Health Psychology, 1,* 119-136.

DeLongis, A., Folkman, S., & Lazarus, R. S. (1988). The impact of daily stress on health and mood: Psychological and social resources as mediators. *Journal of Personality and Social Psychology, 54,* 486-496.

Delphy, C., & Leonard, D. (1992). *Familiar exploitation.* Cambridge, UK: Polity.

Demos, J. (1978). Old age in early New England. *American Journal of Sociology, 84,* 451-476.

Deutsch, M. (1973). *The resolution of conflict.* New Haven, CT: Yale University Press.

Dillard, J. P., & Miller, K. I. (1988). Intimate relationships in task environments. In S. W. Duck (Ed.), *A handbook of personal relationships* (pp. 449-465). New York: John Wiley.

Dobash, R. E., & Dobash, R. P. (1979). *Violence against wives: A case against the patriarchy*. New York: Free Press.

Douglas, A. (1977). *The feminization of American culture*. New York: Knopf.

Duck, S. W. (1986). *Human relationships* (1st ed.). London: Sage.

Duck, S. W. (Ed. with R. C. Silver). (1990a). *Personal relationships and social support*. Newbury Park, CA: Sage.

Duck, S. W. (1990b). Relationships as unfinished business: Out of the frying pan and into the 1990s. *Journal of Social and Personal Relationships, 7,* 5-28.

Duck, S. W. (1991). Diaries and logs. In B. M. Montgomery & S. W. Duck (Eds.), *Studying interpersonal interaction* (pp. 141-161). New York: Guilford.

Duck, S. W., & Miell, D. E. (1986). Charting the development of personal relationships. In R. Gilmour & S. W. Duck (Eds.), *The emerging field of personal relationships* (pp. 133-144). Hillsdale, NJ: Lawrence Erlbaum.

Duck, S. W., & Pond, K. (1989). Friends, Romans, countrymen, lend me your retrospections: Rhetoric and reality in personal relationships. In C. Hendrick (Ed.), *Close relationships* (pp. 17-38). Newbury Park, CA: Sage.

Duck, S. W., Rutt, D. J., Hurst, M. H., & Strejc, H. (1991). Some evident truths about conversation in everyday relationships: All communications are not created equal. *Human Communication Research, 18,* 228-267.

Eckenrode, J. (1984). The impact of chronic and acute stressors on daily reports of mood. *Journal of Personality and Social Psychology, 46,* 907-918.

Eckenrode, J., & Gore, S. (1989). *Stress between work and family*. New York: Plenum.

Eggert, L. L., & Parks, M. R. (1987). Communication network involvement in adolescents' friendships and romantic relationships. In *Communication yearbook* (Vol. 10, pp. 283-322). Newbury Park, CA: Sage.

Erikson, E. (1963). *Childhood and society*. New York: Norton.

Ferree, M. M. (1988). *Negotiating household roles and responsibilities: Resistance, conflict and change*. Paper presented at the National Council on Family Relations, Philadelphia, PA.

Finch, J. (1987). Family obligations and the life course. In A. Bryman, B. Bytheway, P. Allatt, & T. Keil (Eds.), *Rethinking the life cycle*. London: Macmillan.

Finch, J., & Mason, J. (1993). *Negotiating family responsibilities*. London: Routledge.

Fine, G. A., Stitt, J. L., & Finch, M. (1984). Couple tie-signs and interpersonal threat: A field experiment. *Social Psychology Quarterly, 47,* 282-286.

Fineman, S. (Ed.). (1987). *Unemployment: Personal and social consequences*. London: Tavistock.

Finley, N. J., Roberts, D., & Banahan, B. F. (1988). Motivators and inhibitors of attitudes of filial obligation toward aging parents. *The Gerontologist, 28,* 73-78.

Fiore, J., Becker, J., & Coppel, D. A. B. (1983). Social network interactions: A buffer of a stress. *American Journal of Community Psychology, 11,* 423-440.

Fischer, J. L., & Narus, L. R. (1981). Sex roles and intimacy in same and other sex relationships. *Psychology of Women Quarterly, 5,* 385-401.

Fischer, L. R. (1983). Mothers and mothers-in-law. *Journal of Marriage and the Family, 45,* 187-192.

Fitzpatrick, M. A. (1988). *Between husbands and wives: Communication in marriage*. Newbury Park, CA: Sage.

Fletcher, G. J. O., & Fincham, F. D. (1991). Attribution processes in close relationships. In G. J. O. Fletcher & F. D. Fincham (Eds.), *Cognition in close relationships* (pp. 7-35). Hillsdale, NJ: Lawrence Erlbaum.

Fox-Genovese, E. (1991). *Feminism without illusions.* Chapel Hill: University of North Carolina Press.

Garbarino, M. (1976). *Native American heritage.* Boston: Little, Brown.

Gelfand, D. E. (1989). Immigration, aging, and intergenerational relationships. *The Gerontologist, 29,* 366-372.

Giddens, A. (1979). *Central problems in social theory: Action, structure and contradiction in social analysis.* Berkeley: University of California Press.

Giddens, A. (1991). *Modernity and self-identity.* Cambridge, UK: Polity.

Giddens, A. (1992). *The transformation of intimacy.* Cambridge, UK: Polity.

Gilligan, C. (1982). *In a different voice: Psychological theory and women's development.* Cambridge, MA: Harvard University Press.

Ginsburg, G. P. (1986). The structural analysis of primary relationships. In R. Gilmour & S. W. Duck (Eds.), *The emerging field of personal relationships* (pp. 41-62). Hillsdale, NJ: Lawrence Erlbaum.

Ginsburg, G. P. (1988). Rules, scripts and prototypes in personal relationships. In S. W. Duck (Ed.), *Handbook of personal relationships* (pp. 23-39). Chichester: John Wiley.

Glidewell, J. C., Tucker, S., Todt, M., & Cox, S. (1982). Professional support systems: The teaching profession. In A. Nadler, J. D. Fisher, & B. M. DePaulo (Eds.), *New directions in helping: Vol. 3. Applied research in help-seeking and reactions to aid.* New York: Academic Press.

Goffman, E. (1971). *Relations in public: Microstudies of the public order.* New York: Harper & Row.

Goldman, E. (1931). *Living my life.* New York: Knopf.

Goldner, V., Penn, P., Sheinberg, M., & Walker, G. (1990). Love and violence: Gender paradoxes in volatile attachments. *Family Process, 29*(4), 343-364.

Goldsmith, D. (1988). *To talk or not to talk: The flow of information between romantic dyads and networks.* Paper presented at the annual meeting of the Speech Communication Association, New Orleans.

Goldsmith, D. (1990). A dialectic perspective on the expression of autonomy and connection in romantic relationships. *Western Journal of Speech Communication, 54,* 537-556.

Goldsmith, D., & Parks, M. (1990). Communicative strategies for managing the risks of seeking social support. In S. W. Duck (Ed. with R. C. Silver), *Personal relationships and social support* (pp. 104-121). Newbury Park, CA: Sage.

Goode, W. (1963). *World revolution and family patterns.* New York: Free Press.

Gordon, L. (1988). *Heroes of their own lives.* New York: Viking.

Griffith, J. (1985). Social support providers: Who are they, where are they met and the relationship of network characteristics to psychological distress. *Basic and Applied Social Psychology, 6,* 41-61.

Hagemann-White, C. (1984). The societal context of women's role in family relationships and responsibilities. In V. Garms-Homolova, E. M. Hoerning, & D. Shaeffer (Eds.), *Intergenerational relationships* (pp. 133-143). Lewiston, NY: Hogrefe.

Hagestad, G. O. (1984). The continuous bond: A dynamic multigenerational perspective on parent-child relations between adults. In M. Perlmutter (Ed.),

Parent-child relations in child development: The Minnesota Symposium on Child Psychology (pp. 129-158). Hillsdale, NJ: Lawrence Erlbaum.

Hagestad, G. O. (1987). Parent-child relations in later life: Trends and gaps in past research. In J. B. Lancaster, J. Altmann, A. S. Rossi, & L. R. Sherrod (Eds.), *Parenting across the life span: Biosocial dimensions* (pp. 405-433). New York: Aldine de Gruyter.

Hall, D., & Langellier, K. (1988). Storytelling strategies in mother-daughter communication. In B. Bate & A. Taylor (Eds.), *Women communicating* (pp. 107-126). Norwood, NJ: Ablex.

Hall, R. M., & Sandler, B. R. (1982). *The classroom climate: A chilly one for women?* Washington, DC: Project on the Status and Education of Women, Association of American Colleges.

Hall, R. M., & Sandler, B. R. (1984). *Out of the classroom: A chilly campus climate for women.* Washington, DC: Project on the Status and Education of Women, Association of American Colleges.

Hamon, R. R., & Blieszner, R. (1990). Filial responsibility expectations among adult child-older parent pairs. *Journal of Gerontology: Psychological Sciences, 45,* 110-112.

Hanson, K. (1989). "Helped put in a quilt": Men's work and male intimacy in nineteenth-century New England. *Gender and Society, 3*(3), 334-354.

Hanson, S. L., Sauer, W. J., & Seelbach, W. C. (1983). Racial and cohort variations in filial responsibility norms. *The Gerontologist, 23,* 626-631.

Harding, S. (1991). *Whose science? Whose knowledge? Thinking from women's lives.* Ithaca, NY: Cornell University Press.

Hareven, T. K. (1986). American families in transition: Historical perspectives on change. In A. S. Skolnick & J. H. Skolnick (Eds.), *Family in transition.* Boston: Little, Brown.

Harvey, J. H., Agostinelli, G., & Weber, A. L. (1989). Account-making and the formation of expectations about close relationships. *Review of Personality and Social Psychology, 10,* 39-62.

Haskey, J., & Kiernan, K. (1989). Cohabitation in Great Britain: Characteristics and estimated numbers of cohabiting partners. *Population Trends, 58,* 23-32 (London: Her Majesty's Stationery Office).

Hatfield, E., & Rapson, R. L. (1987). Gender differences in love and intimacy: The fantasy vs. the reality. In W. Ricketts & H. L. Gochros (Guest Eds.), In intimate relationships: Some social work perspectives on love. *Journal of Social Work and Human Sexuality, 5,* 15-26.

Hatfield, E., Traupmann, J., Sprecher, S., Utne, M., & Hay, J. (1984). Equity and intimate relations: Recent research. In W. Ickes (Ed.), *Compatible and incompatible relationships* (pp. 1-27). New York: Springer-Verlag.

Hendrick, C. (1988). Roles and gender in relationships. In S. W. Duck (Ed.), *Handbook of personal relationships* (pp. 429-448). New York: John Wiley.

Hess, B. (1972). Friendship. In M. W. Riley, M. Johnson, & A. Foner (Eds.), *Aging and society: A sociology of age stratification.* New York: Russell Sage.

Hetherington, E. M., Cox, M., & Cox, R. (1978). The aftermath of divorce. In J. H. Stevens & M. Matthews (Eds.), *Mother-child/father-child relations.* Washington, DC: National Association for the Education of Young Children.

Hiller, D. V., & Philliber, W. W. (1986). The division of labor in contemporary marriage: Expectations, perceptions, and performance. *Social Problems, 33,* 191-201.

Hinde, R. A. (1979). *Towards understanding relationships.* New York: Academic Press.

Hinde, R. A. (1987). *Individuals, relationships and culture: Links between ethology and the social sciences.* New York: Cambridge University Press.

Hines, M. (1992, April 19). Brain scan reveals basis of sexual differentiation of brain. *Health Information Communication Network News, 5,* 2.

Hirsch, B. J. (1985). Social networks and the ecology of human development: Theory, research and application. In I. G. Sarason & B. R. Sarason (Eds.), *Social support: Theory, research and applications* (pp. 117-171). The Hague, the Netherlands: Martinus Nijhoff.

Hirschman, A. O. (1970). *Exit, voice, and loyalty: Responses to decline in firms, organizations, and states.* Cambridge, MA: Harvard University Press.

Ho, M. K. (1987). *Family therapy with ethnic minorities.* Newbury Park, CA: Sage.

Hochschild, A., with A. Machung. (1989). *The second shift: Working parents and the revolution at home.* New York: Viking/Penguin.

Holland, D. C., & Eisenhart, M. A. (1990). *Educated in romance: Women, achievement, and college culture.* Chicago: University of Chicago Press.

Hopper, R., Knapp, M. L., & Scott, L. (1981). Couples' personal idioms: Exploring intimate talk. *Journal of Communication, 31,* 23-33.

Horowitz, A. (1985). Sons and daughters and caregivers to older parents: Differences in role performance and consequences. *The Gerontologist, 25,* 612-617.

House, J. S., Umberson, D., & Landis, K. (1988). Structures and processes of social support. *Annual Review of Sociology, 14,* 293-318.

Howard, J. A., Blumstein, P., & Schwartz, P. (1986). Sex, power, and influence factors in intimate relationships. *Journal of Personality and Social Psychology, 51,* 102-109.

Hunt, G., & Satterlee, S. (1986). The pub, the village and the people. *Human Organisation, 45,* 62-74.

Imber-Black, E. (1988). Ritual themes in families and family therapy. In E. Imber-Black, J. Roberts, & R. A. Whiting (Eds.), *Rituals in families and family therapy* (pp. 47-83). New York: Norton.

Imber-Black, E., Roberts, J., & Whiting, R. A. (Eds.). (1988). *Rituals in families and family therapy.* New York: Norton.

James, K. (1989). When twos are really threes: The triangular dance in couple conflict. *Australian and New Zealand Journal of Family Therapy, 10*(3), 179-186.

Janeway, E. (1971). *Man's world, woman's place: A study in social mythology.* New York: Dell.

Jencks, C., & Peterson, P. E. (Eds.). (1991). *The urban underclass.* Washington, DC: Brookings Institution.

Jerrome, D. (1984). Good company: The sociological implications of friendship. *Sociological Review, 32,* 696-718.

Johnson, C. L. (1988a). Socially controlled civility. *American Behavioral Scientist, 31,* 685-701.

Johnson, C. L. (1988b). Relationships among family members and friends in later life. In R. M. Milardo (Ed.), *Families and social networks* (pp. 168-189). Beverly Hills, CA: Sage.

Johnson, M. P., Huston, T. L., Gaines, S. O., & Levinger, G. (1992). Patterns of married life among young couples. *Journal of Social and Personal Relationships, 9,* 343-364.

Johnson, M. P., & Leslie, L. (1982). Couple involvement and network structure: A test of the dyadic withdrawal hypothesis. *Social Psychology Quarterly, 45,* 34-43.

Johnson, M. P., & Milardo, R. M. (1984). Network interference in pair relationships: A social psychological recasting of Slater's theory of social regression. *Journal of Marriage and the Family, 46,* 893-899.

Jones, G. P., & Dembo, M. H. (1989). Age and sex role differences in intimate friendships during childhood and adolescence. *Merrill-Palmer Quarterly, 35,* 445-462.

Kanner, A. D., Coyne, J. C., Schaefer, C., & Lazarus, R. S. (1981). Comparison of two modes of stress measurement: Daily hassles and uplifts versus major life events. *Journal of Behavioral Medicine, 4,* 1-39.

Kanter, R. M. (1977). *Work and family in the United States: A critical review and agenda for research and policy.* New York: Russell Sage.

Kaplan, L. J. (1978). *Oneness and separateness: From infant to individual.* New York: Simon & Schuster.

Karpel, M. A., & Strauss, E. S. (1983). *Family evaluation.* New York: Gardner.

Katriel, T., & Philipsen, G. (1981). "What we need is communication": "Communication" as a cultural category in some American speech. *Communication Monographs, 48,* 301-317.

Kaye, L. W., & Applegate, J. S. (1990). Men as elder caregivers: A response to changing families. *American Journal of Orthopsychiatry, 60,* 86-95.

Kemper, T. D. (1968). Third party penetration of local social systems. *Sociometry, 31,* 1-29.

Kessler, R. C., Price, R. H., & Wortman, C. B. (1985). Social factors in psychopathology: Stress, social support, and coping processes. *Annual Review of Psychology, 36,* 351-372.

Kessler, S., & McKenna, W. (1978). *Gender: An ethnomethodological approach.* New York: John Wiley.

Kim, H. J., & Stiff, J. B. (1991). Social networks and the development of close relationships. *Human Communication Research, 18,* 70-91.

Klein, R. (1992, December). *Is the glass half full or half empty? How young couples see their conflicts.* Paper presented at the Women in the Curriculum Series, University of Maine, Orono.

Klinger, E. (1977). *Meaning and void: Inner experience and the incentives in people's lives.* Minneapolis: University of Minnesota Press.

Knapp, M. L., & Hall, J. A. (1992). *Nonverbal communication in human interaction* (3rd ed.). New York: Holt, Rinehart & Winston.

Kogan, N., Lamm, H., & Trommsdorff, G. (1972). Negotiation constraints in the risk-taking domain: Effects of being observed by partners of higher of lower status. *Journal of Personality and Social Psychology, 23,* 143-156.

Krain, M. (1977). A definition of dyadic boundaries and an empirical study of boundary establishment in courtship. *International Journal of Sociology of the Family, 7,* 107-123.

Lakoff, R. (1990). *Talking power: The politics of language.* New York: Basic Books.

Lang, A. M., & Brody, E. M. (1983). Characteristics of middle-aged daughters and help to their elderly mothers. *Journal of Marriage and the Family, 45,* 193-202.

Lannamann, J. (1991). Interpersonal research as ideological practice. *Communication Theory, 1,* 179-203.

Lee, G. R. (1979). Effects of social networks on the family. In W. R. Burr, R. Hill, & F. I. Nye (Eds.), *Contemporary theories about the family: Research-based theories* (pp. 27-56). New York: Free Press.

Leichter, H. J., & Mitchell, W. E. (1967). *Kinship and casework.* New York: Russell Sage.

Leonard, D. (1980). *Sex and generation.* London: Tavistock.

Leslie, L., Huston, T., & Johnson, M. (1986). Parental reactions to dating relationships: Do they make a difference? *Journal of Marriage and the Family, 48,* 57-66.

Levenson, R. W., & Gottman, J. M. (1983). Marital interaction: Physiological linkage and affective exchange. *Journal of Personality and Social Psychology, 45,* 587-597.

Levenson, R. W., & Gottman, J. M. (1985). Physiological and affective predictors of change in relationship satisfaction. *Journal of Personality and Social Psychology, 49,* 85-94.

Lewis, J., & Meredith, B. (1988). *Daughters who care: Daughters caring for mothers at home.* London: Routledge.

Lewis, R. A. (1972). A developmental framework for the analysis of premarital dyadic formation. *Family Process, 11,* 17-48.

Lewis, R. A. (1973). Social reaction and the formation of dyads: An interactionist approach to mate selection. *Sociometry, 36,* 409-418.

Lewis, R. A. (1978). Emotional intimacy among men. *Journal of Social Issues, 34,* 108-121.

Liebow, E. (1967). *Tally's corner.* Boston: Little, Brown.

Locke, H. J., Sabagh, G., & Thomes, M. M. (1957). Interfaith marriages. *Social Problems, 4,* 329-333.

Lorber, J. (1989). Dismantling Noah's arc. In B. Risman & P. Schwartz (Eds.), *Gender in intimate relationships* (pp. 58-67). Belmont, CA: Wadsworth.

Maltz, D. N., & Borker, R. (1982). A cultural approach to male-female miscommunication. In J. J. Gumperz (Ed.), *Language and social identity* (pp. 196-216). Cambridge: Cambridge University Press.

Mandelbaum, J. (1987). Couples sharing stories. *Communication Quarterly, 35,* 14-170.

Manning, F. E. (1983). Cosmos and chaos: Celebration in the modern world. In F. E. Manning (Ed.), *The celebration of society: Perspectives on contemporary cultural performance.* Bowling Green, OH: Bowling Green University Popular Press.

Mansfield, P., & Collard, J. (1988). *The beginning of the rest of your life? A portrait of newly-wed marriage.* London: Macmillan.

178   SOCIAL CONTEXT AND RELATIONSHIPS

Mao, T. (1965). *On contradiction*. Beijing: Foreign Languages Press.
Martin, J., & Roberts, C. (1984). *Women and employment: A lifetime perspective*. London: Her Majesty's Stationery Office.
Masheter, C., & Harris, L. (1986). From divorce to friendship: A study of dialectic relationship development. *Journal of Social and Personal Relationships, 3*, 177-190.
Matthews, J. J. (1984). *Good and mad women*. Sydney: Allen & Unwin.
Maynard, D. W., & Zimmermann, D. H. (1984). Topical talk, ritual, and the social organization of relationships. *Social Psychology Quarterly, 47*, 301-316.
Mazur, E., & Olver, R. R. (1987). Intimacy and structure: Sex differences in imagery of same sex relationships. *Sex Roles, 16*, 539-558.
McCall, G. J. (1970). The social organization of relationships. In G. J. McCall, M. McCall, N. Denzin, & S. Kurth (Eds.), *Social relationships* (pp. 3-34). Chicago: Aldine.
McCall, G. J. (1988). The organizational life cycle of relationships. In S. W. Duck (Ed.), *Handbook of personal relationships* (pp. 467-484). Chichester: John Wiley.
McFall, R. M. (1982). A review and reformulation of the concept of social skills. *Behavioral Assessment, 4*, 1-33.
McGoldrick, M. (1982). Normal families: An ethnic perspective. In F. Walsh (Ed.), *Normal family process* (pp. 167-195). New York: Guilford.
McGoldrick, M. (1988). Ethnicity and the family life cycle. In B. Carter & M. McGoldrick (Eds.), *The changing family life cycle: A framework for family therapy* (2nd ed.). New York: Gardner.
McKee, L., & Bell, C. (1987). His unemployment, her problem: The domestic and marital consequences of male unemployment. In S. Allen, A. Waton, K. Purcell, & S. Wood (Eds.), *The experience of unemployment*. Basingstoke: Macmillan.
Mead, G. H. (1934). *Mind, self, and society*. Chicago: University of Chicago Press.
Medick, H., & Sabean, D. (Eds.). (1984). *Interest and emotion: Essays on the study of family and kinship*. Cambridge: Cambridge University Press.
Merry, S. E. (1989). Mediation in nonindustrial societies. In K. Kressel, D. G. Pruitt, and associates (Eds.), *Mediation research* (pp. 68-90). San Francisco: Jossey-Bass.
Milardo, R. M. (1982). Friendship networks in developing relationships: Converging and diverging social environments. *Social Psychology Quarterly, 45*, 162-172.
Milardo, R. M. (1988). (Ed.). *Families and social networks*. Newbury Park, CA: Sage.
Milardo, R. M., Johnson, M. P., & Huston, T. L. (1983). Developing close relationships: Changing patterns of interactions between pair members and social networks. *Journal of Personality and Social Psychology, 44*, 964-976.
Milardo, R. M., & Klein, R. (1992, November). *Dominance norms and domestic violence: The justification of aggression in close relationships*. Paper presented at the NCFR Pre-Conference Theory Construction and Research Methodology Workshop, Orlando, FL.
Milardo, R. M., & Wellman, B. (1992). The personal is social. *Journal of Social and Personal Relationships, 9*, 339-342.
Miller, J. B. (1986). *Toward a new psychology of women* (2nd ed.). Boston: Beacon.

Mirowsky, J., & Ross, C. E. (1986). Social patterns of distress. *Annual Review of Sociology, 12,* 23-45.

Montgomery, B. M. (1988). Quality communication in personal relationships. In S. W. Duck (Ed.), *Handbook of personal relationships* (pp. 343-366). New York: John Wiley.

Montgomery, B. M. (1992). Communication as the interface between couples and culture. In S. A. Deetz (Ed.), *Communication yearbook* (Vol. 15, pp. 476-508). Newbury Park, CA: Sage.

Moore, S. F., & Myerhoff, B. G. (Eds.). (1977). *Secular ritual.* Assen/Amsterdam, the Netherlands: Van Gorcum.

Morgan, D. (1991). Ideologies of marriage and family life. In D. Clark (Ed.), *Marriage, domestic life and social change.* London: Routledge.

Muir, D. E., & Weinstein, E. A. (1962). The social debt: An investigation of lower-class and middle-class norms of social obligation. *American Sociological Review, 27,* 532-539.

Murdock, G. (1937). Comparative data on the division of labor by sex. *Social Forces, 15,* 551-553.

Mutran, E., & Reitzes, D. C. (1984). Intergenerational support activities and well-being among the elderly: A convergence of exchange and symbolic interaction perspectives. *American Sociological Review, 49,* 117-130.

Napier, A. Y. (1977). *The rejection-intrusion pattern: A central family dynamic.* Unpublished manuscript, University of Wisconsin-Madison, School of Family Resources.

Navran, L. (1967). Communication and adjustment in marriage. *Family Process, 6,* 173-184.

Nydegger, C. N. (1983). Family ties of the aged in cross-cultural perspective. *The Gerontologist, 23,* 26-32.

Nydegger, C. N. (1986). Asymmetrical kin and the problematic son-in-law. In N. Datan, A. L. Greene, & H. W. Reese (Eds.), *Life-span developmental psychology: Intergenerational relations* (pp. 99-123). Hillsdale, NJ: Lawrence Erlbaum.

O'Connor, M. (1989). The Virgin of Guadalupe and the economics of symbolic behavior. *Journal for the Scientific Study of Religion, 28,* 105-119.

O'Connor, P. (1992). *Friendships between women.* London: Harvester Wheatsheaf.

Okin, S. M. (1989). *Gender, justice, and the family.* New York: Basic Books/Harper-Collins.

Olien, M. (1978). *The human myth.* New York: Harper & Row.

Oliker, S. J. (1989). *Best friends and marriage.* Berkeley: University of California Press.

Oring, E. (1984). Dyadic traditions. *Journal of Folklore Research, 21,* 19-28.

Owen, W. (1984). Interpretive themes in relational communication. *Quarterly Journal of Speech, 70,* 274-287.

Oxley, D., Haggard, L. M., Werner, C. M., & Altman, I. (1986). Transactional qualities of neighborhood social networks: A case study of "Christmas Street." *Environment and Behavior, 18,* 640-677.

Pahl, R. E., & Wallace, C. D. (1988). Neither angels in marble nor rebels in red: Privatization and working-class consciousness. In D. Rose (Ed.), *Social stratification and economic change.* London: Hutchinson.

Paine, R. (1969). In search of friendship. *Man* (n.s.), *4,* 505-524.

Parks, M. R., & Adelman, M. B. (1983). Communication networks and the development of romantic relationships: An expansion of uncertainty reduction theory. *Human Communication Research, 10,* 55-79.

Parks, M. R., & Eggert, L. L. (1991). The role of social context in the dynamics of personal relationships. In W. H. Jones & D. Perlman (Eds.), *Advances in personal relationships* (Vol. 2, pp. 1-34). London: Jessica Kingsley.

Parks, M. R., Stan, C. M., & Eggert, L. L. (1983). Romantic involvement and social network involvement. *Social Psychology Quarterly, 46,* 116-131.

Paul, E., & White, K. (1990). The development of intimate relationships in late adolescence. *Adolescence, 25,* 375-400.

Pearlin, L. I. (1983). Role strains and personal stress. In H. Kaplan (Ed.), *Psychosocial stress: Trends in theory and research* (pp. 3-32). New York: Academic Press.

Peplau, L. A., & Gordon, S. L. (1985). Women and men in love: Gender differences in close heterosexual relationships. In V. E. O'Leary, R. K. Unger, & B. S. Wallston (Eds.), *Women, gender, and social psychology* (pp. 257-291). Hillsdale, NJ: Lawrence Erlbaum.

Petronio, S. (1991). Communication boundary management: A theoretical model of managing disclosure of private information between married couples. *Communication Theory, 1,* 311-335.

Piotrkowski, C. S. (1979). *Work and the family system: A naturalistic study of working-class and lower middle-class families.* New York: Free Press.

Pruitt, D. G. (1981). *Negotiation behavior.* New York: Academic Press.

Pruitt, D. G., & Johnson, D. F. (1970). Mediation as an aid to face-saving in negotiation. *Journal of Personality and Social Psychology, 14,* 239-246.

Pruitt, D. G., & Rubin, J. Z. (1986). *Social conflict: Escalation, stalemate, and settlement.* New York: Random House.

Prusank, D. T., Duran, R. L., & DeLillo, D. A. (1993). Interpersonal relationships in women's magazines: Dating and relating in the 1970s and 1980s. *Journal of Social and Personal Relationships, 10.*

Ptacek, J. (1988). Why do men batter their wives? In K. Yllo & M. Bograd (Eds.), *Feminist perspectives on wife abuse* (pp. 133-157). Newbury Park, CA: Sage.

Quinn, W. H. (1983). Personal and family adjustment in later life. *Journal of Marriage and the Family, 45,* 57-73.

Qureshi, H., & Walker, A. (1989). *The caring relationship: Elderly people and their families.* London: Macmillan.

Rands, M. (1988). Changes in social networks following marital separation and divorce. In R. M. Milardo (Ed.), *Families and social networks.* Newbury Park, CA: Sage.

Rawlins, W. R. (1983a). The dialectic of conjunctive freedoms. *Human Communication Research, 9,* 255-266.

Rawlins, W. R. (1983b). Openness as problematic in ongoing friendships: Two conversational dilemmas. *Communication Monographs, 50,* 1-13.

Rawlins, W. R. (1989). A dialectical analysis of the tensions, functions, and strategic challenges of communication in young adult friendships. In J. Anderson (Ed.), *Communication yearbook* (Vol. 12, pp. 157-189). Newbury Park, CA: Sage.

Rawlins, W. R. (1992). *Friendship matters: Communication, dialectics, and the life course.* New York: Walter de Gruyter.

Reis, H. T., Nezlek, J., & Wheeler, L. (1980). Physical attractiveness in social interaction. *Journal of Personality and Social Psychology, 48,* 1204-1217.

Reis, H. T., & Shaver, P. (1988). Intimacy as an interpersonal process. In S. W. Duck (Ed.), *Handbook of personal relationships: Theory, research and interventions* (pp. 367-389). New York: John Wiley.

Reisman, J. M. (1981). Adult friendships. In S. W. Duck & R. Gilmour (Eds.), *Personal relationships: Vol. 2. Developing personal relationships* (pp. 205-230). London: Academic Press.

Reisman, J. M. (1990). Intimacy in same-sex friendships. *Sex Roles, 23*(1-2), 65-82.

Reiss, P. J. (1962). The extended kinship system: Correlates of and attitudes on frequency of interaction. *Marriage and Family Living, 27,* 333-339.

Repetti, R. L. (1989). The effects of daily workload on subsequent behavior during marital interaction: The roles of social withdrawal and spouse support. *Journal of Personality and Social Psychology, 57,* 651-659.

Repetti, R. L. (1992). Social withdrawal as a short-term coping response to daily stressors. In H. S. Friedman (Ed.), *Hostility, coping and health.* Washington, DC: American Psychological Association.

Riegel, K. (1976). The dialectics of human development. *American Psychologist, 31,* 689-700.

Riessman, C. (1990). *Divorce talk: Women and men make sense of personal relationships.* New Brunswick, NJ: Rutgers University Press.

Risman, B. J. (1987). Intimate relationships from a microstructural perspective: Men who mother. *Gender and Society, 1,* 6-32.

Risman, B. J. (1989). Can men mother: Life as a single father. In B. Risman & P. Schwartz (Eds.), *Gender in intimate relationships* (pp. 155-164). Belmont, CA: Wadsworth.

Risman, B. J., & Schwartz, P. (1989). Being gendered: A microstructural view of intimate relations. In B. J. Risman & P. Schwartz (Eds.), *Gender in intimate relationships* (pp. 1-9). Belmont, CA: Wadsworth.

Roberts, J. (1988). Setting the frame: Definition, functions, and typology of rituals. In E. Imber-Black, J. Roberts, & R. A. Whiting (Eds.), *Rituals in families and family therapy* (pp. 3-46). New York: Norton.

Roff, L. L., & Klemmack, D. L. (1986). Norms for employed daughters' and sons' behavior toward frail older parents. *Sex Roles, 34,* 363-368.

Rook, K. S. (1984). The negative side of social interaction: Impact on psychological well-being. *Journal of Personality and Social Psychology, 46,* 1097-1108.

Rook, K. S. (1987). Close relationships: Ties that heal or ties that bind? In W. H. Jones & D. Perlman (Eds.), *Advances in personal relationships* (Vol. 1, pp. 1-35). Greenwich, CT: JAI.

Rubin, J. Z., & Brown, B. R. (1975). *The social psychology of bargaining and negotiation.* New York: Academic Press.

Rubin, L. (1985). *Just friends: The role of friendship in our lives.* New York: Harper & Row.

Ruddick, S. (1989). *Maternal thinking: Towards a politics of peace.* Boston: Beacon.

Rusbult, C. E. (1987). Responses to dissatisfaction in close relationships: The exit-voice-loyalty-neglect model. In D. Perlman & S. W. Duck (Eds.), *Intimate relationships: Development, dynamics, deterioration* (pp. 209-238). London: Sage.

Ryan, M. (1979). *Womanhood in America: From colonial times to the present* (2nd ed.). New York: New Viewpoints.

Sadker, M., & Sadker, D. (1984). *The report card on sex bias*. Washington, DC: Mid-Atlantic Center for Sex Equity.

Safilios-Rothschild, C. (1979). *Sex role socialization and sex discrimination: A synthesis and critique of the literature*. Washington, DC: National Institute of Education.

Sandler, R. M., & Hall, R. M. (1986). *The campus climate revisited: Chilly climate for women faculty, administrators, and graduate students*. Washington, DC: Project on the Status and Education of Women, Association of American Colleges.

Sarsby, J. (1983). *Romantic love and society*. Harmondsworth: Penguin.

Saunders, P. (1990). *A nation of home owners*. London: Unwin Hyman.

Scarf, M. (1987). *Intimate partners*. New York: Random House.

Schaap, C., Buunk, B., & Kerkstra, A. (1988). Marital conflict resolution. In P. Noller & M. A. Fitzpatrick (Eds.), *Perspectives on marital interaction* (pp. 203-244). Clevedon, England: Multilingual Matters.

Schaef, A. W. (1985). *Women's reality*. New York: Harper.

Schneider, B. E., & Gould, M. (1987). Female sexuality: Looking back into the future. In B. B. Hess & M. M. Ferree (Eds.), *Analyzing gender: A handbook of social science research* (pp. 120-153). Newbury Park, CA: Sage.

Schneider, D. M. (1980). *American kinship: A cultural account*. Englewood Cliffs, NJ: Prentice-Hall. (Original work published 1967)

Schorr, A. (1980). *". . . thy father & thy mother . . .": A second look at filial responsibility and family policy*. Washington, DC: Department of Health and Human Services, Government Printing Office.

Scott, C. K., Fuhrman, R. W., & Wyer, R. S. (1991). Information processing in close relationships. In G. J. O. Fletcher & F. D. Fincham (Eds.), *Cognition in close relationships* (pp. 37-67). Hillsdale, NJ: Lawrence Erlbaum.

Scott, J. (1986). Gender: A useful category for historical analysis. *American Historical Review, 91,* 1053-1075.

Seelbach, W. C. (1978). Correlates of aged parents' filial responsibility expectations and realizations. *The Family Coordinator, 27,* 341-350.

Sennett, R. (1977). Destructive Gemeinschaft. In N. Birnbaum (Ed.), *Beyond the crisis*. London: Oxford University Press.

Shanas, E. (1979). The family as a social support system in old age. *The Gerontologist, 19,* 169-174.

Sheppard, B. H., Blumenfeld-Jones, K., & Roth, J. (1989). Informal thirdpartyship: Studies of everyday conflict intervention. In K. Kressel, D. G. Pruitt, and associates (Eds.), *Mediation research* (pp. 166-189). San Francisco: Jossey-Bass.

Sherrod, D. (1989). The influence of gender on same-sex friendships. In C. Hendrick (Ed.), *Close relationships: Vol. 10. Review of personality and social psychology* (pp. 164-186). Newbury Park, CA: Sage.

Shorter, E. (1975). *The making of the modern family*. New York: Basic Books.

Shulman, N. (1975). Life-cycle variations in patterns of close relationships. *Journal of Marriage and the Family, 37,* 813-821.

Snell, W. E., Jr., Hawkins, R. C., II, & Belk, S. S. (1988). Stereotypes about male sexuality and the use of social influence strategies in intimate relationships. *Journal of Clinical and Social Psychology, 7,* 42-48.

Spanier, G. B., & Thompson, L. (1984). *Parting: The aftermath of separation and divorce.* Beverly Hills, CA: Sage.

Stack, C. (1974). *All our kin: Strategies for survival in a black community.* New York: Harper & Row.

Stafford, L., & Canary, D. (1991). Maintenance strategies and romantic relationship type, gender and relational characteristics. *Journal of Social and Personal Relationships, 8,* 217-242.

Stapley, J., & Haveland, J. (1989). Beyond depression: Gender differences in normal adolescents' emotional experiences. *Sex Roles, 20,* 295-308.

Stark, L. P. (1991). Traditional gender role beliefs and individual outcomes: An exploratory analysis. *Sex Roles, 24,* 639-650.

Stein, C. H. (1992). Ties that bind: Three studies of obligation in adult relationships with family. *Journal of Social and Personal Relationships, 9,* 525-547.

Stein, C. H., Bush, E. G., Ross, R. R., & Ward, M. (1992). Mine yours and ours: A configural analysis of the networks of married couples in relation to marital satisfaction and individual well-being. *Journal of Social and Personal Relationships, 9,* 365-383.

Stein, C. H., Gaines, M., Ward, M., Bass, L., & Russner, W. (in preparation). *Felt obligation among college age adults with divorced parents: A qualitative analysis.*

Stein, C. H., & Rappaport, J. (1986). Social network interviews as sources of etic and emic data: A study of young married women. In S. E. Hobfoll (Ed.), *Stress, social support and women* (pp. 47-66). New York: Hemisphere.

Stone, L. (1977). *The family, sex and marriage in England: 1500-1800.* New York: Harper & Row.

Stone, L. (1979). *The family, sex, and marriage in England, 1500-1800.* New York: Harper Colophon.

Straus, M. A., Gelles, R. J., & Steinmetz, S. K. (1980). *Behind closed doors: Violence in the American family.* New York: Anchor.

Surra, C. A. (1985). Courtship types: Variations in interdependence between partners and social networks. *Journal of Personality and Social Psychology, 49,* 357-375.

Surra, C. A. (1988). The influence of the interactive network on developing relationships. In R. M. Milardo (Ed.), *Families and social networks* (pp. 48-82). Beverly Hills, CA: Sage.

Surra, C. A. (1990). Research and theory on mate selection and premarital relationships in the 1980s. *Journal of Marriage and the Family, 52,* 844-865.

Surra, C. A., & Milardo, R. M. (1991). The social psychological context of developing relationships: Interactive and psychological networks. In W. H. Jones & D. Perlman (Eds.), *Advances in personal relationships* (Vol. 3, pp. 1-36). London: Jessica Kingsley.

Swain, S. (1989). Covert intimacy: Closeness in men's friendships. In B. J. Risman & P. Schwartz (Eds.), *Gender in intimate relationships* (pp. 71-86). Belmont, CA: Wadsworth.

Szinovatz, M. E. (1984). Changing family roles and interactions. In B. B. Hess & M. B. Sussman (Eds.), *Women and the family: Two decades of change* (pp. 164-201). New York: Hawthorne.

Tannen, D. (1990). *You just don't understand: Women and men in conversation.* New York: Morrow.

Tavris, C. (1992). *The mismeasure of woman.* New York: Simon & Schuster.

Tennen, H., Suls, J., & Affleck, G. (1991). Personality and daily experience: The promise and the challenge. *Journal of Personality, 59,* 313-338.

Thompson, E. H., Jr. (1991). The maleness of violence in dating relationships: An appraisal of stereotypes. *Sex Roles, 24*(5-6), 261-278.

Thompson, L., & Walker, A. J. (1989). Gender in families: Women and men in marriage, work, and parenthood. *Journal of Marriage and the Family, 51,* 845-871.

Thomson, E., & Colella, V. (1992). Cohabitation and marital stability: Quality or commitment. *Journal of Marriage and the Family, 54,* 259-267.

Thorbecke, W., & Grotevant, H. D. (1982). Gender differences in adolescent interpersonal identity formation. *Journal of Youth and Adolescence, 11*(6), 479-492.

Ting-Toomey, S. (1991). Intimacy expression in three cultures: France, Japan, and the United States. *International Journal of Intercultural Relations, 15,* 29-46.

Tognoli, J. (1980). Male friendship and intimacy over the life span. *Family Relations, 29,* 273-279.

Tonti, M. (1988). Relationships among adult siblings who care for their aged parents. In M. D. Kahn & K. G. Lewis (Eds.), *Siblings in therapy* (pp. 417-434). New York: Norton.

Traupmann, J., & Hatfield, E. (1981). Love and its effect on mental and physical health. In R. Fogel, E. Hatfield, S. Kiesler, & E. Shanas (Eds.), *Aging: Stability and change in the family* (pp. 253-274). New York: Academic Press.

Troll, L. E. (1971). The family of later life: A decade review. *Journal of Marriage and the Family, 33,* 263-290.

Turner, V. (1967). *The forest of symbols: Aspects of Ndembu ritual.* Ithaca, NY: Cornell University Press.

Van Gennep, A. (1909). *Les rites de passage* (M. B. Uizedom & G. L. Caffee, Trans.). London: Routledge & Kegan Paul. (Republished by University of Chicago Press, 1960)

VanYperen, N. W., & Buunk, B. P. (1991). Equity theory and exchange and communal orientation from a cross-national perspective. *The Journal of Social Psychology, 131*(1), 5-20.

Vuchinich, S. (1987). Starting and stopping spontaneous family conflicts. *Journal of Marriage and the Family, 43,* 785-788.

Wake, S., & Sporakowski, M. (1972). An intergenerational comparison of attitudes toward supporting aged parents. *Journal of Marriage and the Family, 34,* 42-48.

Walker, A. J., Pratt, C. C., Shin, H., & Jones, L. L. (1990). Motives for parental caregiving and relationship quality. *Family Relations, 39,* 51-56.

Wamboldt, F. S., & Reiss, D. (1989). Defining a family heritage and a new relationship identity: Two central tasks in the making of a marriage. *Family Process, 28,* 317-335.

Warner, R. (1991). Incorporating time. In B. Montgomery & S. Duck (Eds.), *Studying interpersonal interaction.* New York: Guilford.

Weeden, C. (1987). *Feminist practice and poststructuralist theory.* Oxford: Basil Blackwood.

Weiss, L., & Lowenthal, M. F. (1975). Life-course perspective on friendship. In M. Thurnher & D. Chiriboga (Eds.), *Four stages of life* (pp. 48-61). San Francisco: Jossey-Bass.

Weiss, R. L., & Heyman, R. E. (1990). Observation of marital interaction. In F. D. Fincham & T. N. Bradbury (Eds.), *The psychology of marriage* (pp. 87-117). New York: Guilford.

Wellman, B. (1985). Domestic work, paid work and net work. In S. W. Duck & D. Perlman (Eds.), *Understanding personal relationships.* Beverly Hills, CA: Sage.

Wellman, B. (1992). Men in networks: Private communities, domestic friendships. In P. Nardi (Ed.), *Men's friendships.* Newbury Park, CA: Sage.

Wellman, B., & Wellman, B. (1992). Domestic affairs and network relations. *Journal of Social and Personal Relationships, 9,* 385-409.

Welter, B. (1966). The cult of true womanhood: 1820-1860. *American Quarterly, 18,* 151-174.

Werner, C. M. (1989). *Celebrations in family relationships.* Paper presented at the meeting of the American Psychological Association, New Orleans, LA.

Werner, C. M. (1992). [Christmas decorations]. Unpublished raw data.

Werner, C. M., Altman, I., & Oxley, D. (1985). Temporal aspects of homes: A transactional perspective. In I. Altman & C. M. Werner (Eds.), *Home environments: Vol. 8. Human behavior and environment: Advances in theory and research* (pp. 1-32). Beverly Hills, CA: Sage.

Werner, C. M., Altman, I., Oxley, D., & Haggard, L. M. (1987). People, place, and time: A transactional analysis of neighborhoods. In W. H. Jones & D. Perlman (Eds.), *Advances in personal relationships* (pp. 243-275). Greenwich, CT: JAI.

Werner, C., Brown, B., Altman, I., & Staples, B. (1992). Close relationship in their physical and social contexts: A transactional perspective. *Journal of Social and Personal Relationships, 9,* 411-431.

Werner, C. M., & Haggard, L. M. (1985). Temporal qualities of interpersonal relationships. In G. R. Miller & M. L. Knapp (Eds.), *Handbook of interpersonal communication* (pp. 59-99). Beverly Hills, CA: Sage.

Werner, C. M., Haggard, L. M., Altman, I., & Oxley, D. (1988). Temporal qualities of rituals and celebrations: A comparison of Christmas Street and Zuni Shalako. In J. E. McGrath (Ed.), *The social psychology of time* (pp. 203-232). Newbury Park, CA: Sage.

Werner, C. M., Peterson-Lewis, S., & Brown, B. B. (1989). Inferences about homeowners' sociability: Impact of Christmas decorations and other cues. *Journal of Environmental Psychology, 9,* 279-296.

Werner C. M., Turner, J., Twitchell, F. S., Shipmann, K., Dickson, B., Bruschke, G. V., & von Bismarck, W. B. (1992). *Commitment, behavior, and attitude change: A strategy for increasing long-term recycling.* Unpublished manuscript, University of Utah, Salt Lake City.

West, C., & Zimmerman, D. H. (1987). "Doing gender." *Gender and Society, 1,* 125-151.

Wheeler, L., & Nezlek, J. (1977). Sex differences in social participation. *Journal of Personality and Social Psychology, 35,* 742-754.

Wheeler, L., & Reis, H. T. (1991). Self-recording of everyday life events: Origins, types, and uses. *Journal of Personality, 59,* 339-354.

White, B. (1989). Gender differences in marital communication patterns. *Family Process, 28,* 89-106.

White, K., Speisman, M. J., Jackson, D., Bartis, S., & Costos, D. (1986). Intimacy maturity and its correlates in young married couples. *Journal of Personality and Social Psychology, 50,* 152-162.

Whiteside, M. F. (1988). Creation of family identity through ritual performance in early remarriage. In E. Imber-Black, J. Roberts, & R. A. Whiting (Eds.), *Rituals in families and family therapy* (pp. 276-304). New York: Norton.

Williams, D. G. (1985). Gender, masculinity-femininity, and emotional intimacy in same-sex friendship. *Sex Roles, 12,* 587-600.

Williams, D. G. (1988). Gender, marriage, and psychosocial well-being. *Journal of Family Issues, 9,* 452-468.

Williams, R. G. A. (1983). Kinship and migration strategies among settled Londoners. *British Journal of Sociology, 34,* 386-415.

Wills, T. A., Weiss, R. L., & Patterson, G. R. (1974). A behavioral analysis of the determinants of marital satisfaction. *Journal of Consulting and Clinical Psychology, 42,* 802-811.

Winstead, B. A. (1986). Sex differences in same-sex friendships. In V. J. Derlega & B. A. Winstead (Eds.), *Friendship and social interaction* (pp. 81-99). New York: Springer-Verlag.

Wolin, S. J., & Bennett, L. A. (1984). Family rituals. *Family Process, 23,* 401-420.

Wood, J. T. (1986). Different voices in relationship crises: An extension of Gilligan's theory. *American Behavioral Scientist, 29,* 273-301.

Wood, J. T. (1993). Enlarging conceptual boundaries: A critique of research on interpersonal communication. In S. P. Bowen & N. J. Wyatt (Eds.), *Transforming visions: Feminist critiques in communication studies.* Cresskill, NJ: Hampton.

Wood, J. T. (in press). Engendered identities: Shaping voice and mind through gender. In D. R. Vocate (Ed.), *Intrapersonal communication: Different voices, different minds.* Hillsdale, NJ: Lawrence Erlbaum.

Wood, J. T., Dendy, L., Dordek, E., Germany, M., & Varallo, S. (in press). The dialectic of difference: A thematic analysis of intimates' meanings for differences. In K. Carter & M. Presnell (Eds.), *Interpretive approaches to interpersonal communication.* New York: State University of New York Press.

Wood, J. T., & Lenze, L. F. (1991a). Strategies to enhance gender sensitivity in communication education. *Communication Education, 40,* 16-21.

Wood, J. T., & Lenze, L. F. (1991b). Gender and the development of self: Inclusive pedagogy in interpersonal communication. *Women's Studies in Communication, 14*(1), 1-23.

Wortley, D. B., & Amatea, E. S. (1982). Mapping adult life changes: A conceptual framework for organizing adult development theory. *Personnel and Guidance Journal, 60,* 476-482.

Wright, P. H. (1982). Men's friendships, women's friendships, and the alleged inferiority of the latter. *Sex Roles, 8,* 1-20.

Name Index

Subject Index

194

About the Contributors

Graham Allan is a Reader in Sociology at the University of Southampton, England. His main research interests are in informal social relationships and domestic life. His publications include a *Sociology of Friendship and Kinship, Family Life, Friendship: Developing a Sociological Perspective,* and *Home and Family* (with Graham Crow). He is currently engaged in research into social isolation and is coauthoring a book on the sociology of community life.

Irwin Altman is Distinguished Professor at the University of Utah. His research interests focus on cross-cultural aspects of interpersonal relationships, with particular emphasis on temporal, environmental, and social contexts of relationships. For several years he has been conducting ethnographic research on dyadic and communal relationships among polygynous families in the United States.

Leslie A. Baxter is Professor in the Department of Rhetoric and Communication at the University of California at Davis. She has written over 50 refereed articles and book chapters on communication in personal relationships.

Niall Bolger is Assistant Professor in the Social-Personality Psychology Program at New York University. He obtained a B.A. in psychology at Trinity College, Dublin, and an M.S. and Ph.D. at Cornell University. His research interests include the social psychology of daily life, social and personality processes in health and illness, and methods for the analysis of temporal data.

Barbara B. Brown is Associate Professor in the Environment and Behavior area of the Family and Consumer Studies Department at the University of Utah. Her work focuses on applying ideas about attachment, privacy regulation, and territoriality to social and physical aspects of human behavior. These applications have included work on residential burglary, university dropouts, and problems of residential life, from shared housing to natural disasters.

Steve Duck is the founding editor of the *Journal of Social and Personal Relationship,* the editor of *Wiley Handbook of Personal Relationships,* and the editor or author of 25 other books on personal relationships. He also founded the International Network on Personal Relationships, the professional organization for the field, and two series of international conferences on relationships. He is presently the David and Amy Starch Research Professor at the University of Iowa, Iowa City.

Joseph Ginat is in the Department of Land of Israel Studies at the University of Haifa, Israel.

Shannon Kelleher is a psychology major in the College of Arts and Sciences at New York University.

Renate Klein is a postdoctoral fellow at the University of Maine and is currently on leave from the University of Cologne, Germany. Her research interests include social conflict and negotiation.

Robert M. Milardo is Associate Professor of Family Relationships at the University of Maine. He is associate editor of the

Journal of Social and Personal Relationships and coauthor of *Families and Social Networks* (Sage).

Catherine H. Stein is Associate Professor in the Psychology Department at Bowling Green State University. She is interested in the influence of social networks and family relationships on individual mental health and well-being. She is a clinical-community psychologist and has written a number of papers in the area of social relationships.

Carol M. Werner (Ph.D., Ohio State University) is Professor of Psychology at the University of Utah. She is a social-environmental psychologist who studies how people use their environments to foster effective social interaction. She is also interested in the role of service in the university curriculum.

Julia T. Wood is Professor in the Department of Communication at the University of North Carolina at Chapel Hill, where she teaches and conducts research on close relationships, gender and communication, and feminist theory. Within these areas she has written or coauthored eight books, coedited three other books, and published more than 50 articles in journals in communication, women's studies, and the humanities.

Visions of the Future:
HR Strategies for the New Millennium

Marc G. Singer
Editor

PREFACE

Much has been written about the need for human resources practitioners to become strategic partners in their organizations. The most important elements of strategic planning are the ability to identify emerging trends and understand how these trends will affect the way we do our business.

We are extraordinarily grateful for the wealth of talent found in the membership of the Society for Human Resource Management's national committees. These professionals have looked ahead, and in their own area of expertise they are presenting to us likely scenarios for the near future. Under the guidance of Dr. Marc G. Singer, past SHRM Research Committee Chair, and with invaluable assistance from SHRM staff, SHRM's committees selected the issues most likely to have the highest impact on the field of human resource management in the next century. The main purpose of this book is to cause the reader to become ever vigilant for change in the environment and how this change will impact human resources. How quickly we identify the trends, and how ready we are to respond to them, will determine to a great degree how credible and successful we are in our respective organizations.

Here, then, is the collective effort of many professionals. Enjoy and utilize the insights offered to make your world the envy of all around you. Our wish is that this book will influence you to become future-focused.

Michael J. Lotito, SPHR
Chair 2000

Ommy Strauch, SPHR
Vice President for Committees 1999–2000

ACKNOWLEDGMENTS

Predicting the future of Human Resources is at best a risky business. Academicians, practitioners, and researchers offer varying opinions about the issues that will have the greatest impact on human resource managers over the next decade. HR writings abound in areas such as government rules and regulations, the future role of unions, core competencies, costing HR, measurement, accountability, changing workforce demographics, and global impacts. The single constant that underlies these various perspectives appears to be the probability that the role of human resource management will undergo a significant transformation in the near future.

In an effort to identify some of the key issues facing the human resource profession during the early years of the millennium, professional volunteer members of SHRM's functional committees combined their numerous talents and energies. The result of this synergy is this book, *Visions of the Future: HR Strategies for the New Millennium*. I am especially grateful to Michael Lotito, SHRM Chair, whose leadership and support during the initial stages of the book enabled the commencement of this project, and to Ommy Strauch, Vice President for Committees, for her continuing assistance and encouragement during the project's completion phase. I am extremely thankful to the 1998 and 1999 SHRM committee chairs for their assistance in coordinating the efforts of their committees and for diligently monitoring their authors' contributions. I extend my thanks to the staff at SHRM who edited, formatted, and produced the final version of this project. Finally, I extend a special thank you to the members of the various committees and the authors for their time and efforts in writing this book.

Marc G. Singer
Editor
March 2000

TABLE OF CONTENTS

TABLE OF CONTENTS

Visions of the Future:
HR Strategies for the New Millennium

COMING OF AGE

Michael R. Losey
Society for Human Resource Management

The human resource management profession will profoundly change in the next century, as the United States and other developed countries evolve from manufacturing and service-based economies to knowledge-based ones. The industrial revolution created the human resource profession, and the twenty-first century workplace will require it to continue to transform itself. In the new millennium, human resource professionals must be fully accepted strategic business partners, leading their organizations through yet unidentified challenges in a rapidly changing global workplace. They will need to be more proactive in the design and implementation of workplace practices that will attract, retain, and motivate a shrinking pool of qualified workers.

In taking on that role, human resource professionals are now compelled to learn new skills that go beyond complex administration or being "gatekeepers." Their primary responsibilities have been to ensure compliance with labor contracts and federal and state laws, and to administer company policies and practices. In the twenty-first century, human resource professionals will be required to anticipate the needs of an increasingly white-collar workforce and plan strategically to meet those needs.

The trend is already happening. Companies are now realizing that the human resource function has a direct impact on their bottom lines and must be linked to core business strategies. Now, more than ever before, CEOs are asking, "Who is running this part of our company? Is that person competent?" There is a growing recognition that bona fide human resource professionals must understand economic, political, social, cultural, and demographic trends. They must also master technological innovations, changing work values, skill shortages, and global trends and practices, as well as government mandates in labor laws, affirmative action, health care, and privacy—to mention but a few areas of required competency. And, increasingly, human resource professionals must understand the business of business. Each day, the number of workplace issues in which human resource professionals must play a role increases, and their involvement in senior-level decision-making has become central to many organizations.

Yes, the human resource profession is now coming of age. In the new millennium, the profession will not require human resource professionals but human resource *leaders*. Higher levels of competencies will be required. The result will be higher barriers of entrance to the profession—as it should be in any demanding profession.

The H in HR—for History

To understand the future of the human resource profession, it is important to understand it through the lens of its history. It is a brief history, because the profession did not truly exist until the late nineteenth and early twentieth centuries, when the industrial revolution was at its peak.

Before the industrial revolution and the onset of mass production, there was little need for a profession dedicated to managing a workforce. As many as 90 percent of the people working in the United States were farmers. The remaining workers were tradesmen and craftsmen in business for themselves. There was no discussion about what the children would grow up to be. Farmers' sons knew what they would grow up to be: farmers. Daughters would become wives and mothers and care for the home. And they all learned their skills through their families.

Those vying to enter a trade were usually required to complete an extensive apprenticeship program under the tutelage of a master tradesman. These working relationships were close, personal relationships that rarely needed the intervention of a third party. Skilled craftsmen and apprentices worked in small shops or at home. There was little need for unions, workers' compensation, or labor laws on the family farm or in the small craft shop because workplace issues could be addressed through these personal relationships.

The industrial revolution, however, changed the nature of work. Now, through the application of electricity and other power sources, standardization of parts and tools, and improvements in processes, mass production was possible. For the first time, business owners could employ many workers in one location. Companies that designed a better product at less cost could use the railroad for efficiently shipping mass quantities of goods to previously out-of-reach markets, driving the demand for more goods and more workers. To feed that demand, immigration into the United States rose to an all-time high, and the most diverse workforce in the world began to take shape.

Unfortunately, though, abuses to workers were also at an all-time high. Labor laws such as minimum wage rate protection, overtime, workers' compensation, health and safety, or equal employment opportunity did not exist. Employers had little interest in their workers' personal lives, working conditions, or job satisfaction. Many companies were family-owned or dominated by one individual who believed that the employees' lots had improved through their employment. Any attempts to suggest changes were viewed as a threat to the owner's financial and personal interests. Many employers considered low-skilled employees in a mass production work environment as expendable.

Henry Ford allegedly commented that he didn't know why his employees insisted on bringing their heads to work when all he needed was their hands and feet. Ford's 380 percent turnover rate in 1913, which essentially crippled his company's ability to grow in an emerging industry, was a direct result of his attitude toward line workers and was driven by working conditions that were unacceptable at any wage. He agreed to double the workers' daily wage rate to five dollars so that he could stem turnover and buy employee loyalty, not so that "his workers could buy his cars" as some have suggested.

In many companies like the Ford Motor Company, the personnel people who previously had been given the largely administrative job of hiring low-wage, unskilled employees now saw that the well-being of employees had become much more important than how much they were paid. This became especially apparent as unions became more of a force to reckon with and as the nation's state and federal laws began to provide added protections to the interests of organized labor.

Many employers viewed the growing "union threat" as socialistic or radical, rather than as a self-preserving interest of workers in banding together to demand safer working conditions, humane treatment, and fair wages. And before the prohibition of unfair labor practices as we know them today, anti-union efforts were sometimes ruthlessly led by personnel representatives, some with security or police backgrounds. Industry viewed unions as its biggest and most powerful competitors because a union could shut down the employer faster or possibly disadvantage it more than any business competitor. This reality became a very real risk, and with risk comes interest and attention. The human resource profession became more important, and for the first time it mattered who was in the personnel job.

This was the environment that led to the rise of the modern union in the United States and, shortly thereafter, the human resource management profession. Unions rallied workers together to demand safer working conditions, humane treatment, and fair wages. They quickly became a force to be reckoned with, and while the political, social, and economic balance of power has shifted over time between unions and employer, unions have left an indelible mark on the American workplace.

The National Labor Relations Act, the Fair Labor Standards Act, the Taft-Hartley Act, the Equal Pay Act, the 1964 Civil Rights Act, the Age Discrimination in Employment Act, ERISA, the EOAA, OSHA, COBRA, the Americans with Disabilities Act, the Family and Medical Leave Act, and the Older Workers Protection Act, among others, have all been enacted, either directly or indirectly, because of the presence of the modern union in the American workplace.

Ironically, it is the passage of these laws that has aided in the steady decline of union membership since the mid-1950s. Today, only about 14 percent of the U.S. workforce is unionized, whereas in the late 1940s through the mid-1950s, one out of three workers were union members. These laws expanded protections to all workers, yet to some extent also usurped unions' roles in protecting workers. These legislative protections, along with the changing nature of the workforce, have dramatically affected the human resource profession.

Today, we are witnessing a historic social and economic shift into a knowledge-based economy, where we certainly want the employees to bring their heads to work. Today, it is not how many good parts you can make in an hour; it is how many good decisions you can make. Today, intellectual capital and the individual can make the crucial difference to an organization's success or failure.

The Future

What will all of this mean to the future of the workplace and the human resource profession?

Some may argue that the labor movement has become a dinosaur that will not last far into the next millennium. Falling membership rolls, the existence of federal labor laws that protect workers, and a growing white-collar workforce suggest that unions will become obsolete in the workplace of the twenty-first century.

My advice—don't count the unions out. A revitalization of the labor movement is taking place. We will see its survival through the increased unionization of white-collar and service-sector employees. Just this past year, physicians, who have a long-standing conservative outlook, voted to unionize to counter the powerful grip of health maintenance organizations on their fees and their practices. Temporary employees at Microsoft have also made moves to form a union. And the labor movement has moved to college campuses. At Stanford University, highly educated graduate assistants recently voted to join a union. At Dartmouth, undergraduates have focused their attention on fighting for a living wage for unskilled workers.

Yes, there will be a labor movement in the new millennium. But an increasing number of tomorrow's unions will consist of highly educated white-collar workers with very specific work skills. They will not look like or act like the old blue-collar unions of the past. Their emphasis will be to establish terms and conditions of employment, and at contract time they will act very much like a traditional union—yet with the clout of skilled workers. They will also add new complexity to the workplace, as unions representing bright and curious engineers, scientists, programmers and others second-guess company decisions on such issues as how their pensions are invested.

Tomorrow's union workers may not depend on the union to turn each element of the employment relationship into an actionable grievance. Their highly sought skills will enable them to leave a problematic employer easily. As a result, they will resolve many employment-related issues themselves, just as technical and professional employees do today. Collectively, though, the new unions will advance the interests of their membership, but their goals will be increasingly less oriented to cents per hour and more directed toward fair treatment, work and family, education, training, and other issues of concern to a better-educated and more sophisticated workforce.

Human resource professionals, therefore, will need to learn new skills to handle negotiations and arbitration with these new unions and their new members. Human resource professionals seeking to keep their workplace union-free will have to plan accordingly to anticipate and accommodate workers' wants and needs.

The face of the workplace will change in the twenty-first century. It will be older, more diverse, and more female. There will be fewer qualified workers as the net additions to the workforce decrease. Human resource professionals may find themselves allocating more dollars to their training budgets than ever before to retrain employees when new employees are not available, or to make up for the widening gap between what skills employers will need and what skills are taught in our schools.

As the face of the workplace changes, human resource professionals will continue to grapple with work/life issues. It will become more vital than ever to design a workplace (and with it benefit and compensation packages) that will not only attract and retain scarce workers, but also permit them to contribute in ways that add to their fulfillment of their own potential.

Labor, Social Security, and immigration laws will also have to be changed to reflect the new workforce needs if the United States is to remain an economic world leader. To accomplish these changes, human resource professionals must become a more active voice in reflecting the reality of the workplace of today and tomorrow. More important, they will have to become change-makers, actively participating in the legislative process at both the state and federal levels; few professions are affected as much by legislative changes as is human resource management.

Technology will be another factor to be reckoned with in the twenty-first century. Not only will it demand more skilled workers, it will enable the workplace to become more virtual.

The number of U.S. workers who telecommute has increased in recent years and the trend will continue. Technology will also allow for more workers to become contingent workers, or "free agents." Human resource professionals will have to develop practices that ensure that these workers are "connected" to the workplace by more than just a dedicated line.

Many human resource professionals may find themselves fostering a life-long learning environment in their workplaces to keep workers up-to-date on the myriad technological innovations. This may mean more extensive and cost-effective training programs, or partnerships with local colleges and universities, or both.

Technology will also affect the human resource profession itself. More effective use of the Internet and intranets, and the increasing sophistication of human relations information systems that can effectively track compensation and benefit packages and federal rules and regulations, will demand higher-skilled human resource professionals, while also easing the administrative burdens historically associated with the field. Technology will also permit the increased outsourcing of many of the administrative human resource functions, allowing corporate human resource professionals to become strategic thinkers, planners, and implementers of new ideas and programs.

The workplace of the new millennium will also transcend international borders. The 1990s have witnessed a surge of global mergers and acquisitions, and this globalization will require tomorrow's human resource professionals to consider a whole new set of challenges associated with working in diverse cultures. Language, societal norms, compensation, employment, retirement, and work/family accommodations and expectations are just a few of the issues human resource professionals will have to consider in a global light.

The following chapters in this SHRM-sponsored book provide more detail on the changes—and the challenges—the profession and SHRM face in the new millennium. It is precisely those challenges that will make the human resource profession a vital component in an organization's bottom line.

COMPENSATION AND BENEFITS

Raylana S. Anderson
Compensation and Benefits Committee

Today's most critical Human Resources Compensation and Benefits challenge is the development and ongoing, effective implementation of compensation and benefit programs. These programs must support the desires of both the organization and the employee for individual responsibility and organizational/career connections.

Underlying Issues

Several issues underlie the development of this critical challenge. In 1999 corporations recognized a looming talent shortage at the highest levels. A survey conducted by Byham (1999) reported that the average company expected a 33 percent turnover of its executives in the following five years. One-third of these companies were not confident that they could find suitable replacements. Furthermore, three-fourths of the corporate officers surveyed said that their companies then had insufficient talent or were chronically short of talent.

A final survey finding served to identify the likely long-term impact of this situation. That is, half of the 500 respondents surveyed felt that their companies were not doing effective succession planning and were unprepared to replace key executives (Byham 1999). Certainly, these findings provided information to support a shift in methods of retaining corporate employees, including benefits and compensation practices.

This critical shortage of key management/leadership talent did not occur in a vacuum. For the most part, it resulted from intentional organizational efforts focused on short-term, operational (rather than long-term, strategic) concerns—to control short-term costs, increase short-term productivity, and so forth.

Significant domestic and foreign economic factors (e.g., corporate buy-outs, expansion and uncertainty of international trade and industries, international monetary security, varying labor costs across borders) contributed to organizations' leading their employees and operations down a short-term path.

Organizations in the late 1990s were still stripping out managerial layers and reducing their workforces. The results of these actions included several important practices that have since contributed to the need for change to a long-term, employee-employer relationship based upon meeting both corporate and individual needs.

In the late 1990s, people were working frantically to keep businesses afloat, leaving little or no time and energy to apply a broad perspective on the changing marketplace, customers, and other factors affecting the organization. In this short-term survival mode, businesses were not developing backups for key managerial/leadership roles; they were eliminating "middle" managers and "assistant to" positions (Grossman 1999).

As organizations eliminated middle management roles, individuals remaining at low-level management ranks lost gradual opportunities for growth. And organizations began to recognize seemingly overwhelming gaps between skills needed to progress from one remaining job within the organization to the next (Grossman 1999). As a result, they routinely began to feel it necessary to turn to outside talent to fill top management roles.

As a part of this short-term business focus, supported by the elimination of middle management, organizations increasingly failed to recognize the value of skills (e.g., critical thinking, decision-making, problem-solving) and behaviors (teamwork, collaboration, coaching, developing) that are critical for organizational success in the twenty-first century. Furthermore, individuals who demonstrated these seemingly unusual and short-term unproductive skills were not appropriately rewarded. Corporate rewards, including pay, were provided to individuals with technical skills and competence, often at the expense of, or to the exclusion of, competence in civility and in management/leadership (Grossman 1999).

While these active organizational influences were having an impact on corporate decision-making, other forces also have been at work in the labor market. Women have returned to the workforce in dramatic numbers, and fully 50 percent of today's workforce are women, representing more than 85 percent of all working-age women (Huitt 1998). Employee trends recognized in the late 1990s also are affecting today's organizations. The growth of the labor force has slowed down. The mix of the labor force in terms of race, culture, age, and gender, has changed. People are having children relatively late in life (after they have begun their working careers), forcing work/life choices that are significant to both themselves and their employers. Alternative (i.e., not full-time, regular) employment has continued to develop from the "contingent" workplace ideas of the late 1990s (Rappaport, Bogosian, and Klann 1998).

Several additional trends complete this description of today's work environment and help us recognize important differences between today and the late twentieth century. The pace of change from the agricultural/manufacturing age into the "full" information age continues to accelerate. As of the year 2000, fewer than 13 percent of U.S. workers were involved in agriculture or manufacturing, while more than 50 percent were involved in information (Huitt 1998).

According to Huitt (1998), at the turn of the century, businesses owned by women represented 50 percent of all U.S. businesses. These women-owned businesses were successful and employed more than 18.5 million people—more than 26 percent of the workforce and more people than are employed by all Fortune 500 companies combined. Contrary to then-popular beliefs, the late 1990s demonstrated that women in top management/leadership roles performed well. For example, women's effectiveness as managers, leaders, and teammates outstripped the abilities of their male counterparts in 28 of 31 managerial skill areas (Huitt 1998). Furthermore, workers continuing to enter the workplace today are different from their predecessors. GenXers (now ages 30 to 40) place a high value on education, want technology to support their work, and want time off and work/life flexibility (Rappaport, Bogosian, and Klann 1998). GenYers (now ages 16 to 30) are primary consumers of leisure and entertainment products (Halverson 1998), are more likely than previous generations to express opinions and ask questions, are more accepting of ethnic and cultural differences, are less likely to show prejudice toward races, and are more inclined to demonstrate a sense of personal responsibility (HoraceMann 1996).

In some way, as a reaction to massive corporate job restructuring, layoffs, and reductions in force in the late 1990s, working individuals have exercised their collective strength to influence key legislation and corporate practices. Today's organizational, compensation, and benefits environment is characterized by a Social Security system that includes a significant degree of individual direction on investment of funds, individually portable long-term savings/pension plan benefits, and widespread access to medical savings accounts (MSAs), long-term care (LTC) insurance, and other programs important to individuals.

What Does This Mean Today?

Meeting today's critical compensation and benefits challenges means hard work must continue. It is necessary to develop and implement compensation and benefit programs that support the desires of organizations and employees for both individual responsibility and organizational/career connections. The good news is that a review of these issues and trends can serve as a broad guideline for effective compensation and benefits decision-making in 2010. Furthermore, to meet the challenge, we can build upon the foresight of certain forward-thinking organizations that were beginning to develop compensation, benefits, and work/life practices in the midst of the turmoil outlined above. Broadly, two significant practices are incorporated into today's successful organizational HR roles. One is compensation programs based upon results, and the other is maximum flexibility (i.e., individual responsibility/choice) in benefit program offerings. HR systems, which reinforce individuals' connections to organizations, support these practices on a daily basis. These systems include HR roles to routinely strengthen supervisors' management/leadership skills and to maintain routine contact with individuals who work off-site, off-hours, and so on.

Since the late 1990s, in part through lobbying efforts of SHRM and its members, Congress's attention has moved to recognize and remove regulatory barriers to ongoing organizational and individual success. Congress has acted to eliminate many of these barriers, resulting in a current regulatory environment that provides the following elements:

- Compensation laws and regulations, under a revision of the 1938 Fair Labor Standards Act (FLSA), that support organizational and individual flexibility and responsibility.

- 100 percent deductibility of health-related insurance costs for self-employed individuals.

- Permanent access to medical savings accounts (MSAs).

- Maintenance of tax-favored status for group benefit programs sponsored by organizations.
- Regulations that support cooperation with appropriate levels of liability among businesses, individuals, and communities in support of individual health/wellness.
- Significant levels of both portability of long-term financial/pension benefits, and a level of individual direction of Social Security benefit funds in the financial market.

These regulatory changes support the ability of today's organizations and working individuals to be mutually successful. (The details of their development are not a part of this writing.)

Telework—An Important, Intervening Phenomenon

While Telework is generally viewed as an employment practice, its evolution in modern workplaces has affected decision-making on compensation and benefits. For this reason, a brief description of Telework is important. In describing the "dejobbing" of the workforce, Huitt (1998) established the current description of Telework to include temporary full-time and part-time jobs, home-based business, entrepreneurship, and increased personal responsibility for work. It is important to note that individuals who independently and periodically contract their services to organizations and whose compensation and other rewards are based upon completion of agreed-upon results are included in the Telework/dejobbed workforce.

Compensation Practices

The late 1990s focus on technical skills competence led many organizations to offer compensation packages to individuals that were significantly out of line with established compensation structures. Creativity focused on providing these technology-savvy individuals with more compensation than they could obtain through other sources (i.e., more than they were making at a competitor; more than they might make after a competitive counteroffer; more than they might make if they checked the Web a few weeks from hire).

At the same time that organizations focused on compensation packages for technical skills competence, they began labeling workers as "contingent" nonemployees to avoid organizational compensation and benefit commitments. The Microsoft decision (*Vizcaino v. U.S. District Court for the Western District of Washington*, 1998) and its implications resounded through corporate structure and encouraged individuals to question their work/organizational relationships. In its 1998 *Alternative Staffing Survey*, SHRM reported:

- Nearly three out of four organizations surveyed (74%) used alternative workers to supplement their workforces.
- Nearly eight out of ten respondents (79%) reported that workers from temporary agencies were among their organizations' alternative workers.

Notably, these workers would not, in 1998, have been considered "employees," to whom an organization's own compensation and benefit programs would be offered. In fact, seven out of ten respondents in the SHRM 1998 *Alternative Staffing Survey* said they did not offer any organizational benefits to alternative workers, although these organizations did indicate a preference for using alternative workers from agencies that provided benefits to these individuals. Today, the arbitrary label lines have blurred, and organizations are meeting the compensation and benefits challenges that have been highlighted. As indicated, the broad compensation strategy is to reward individuals based on their performance toward achieving organizational results.

One compensation technique, developed to support compensation for results in a variety of settings and schedules, is the idea of work modules (Coleman 1998). As a practical matter, corporate and HR experience have demonstrated that a four-hour work module is the most effective. Four hours is about the shortest unit of time that is economically or psychologically viable for accomplishing meaningful work.

At appropriate times within corporate staffing evaluation cycles, work is reviewed to determine whether it can be modularized. If modules are appropriate, work, expected results, and related rewards are defined. Individuals within the organization's available, nonregular labor force are notified, and they use a variety of electronic means to offer their services and make commitments to complete available work modules. Compensation professionals monitor this "bidding" process, negotiate final work agreements, monitor timely and accurate completion of the work in cooperation with departmental leaders, and compensate individuals according to agreed-upon parameters. The role of HR professionals within the organization is to support critical connections, as well as to provide important business information.

Module-based work has also been developed as a means of offering work/life flexibility to organizations' regular, full-time employees. Rather than being penalized for missing time "at work," individuals maintain a means for demonstrating work completion/results, regardless of their location. Employees can choose to "leave work" to attend important personal events or meetings and can avoid the negative impact of once-prevalent perceptions that individuals not "at work" were not productive. Results, not face time or location, are the basis for determining productivity and compensation.

Modules are not today's only technique for tying compensation to performance/results. Compensation and employment professionals in today's organizations cooperate to monitor a variety and a multitude of contract relationships with individuals whose formal employment relationship is not with single organizations. These individuals are often established, successful entrepreneurs whose skills, whether in technical or management/leadership arenas, are valuable to complete a specific project or for a specified period. Bringing these individuals into an organization is a matter of negotiating time, fees, authority, responsibility, and expected results. HR/compensation professionals monitor these negotiations, which are successful only if they are based upon clear communication of expectations and responsibilities.

Compensation decision-making has also been affected by organizations' ongoing development of continuous learning environments, including "corporate universities," an increasingly popular and meaningful benefit plan. These universities have been created in an effort to retain GenXers who expect opportunities for continuous education, to develop technical as well as management/leadership skills in employees and staff pool participants, to support leadership succession management, and, at times, to generate revenue outside of the organization.

The completion of training or development programs within the university or other organizational learning structure is the responsibility of individuals. They review organizational goals and plans and then select a training/development curriculum. It is the responsibility of compensation professionals, in cooperation with employment/training staff and top executives, to monitor training programs and related employee/individual rewards. It is each individual's responsibility to review the available curriculum, enroll, and complete specific programs. Compensation is one reward that has been built into individuals' completion of courses.

Benefits

No longer is the privatizing of some portion of an individual's Social Security benefits major news; the practice is now routine. Employers have been assured, through legislation and accompanying regulations and court decisions, that education for their employees about available Social Security investment options can be provided without liability. For individuals in today's workforce, efforts to make long-term financial plans, including pensions, truly portable, have also been successful.

These practices, along with equity in the full deductibility of health and related insurance costs for self-employed individuals, supports organizations' ability to meet today's challenges. The work/life needs of increasingly diverse employees pushed the trend toward individual choice and responsibility, and flexibility in benefits and non-financial rewards, to tidal wave proportions.

As of 1998, the *SHRM Benefits Survey* reported that flexible benefits (i.e., full cafeteria plans) were offered by just 29 percent of U.S. organizations. The growing and sustained value of flexible benefit programs provided the opportunity to create a win-win situation between organizations and individuals. As a result:

- Organizations maintain the ability to budget total benefit expense by offering eligible individuals a certain sum of dollars from which benefit selections may be made from among those provided by the organization.

- Eligible individuals have the responsibility for learning about available selections and for making appropriate choices.

The same 1998 *SHRM Benefits Survey* documented only initial creativity in offerings of family-friendly, personal service benefits. These benefit offerings were relatively new in 1998 and were initiated to support employees' desires for opportunities to meet work/life objectives (e.g., more "free" time). Meeting these needs also has provided opportunities for organizations to connect with individuals.

Benefit offerings noted in the 1998 *SHRM Benefits Survey* included the following:

Benefit Plan	Percent of Employers Offering the Plan
Dependent care spending accounts	59%
Health care premium spending accounts	46%
Medical flexible spending accounts	57%
Domestic partner benefits	7%
Adoption assistance	12%
Relocation benefits (spousal assistance)	67% (23%)
Long-term care insurance	32%
Educational assistance	87%
Retirement planning services	40%

Note: Adapted with permission from Society for Human Resource Management, *SHRM Benefits Survey*, 1998, pp. 11–42.

In addition to increasing the prevalence of benefit plans, today's benefit programs have been developed to incorporate features and tools that support meeting this critical challenge. Benefit professionals have designed and implemented programs that maximize the application of regulatory flexibility and tax-preferred arrangements. Programs now include comprehensive, ongoing communication to employees about the availability and value of benefits offered to them.

Special plans are incorporated into benefit programs to support mutually productive employer/employee connections. One example is a comprehensive disease management plan that incorporates individual medical support while an individual is unable to work and HR/benefit return-to-work coaching for individuals who have been off of work because of catastrophic illnesses or injuries.

Continuing a trend begun in the 1990s, eldercare and childcare, as well as health/wellness programs, are offered in cooperation with viable community organizations and resources. Coverage in group health benefit plans, with support from the insurance industry, state legislatures, and Congress, routinely includes coverage for "alternative" treatments such as therapeutic massage, acupuncture, herbs, nutritional counseling, guided meditation, and over-the-counter drugs. Childcare and/or eldercare, and an increasing array of personal/concierge services, are routinely offered by today's employers.

As described above, training/development has been incorporated into a true organizational benefit program that supports individual learning. Curricula are routinely monitored to be sure available programs include those that are:

- important to organizations (e.g., basic organizational business and financial programs).

- important to both organizations and individuals (e.g., management, team-building, leadership programs).

- important to individuals with necessary ambition, interests, and abilities. These programs may include technical courses on subjects directly related to individuals' jobs or may provide opportunities for individuals to continue learning about any number of topics.

Nonfinancial reward programs are still being created. These personal benefits have grown in type and number from those offered in the late 1990s (e.g., childcare/eldercare referral service; wellness resources and information; casual dress days; concierge services; dry cleaning services). Individual choices are routinely encouraged, through use of paid time off (PTO) banks. Key employees with outside interests (e.g., community, education) are retained, in part, through opportunities for time off of work for community and related service and through both paid and unpaid sabbaticals. The availability of other benefit plans has grown in support of employee retention efforts and meeting today's critical challenge.

Aspects of employee assistance programs (EAPs), which have been available for years, have been incorporated into the fabric of organizations. Externally, EAPs continue to offer personal counseling services to employees and other staff to meet a variety of needs. Internally, EAP-like benefit plans have been created. Professionals offering services within these plans offer organizations, employees, and staff services to meet the specific challenge of promoting connections.

The primary value offered by an EAP benefit program is maintaining and strengthening necessary connections within organizations. These benefit professionals create and monitor individual executive coaching in succession management. They may also interact with employees to watch for, and work through, signs of burnout before an individual leaves the organization. Responsibilities of organizational EAP professionals may also include delivery of daily services to all individuals whose work is related to the organization.

Orientation is a benefit program that lasts six months to one year. During this period, individuals are provided specialized, one-on-one attention to attach them to the organization. At the same time, organizations clearly outline expectations for the individual. Such expectations focus on each individual's responsibilities, which may include:

- meeting performance expectations.

- active participation in work, whether work is done with or without the cooperation of team members.

- dedication to set and meet progressive educational training and development objectives, through participation in external and/or internal programs.

Summary

The workforce is more diverse than ever, and this diversity continues to shape external and regulatory change, as well as private, organizational change. Those organizations that recruit, retain, and develop managers/leaders to look ahead, plan for meeting the pace of change, and lead and develop the individuals around them will succeed. A significant part of that success will be the implementation of compensation programs based on results and benefit programs that support individual responsibility, choice, and flexibility.

The specific challenge for HR professionals in this field is to maintain and blend sound business knowledge with human behavior and technical skills/competence.

Recommended Actions

Universals

- Know your key business objectives.
- Know your employees' key needs, wants, and motivators.

Compensation/Benefits

- Create and maintain a comprehensive, flexible, total compensation program.
- Blend critical recruiting and training (technical and management) into a total compensation perspective.
- Focus rewards (compensation, benefits) on work (i.e., productivity, results), not on face time. Communicate with all employees and train them to accept and understand this focus.
- Ensure constant communication with all employees and affiliated individuals (when they are working with your company).
- Monitor research on effectiveness of "alternative" and preventive health care. Adopt periodic changes to your plans.
- Remember and plan means to benefit employees with families, as well as singles. Consider plans (e.g., use of paid time off) that support personal commitment to professional or community organizations.
- Develop and monitor databases of available, competent independent contractors. Maintain contact with them (as a part of their reward structure). Develop electronic (i.e., efficient) means to announce available work, accept "bids," and monitor/compensate for results.
- Monitor work to identify modules. Compensate and reward completion of modules appropriately.
- Incorporate comprehensive (chronic) disease—and health—management into group benefit plans.
- Monitor the impact of total compensation programs, including employee satisfaction, as well as costs and utilization. Build individual flexibility/responsibility into the program.

References

Byham, W. C. "Grooming next-millennium leaders." *HR Magazine* 44(2) (1999): 46-70.

Coleman, D. R. "Baby boom to baby bust: Flexible work options for older workers." *Benefits Quarterly*, 14(4) (1998): 18-28.

Grossman, R. J. "Heirs unapparent." *HR Magazine*, 44(2) (1999): 36-44.

Halverson, G. "Power buyers: Boomers and generation Y." *Christian Science Monitor*, 9 March 1998 [on-line]. Available at www.csmonitor.com/durable/1998/03/09/econ/econ.6.html).

HoraceMann Educators Corporation. 1996 educator survey fact sheet [on-line]. Available at www.horacemann.com/html/educator/esurvey7.html).

Huitt, W. G. "The workplace and the transition to the information age: How it impacts and is impacted by women." Paper presented at the 3rd Annual Women's Studies Conference, Valdosta, Georgia, March 1998.

Rappaport, A. M.; Bogosian, C. A; and Klann, C. A. "Population trends and the labor force in the years ahead." *Benefits Quarterly* 14(4) (1998): 8-17.

Society for Human Resource Management Issues Management Program. *SHRM Benefits Survey.* Alexandria, Virginia: Society for Human Resource Management, 1998.

Society for Human Resource Management Issues Management Program. *SHRM Alternative Staffing Survey.* Alexandria, Virginia: Society for Human Resource Management, 1998.

Vizcaino v. U.S. District Court for the Western District of Washington, No. 98-71388 (W.D. Wash. 1998).

Supplemental Readings

Pritchard, K. H. *Telework: Compensation Issues.* SHRM White Paper #61512. Alexandria, Virginia: Society for Human Resource Management, December 1998.

Pritchard, K. H. *Telework: Selected references and resources.* SHRM White Paper #61515. Alexandria, Virginia: Society for Human Resource Management, December 1998.

REINVENTING PUBLIC POLICY THROUGH STATE AND LOCAL CONTROL

Debbra M. Buerkle
Legislative Action Committee

In the 1990s, changes in federal laws dominated the reading material of in-baskets for HR directors nationwide. The pendulum is swinging back, and HR professionals will see an increased volume of local ordinances and state laws governing how they define and carry out employment policy and employee-employer relationships. Since 1994, passage of employment-related laws at the state level has increased dramatically. HR professionals should prepare to face a continued surge of "customized" public policy geared to legislate how employers "do business" at the state and local levels.

What is causing this shift from nearly exclusive federal policymaking to high-gear production and dissemination of state and local public policy affecting employment? According to Edward Potter's (1995, p. 6) white paper, "No longer can competitiveness be viewed as a macroeconomic contest between nations. It is a struggle fought daily by employers and employees in the operating units of American companies."

In the 1930s and 1940s, when competitiveness affected our national economic viability and military security, many of the original employment-related regulations affecting employers, including Social Security and the Fair Labor Standards Act, were put into place. Also, the federal government was vigorously working to effect economic and social reform. Why use employers as the vehicle for these reforms? It is allowed under the Interstate Commerce clause of the Constitution. Employers have money and also have influence at the local level. Our government knows it can't afford to continue its efforts to enact and enforce social change by being the "national enforcer"—it must shift the burden by encouraging state and local governments and agencies to carry out the social, economic, and political agendas of the times.

The Occupational Safety and Health Administration (OSHA) is an example of an agency that has made a shift from enforcement to encouragement. Most recently, the agency introduced administrative changes ushering in a customer-friendly approach to enforcement and compliance that provides incentives to local agencies for effecting goals at the local level. In fact, a press release (1998) from OSHA announcing its new award-winning enforcement partnership program also reported that the agency was expanding nationwide as the cooperative compliance program (CCP) and that it was being offered to 12,250 employers. OSHA's Maine 200 program, the prototype for CCP, won the prestigious Innovation in American Government Award from the Ford Foundation as well as the Hammer Award from Vice President Al Gore's National Performance Review in 1998. While some say this is just another method of enforcing a federally mandated agenda, others pronounce the trend "effective" because it is happening within and through local control. Regardless of whether it's effective, it is demonstrating the shift from federal control to regionalized control.

Another reason for the shift is pressure arising from American small businesses to specifically address their social and economic concerns. It is likely that laws and ordinances will be developed to fuel the continued growth and competitive opportunity afforded these smaller businesses. According to the National Federation of Independent Businesses (NFIB) (1999):

Congress and the president need to be more aware of the fact that the burden of federal regulations falls disproportionately on small business. The idea of one-size-fits-all regulation is unrealistic and costly. In fact, the regulatory cost per employee to small firms is approximately 50 percent more than the cost to large firms. Small businesses employ 53 percent of the work force, but shoulder 63 percent of the total business regulatory costs. Firms with 20 to 49 employees spend, on average, 19 cents out of every revenue dollar on regulatory costs. When we hear "regulations" we don't necessarily remember all of the paperwork that comes with them. Tax compliance and payroll record keeping are the two largest components of the regulatory burden today. Firms with less than 10 employees report that their tax and payroll costs represent about 80 percent of their total regulatory burden. In fact, firms with under 50 employees spend close to five percent of their revenue on tax compliance costs alone.

Local governments also have pressures to compete. In recent years, cities and counties have created their own minimum wage requirements (enforced with businesses that provide services and resources to those local government entities) to ensure competitiveness with larger employers or unions.

In order to be responsive to their constituents, state legislatures are contending with questions of employment practices such as reference-checking, employee conduct (violence in the workplace), credit-checking, retraining welfare and displaced workers, and English-only language use in the workplace. Another trend at the state level, a proliferation of benefit mandates for insurers and employers, makes doing business across state lines an administrative nightmare. Discussion is also prevalent about local ordinances supporting or disallowing discrimination based on sexual orientation. All of these topics, and more, will be evaluated for applicability in the workplace at the local or regional level because of pressures from both local governments and businesses residing in and operating within that state.

How will human resources be affected by the increased state and local attempts to define and customize public employment policy in a way that more directly serves local constituencies? The following are six ways:

1. **Employers will put increased pressure on their HR leadership to participate in grassroots efforts to design legislation favorable to their industry or core business at the state and local levels.** HR profession advocates will find themselves needing to form coalitions and alliances with existing state and local public policy influences, such as the Chamber of Commerce, in order to formulate effective policy initiatives or responses to proposed legislation. Individuals who think that grassroots participation is a waste of time will be left in the dust of those who race forward to create controls that are favorable for their *businesses.*

2. **More emphasis will be placed on *where profits originate* (to prevent an eroded tax base in the wake of Internet/global commerce), forcing different ways of compensating and accounting for workforce production and productivity.** Legislation governing payroll and sales taxes at the state and local levels will increase to prevent the erosion of the regional tax base. Look for local responses to Internet commerce, especially the question of what's taxable, and which governments benefit from that taxation.

3. **Nearly every HR professional will need "international" experience and professional resources supporting doing business with non-U.S. business partners, contractors, and employees.** Right now, we're seeing an increase in cities creating a "living" or minimum wage for payment of employees living locally or doing business with a local government. As global competitiveness increases and a "local" company's workforces and product distribution networks extend globally, HR professionals may be tracking much more than just U.S.-legislated regional "living wage" requirements; they'll have to have access to and be able to respond to wage and benefit issues in every region of the world.

4. **The changes in workforce demographics will render many U.S. discrimination laws useless, especially if employees are citizens of, and residing in, other countries while working for your firm.** These changes will encourage a proliferation of new laws governing how local/state-based firms must treat local and nonlocal workers. They will include which employees are considered part of the local workforce, and therefore are subject to local employment practice legislation (especially the aging workforce). This will also mean significant legislative reactions to the intergeneration equity issues that will emerge as the "boomer" generation continues to age. According to the U.S. Census Bureau, America's older population will more than double by 2050, from 33.9 million to 80 million. By that year, as many as one in five Americans could be senior citizens, and many of those will still be active in the workforce.

5. **Futurists and HR professionals seem to agree that businesses will continue to stay slim by assigning functions to subcontractors. Because more people will be paid from individual or small-business employment contracts, questions about which/whose laws apply to those contracts must be answered.** Legislation at the state and local levels will most likely be what raises these questions. And most likely, the HR professional will be the one to answer them. Think of this situation: A software development firm is having difficulty finding the requisite-skilled employees it needs. It finds a variety of skilled "free agents" and contracts for their time and work product individually from where they live in Malaysia, Singapore, Pakistan, and Romania. Work products and communication about work are sent back and forth over the Internet, or by phone or fax. Your company is going to be more concerned about questions of security, contractual compliance, work-product ownership, and product quality than with questions about timekeeping and exempt/nonexempt status. "Traditional" Department of Labor wage and hour concerns may not even be relevant anymore. This is a very real situation, and if it's not

already happening in your organization, it probably will be soon. HR professionals will need to develop creative *and* compliant strategies to address global business issues affecting their profession and their organization.

6. **HR professionals will need to align more closely with local medical professionals and insurance professionals servicing their workforce in order to comply with a proliferation of more vigorous laws supporting healthy ecosystems within and around the workplace—and not just "the" workplace, but all workplaces used by your workers.** This will especially be necessary in states that legislate 24-hour benefit programs (those plans that cover both personal and occupational-related medical conditions) to adequately insure the huge population of home-based businesses. Insurance portability issues and health care plan eligibility (especially with regard to community and age-based underwriting) will be increasingly legislated at the local and regional levels in order to respond to the needs of smaller, entrepreneurial businesses.

Exploring these six areas in more depth highlights the readiness and responsiveness of HR professionals.

1. **HR professionals will face increased pressure to participate in grassroots efforts to design legislation favorable to their industry or core business at the state and local levels.**

    Competencies required:

    (a) Cognizance of your organization's industry trends and resources, and a comprehensive local personal contact network to tap into the local and regional legislative process. For example, a manufacturer of computer peripheral equipment will have industry ties to the American Electronics Association (AEA), the local employers' association, and the local Chamber of Commerce. HR professionals in this type of industry sector would need to be grassroots participants within the local Chamber and should be familiar with the lobby supporting the AEA at the state level.

    (b) Good networking skills, as well as the ability to find and filter information pertaining to the HR profession within your particular industry.

    (c) A clear understanding of the legislative infrastructure in your state, county, and city governments.

    (d) The ability to develop and maintain positive relationships with industry sector representatives and professional lobbyists in order to keep abreast of legislation affecting your employer.

2. **HR professionals will be required to understand *where profits originate* (to prevent an eroded tax base in the wake of Internet/global commerce) and to develop different ways of compensating and accounting for workforce production and productivity.**

    Competencies required:

    (a) A comprehensive understanding of the business strategy affecting your organization.

(b) An ability to find, discern, and use compensation data resources in a way that integrates effectively with productivity and quality concerns of the organization.

(c) An understanding of the laws, both local/regional and federal, affecting compensation design and delivery.

(d) An understanding of tax law as it relates to profitability in the organization, as well as to compensation *and benefits*.

3. **Nearly every HR professional will need "international" experience and professional resources supporting doing business with non-U.S. business partners, contractors, and employees.**

Competencies required:

(a) An ability to discern and secure applicable data and resources pertaining to other countries' national and regional compensation and practices, as well as a knowledge of any non-U.S. laws that govern doing business within other countries where the your organization or employees may be located.

(b) A comprehensive resource person available to assist with development of contracts and contractor agreements with nationals from other parts of the world.

(c) An understanding of the applicability of benefits programs to employees or contractors within those countries where your firm does business.

4. **The changes in workforce demographics will render many U.S. discrimination laws useless, especially if employees are citizens of and residing in other countries while working for your firm. The aging of the U.S. workforce will lead to legislation affecting intergeneration equity.**

Competencies required:

(a) An understanding of your region/state and city's demographics and your organization's commitment to reflect those demographics.

(b) An understanding of the impact of an aging workforce on scheduling, ergonomic, and workplace health and safety requirements, and essential functions.

(c) An understanding of multi-audience communication problems and the ability to develop innovative approaches to ensure understanding of company policy and communiqués throughout the organization.

(d) The ability to discern the impact of diverse demographics on your organization's training and development needs, and especially the cultural expectations relating to interpersonal relationship skills.

(e) An ability to discern and communicate the potential impact of proposed changes in EEO regulations and legislation on your organization *before* changes in legislation occur.

5. **Businesses will continue to stay slim by assigning functions to subcontractors. Because more people will be paid from individual or small-business employment contracts, questions about which/whose laws apply to those contracts must be answered.**

Competencies required:

(a) An understanding of current tax codes and laws affecting contractor relationships.

(b) The ability to develop and maintain effective and fair policies and practices affecting contractor relationships within your organization.

(c) The ability to discern your organization's or industry's needs with regard to use of subcontractors, small businesses, and *minority enterprises and the ability to locate and assist in prequalifying these resource providers for contracting purposes.*

6. **HR professionals will need to align more closely with local medical professionals and insurance professionals servicing their workforce in order to comply with a proliferation of more vigorous laws supporting healthy ecosystems within and around the workplace.**

Competencies required:

(a) A thorough understanding of the work environments affecting your organization's employees.

(b) A thorough understanding of the risk factors affecting those environments.

(c) The ability to discern preventative approaches to reducing risk in each of the applicable work environments.

(d) An understanding of the laws and regulations applying to your organization's work environments.

It's always difficult to hold up the crystal ball and prognosticate events—especially where politics are involved. But the trend of increased state and local legislation and regulatory impact will continue. This will happen in part as a response to perceived federal overregulation, but more likely as the federal government itself scales back efforts to promulgate national-level controls and looks to the states to provide the funds and the labor to carry out policies that will effect social and political change. On behalf of their profession, and the businesses they represent, HR professionals will be increasingly challenged to respond to legislation and controls proposed at the state and local levels.

Recommended Actions

- Identify and monitor resources that publish demographic statistics for your metropolitan statistical area or region.
- Know your state legislators and their staff.

- Bookmark federal and state legislative information sites and monitor their summaries on the Internet.
- Maintain your membership in SHRM and become a grassroots member.
- Join the local Chamber of Commerce and maintain relationships with that group's members.
- Know your congressional representatives and their staff.
- Never assume that you can't make an impact on public policy.
- Attend your city council or county commissioners meetings periodically.
- Keep a file of newspaper, trade journal, and other research source news that highlights employment-related public policy issues at the state, local, and federal levels.
- Network with people to discuss trends and ascertain public opinion that may influence grassroots legislation, and stay involved!

References

National Federation of Independent Businesses. "What ever happened to regulatory reform?" February 1999 [on-line]. Available at http://www.nfibonline.com.

Occupational Safety and Health Administration press release. 1998. [on-line]. Available at http://www.osha.gov/media/oshnews.

Potter, E. *The Proper Federal Role in Workplace Policy*. White paper. Washington, D.C.: Center for Employment Policy, 1995.

COMPETENCY-BASED APPROACH TO LEVERAGING TALENT*

Robyn Burke
Human Resource Development Committee

Introduction: Skills Shortage Magnified

As competitive pressures, the pace of change, technological innovation, and the fast flow of information continue to increase, so does the demand for specialized knowledge and skills. Consequently, human resource professionals must address an intensifying challenge to attract and retain capable, qualified human resources. With this dynamic business environment, employers are forced to take creative, aggressive measures to persevere through the labor shortage difficulties and to build the competencies required for the future. The greatest challenges are the absence of skilled workers and an aging and increasingly mobile workforce.

Clearly, there are not enough skilled workers to fill the 1,239,557 job vacancies (America's Job Bank 1999). The majority of these job opportunities will continue to be within the professional/specialty/technical occupations. Futurists predict that 60 percent of all jobs will require skills possessed by only 20 percent of today's workforce (Saratoga Institute 1997, as cited by Interim Services 1999). Computer-related and teaching jobs will comprise more than 15 percent of all new jobs between 1996 and 2006. And of the twenty-five fastest growing occupations, eighteen will require a minimum of a bachelor's degree (Pilot 1998). The gap between current skills and needed skills is widening. This skill shortage is resulting in a constant requirement and market for talent (Talent Alliance, as cited by Interim Services 1999).

In addition, because our labor pool is older, the widening of the gap is accelerating. The number of workers ages forty and older is growing at a rapid rate, with a significant number in the over-fifty-five population. The increasing percentage of available workers over age fifty-five has caused the labor pool to grow at a snail's pace. Most businesses today do not tap into the talent available through this older, but very employable, resource. The resulting challenge for employers today is how to create a large enough pool of skilled workers.

Retention: A Compelling Issue

Before you develop a human resource strategy that will best equip you to attract and develop the necessary talent, consider not only the challenge of finding the skills in a labor market that is falling way behind, but also how to keep and leverage this qualified pool when you need it. Retention, career development, and sources for finding the talent in a timely manner have a major impact on your ability to tap into a talent pool when needed.

---

* The author would like to thank Diana Osinski, Shelly Prochaska, and Jack Kondrasuk, members of SHRM's national Human Resource Development Committee, for their support, ideas, and assistance in writing, researching, and editing this chapter.

Retention presents greater challenges than ever before; 280 million workers have changed jobs since 1980. Labor is being redeployed at an unprecedented scale and pace, straining the current system and threatening corporations' abilities to execute their business strategies. In this market, highly skilled employees see themselves as free agents. They are a scarce, and therefore costly, resource (Saratoga Institute 1997, as cited by Interim Services 1999). Because of their scarcity, recruiting and sourcing talent has become a huge business of its own.

The sources for qualified workers to perform core business processes and key business support services are many and varied, and tapping them is necessary to bridge the wide gap. Workers are being obtained from many nontraditional labor and recruiting sources because of the labor shortage, including use of immigrants, exporting/packaging of work, outsourcing, and use of contingent workers. These sources translate to means of survival for employers coping with the deficiency of knowledge and skills.

The Human Resource Development Strategy of the Twenty-First Century

The above factors are contributing to the greatest human resources challenge for the twenty-first century—specifically, how can essential talent and skills be leveraged in this fluctuating market with a severe shortage of qualified workers who look older and are harder to find and keep? This complex labor market has forced businesses to take creative measures to tackle the challenge. It has shifted the role of human resources from a back room support function to a key contributor in achieving crucial business results. Knowledge has become the only source of long-term, sustainable, competitive advantage, but knowledge can only be employed through the skills of individuals (Horne 1998).

Tapping this knowledge base means everything. Wallace (1998), as cited by Verespej (1998), maintained that organizations continue to combine emerging technologies with creative employment arrangements, contingency-based pay, customer and supplier partnerships, and other mechanisms that enable them to tap seamlessly into talented employees anywhere at anytime. This new, emerging workforce is more complex. There are core workers who possess the requisite knowledge and skills to deliver key business process; hired guns who specialize in certain technologies or support processes; and contingent workers who serve to supplement the core workforce during peaks and valleys. Therefore, today's employee has many options as to how to relate to a company (Verespej 1998). And companies have to plan strategically how to optimize this workforce mix in such a way as to leverage the right talent at the right time.

Focus Your Human Resource Development Strategy on Competency-Building

The net result of these challenges is that employers are faced with making a strategic decision. Employers must consider what spot along the competency development spectrum best suits their needs. Will you:

- contribute to the continuing inequitable workforce situation by narrowing consideration of who is employable? This choice perpetuates the undereducation, lack of skills, and barriers for the older worker.

- proactively develop a compelling strategy to engage and ensure that the potential work pool obtains critical education and knowledge and that these people become a large percentage of the labor pool?

The choices employers make today will determine their success in 2020 and, to a great extent, affect both the U.S. and world economies. Therefore, employers must assume leadership to ensure the existence of a capable workforce.

A proactive strategy begins with organizations assessing and recognizing what they are not and being willing to reassign less strategic, noncore processes. At the same time, they must fully dedicate the development of their internal human resources toward building competencies that will equip them to maintain a competitive advantage in serving customers.

So what is a competency? Be sure that your organizational members and human resources practitioners agree on its definition and application. It is more than knowledge, skills, talent, and attributes; it is a cluster or an accumulation of any and all of the above. The distinguishing element is that a competency correlates directly to the successful (or unsuccessful) performance of a job, role, or responsibility. What distinguishes a competency is that it address whether a person will be able to perform in a certain situation. Thus, it can be measured against well-accepted standards and can be improved through training and development (Parry 1998).

A focused, competency-based approach allows businesses to identify activities and services that are not essential to the business. Once identified, these services become prime candidates for outsourcing, exporting, or use of contingent workers or other sources that do possess and attract those necessary talents and skills. The suppliers of these secondary processes have the freedom to focus on cultivating core competencies that are required to deliver business support services (Sharp 1997).

When you tap into these nontraditional talent sources for the delivery of noncore processes, the outside service providers may offer a career path, appropriate and timely training, and a competitive compensation package to leverage the essential knowledge and skills needed to develop an organization's set of core competencies. Consequently, this partnership approach allows organizations to gain access to individuals with specialized skills that an employer might otherwise find both expensive and difficult to attract. Because there is a shortage of skilled workers, and skilled workers tend to be ambitious, they are more likely to take jobs that offer career paths, training, challenging assignments, and self-development (Sharp 1997). Furthermore, this partnership approach allows these support service providers to invest in building a larger qualified pool.

The Impact of Your Choice

The most important implication of these workforce challenges to businesses today is that they force employers to create mechanisms that permit individuals to be upwardly mobile. The quality of the future labor pool depends on the knowledge and skills acquired by today's students. Employers have a compelling interest in the health of the educational system (SHRM Visions 1998) and its capacity to develop this knowledge base. A nation with a large number of workers who are unemployable or capable of working only in the most menial, low-wage jobs will be a nation fraught with social tension and burdened by expensive demands of social welfare programs. The driving force of upward mobility depends simply on education—education that starts in the public school system (D'Amico 1997) and continues diligently with employers.

Acknowledging that the largest percentage of the labor pool is underskilled gives employers a reason to consider seriously how to engage this untapped source. Businesses that endeavor to tap into this underutilized segment of the workforce will be the premier employers in 2020. The solution is not new or complex. Specifically, employers need to consider the urgency of the following:

- Employees are the learning capacity of organizations.
- Underskilled and older workers are a crucial source of untapped talent.
- Learning opportunities develop the competencies of lower-skilled employees and enable them to become key contributors to the core processes.
- Literacy programs, skills training, and interesting project work engage individuals and enable them to learn.
- Motivating and retaining the *entire* team, both the employees from within the company and the employees from outside sources is critical. Providing incentives and recognition for the "outsiders" is not practiced by many employers, but it is crucial to achieving desired results, and therefore it needs to be included in the retention strategy.

Whether the job is for the core employer or the supplier of business support services, individuals require a broader set of competencies beyond reading, writing, math, solving basic problems, and behaving dependably. Today, more than 50 percent of jobs require more than these basic skills, and the percentage will continue to grow. The broader set, which can be developed through multiple learning experiences, includes managing more complex projects through defining problems; quickly assimilating relevant data; reorganizing information; discussing findings; and working collaboratively with others to find, develop, and implement the best solutions (Mower 1997).

Employers who accept the critical responsibility to provide learning opportunities for developing both the basic and broader sets of competencies will boost overall employability. That is, they will create the capability for attracting, constructing, and developing productive skills and competencies that will allow individuals to find, initiate, and enrich jobs, and thus to obtain rewarding careers (Ducci IFTDO). Now the proposition shifts to how best to boost employability with a labor pool that is not skilled enough, is older, is more mobile, and is retained from multiple external sources.

Target the Talent and Develop It

The answer is to focus human resource development opportunities around key processes. Depending on the type of business, key processes may be manufacturing of specific products, researching and developing of products, packaging of products, or sales and marketing. The time has come to commit to identifying and developing the set of competencies needed through offering an appropriate blend of learning opportunities. It requires an approach that targets the underlying competencies needed to achieve high performance and later provides the necessary skills-building. The competencies will lay the solid foundation needed for effective skills instruction (Parry 1998). In addition, such a commitment demands the engagement of external sources to allow access to competencies required to deliver supporting services.

Use a Competency-Based Approach to Human Resource Development

Given the complexity, diversity, and global nature of the emerging workforce, coupled with the shortage of skilled workers, employers are facing challenges to ensure that the necessary skills are there when needed. Where should an organization begin? The best place to start is to assess and decide which three to five processes are core to the business. Once these are clearly defined and understood, begin structuring the talent of the organization around those processes so that individuals focus on the calibration and improvement of those processes. In addition to organizing the human resources, consider the possibility of introducing information solutions and software to process and rearrange the workflow and talent (Verespej 1998). As a result of focusing on the core processes, companies can target the competencies/talents needed to enable them to achieve business results. Furthermore, companies may utilize other workforce talent sources such as immigration, exportation of work, contingent workers, or outsourcing to contend with the many less important, but necessary, processes.

The goal is to ensure access to an adequately qualified labor pool and to cultivate the talent needed in a tough, tight, competitive market. This can only be accomplished by focusing on what the business is and needs to be all about. Furthermore, it means allowing other businesses to make a living by delivering the less important or specialized processes. The less important processes are likely to be some other organization's core processes, such as sales and marketing, packaging, researching or analyzing, or delivering. It can be costly to "give up" these secondary processes, but not as costly as trying to sustain the capability internally.

This competency-based approach allows employees to be trained and to enjoy careers with either the "core" company or the supplier company, which by virtue of supplying one of the noncore processes has a core of its own. Both employers in this scenario have a tremendous opportunity to attract, hire, retain, develop, motivate, and leverage a talent pool of workers. Both employers have careers to offer to workers. A focus on key processes provides a clear definition of the set of competencies required for success.

Agencies supplying temporary workers, and businesses themselves, have a responsibility to operate schools and training facilities to address skill gaps, notably in the skilled blue-collar labor area. The development activities need to include short courses, training, and certification to meet that demand (Coates 1997). Suppliers that are used to bridge the skills gap in the computer-related field must develop a rigorous plan for growing the talent pool. Therefore, the combined provision of training and project learning experiences will enable these organizations to test, certify, and meet the quality standards required by the organization's client base. These combined learning experiences may open the door to career opportunities for the underemployed, older, and underskilled labor pool.

Equip Contributors with the Competencies to Flex

As mentioned earlier, the broader competency set required by most businesses today is the ability to flex with changes by managing successfully in a complex, multiple-project-based environment. We are witnessing the disappearance of the job as we know it. People are assigned to projects or programs rather than jobs. A job will consist of working on a project or program for a certain period of time, instead of doing the same tasks routinely and repeatedly (Verespej 1998). Many routine tasks have been or will be automated, or are/will be provided by a supplier who can perform those tasks more efficiently. Therefore, using projects as a training ground for project management skill development optimizes the transfer of learning to the workplace and at the same time provides professional skill development and the achievement of business and operational objectives. Employers must be savvy about providing this education and establishing parameters for the type and selection of appropriate projects, project sponsorship, and learning goals. The project management skill set has rapidly become the critical competency set for individuals to achieve high performance of core processes. Employers need to have the flexibility and elasticity to assign individuals to different projects throughout their careers.

Employers and individuals must take joint responsibility for developing the core competencies. Those interested in becoming contributors and enhancing skills will require a rigorous learning plan. The plan may include development through formal training and certification, challenging projects, mentoring, and self-paced learning via tools such as interactive multimedia-based training, video/satellite technology, and Web-based training. These tools can incorporate situational responses and help assess and develop competencies. Before an individual can participate in pursuing these learning opportunities, employers must help by providing training on how to utilize these resources effectively and implementing creative solutions for gaining access to them.

The Employers' Responsibility

This chapter has examined the many challenges employers face today. The reality is that employers have to do more to continue education and improve the employability and upward mobility of the unskilled workforce, whose demographic makeup presents an additional challenge of its own. The recommendations for leveraging the talents and skills required in this highly professional technical workplace stem from taking a fundamental and diligent review of the businesses' core processes and the set of competencies needed to deliver those processes. Thereafter, the emphasis is about retaining and developing the competencies around these processes.

Use Competencies to Integrate Your HRD Strategy to the Business Strategy

The approaches are similar whether you are an employer providing the business product or service or a supplier of the support services. Specifically, the human resource development practitioner must:

- demonstrate that human resources are your business' future learning capacity. The "operations group" still might not buy it. With competencies, you will be able to measure the difference in performance results.

- offer formal training, specifically skills instruction, to the extent necessary to deliver core processes successfully. This may include:

  - schools and training facilities.

  - literacy programs such as reading, writing, math, and computer literacy.

  - short courses, certifications, post-secondary education.

  - English as a second language or other languages appropriate to supporting the core business processes.

- focus learning experiences only on the set of competencies needed for high performance of core processes. Let your vendors provide your employees with the peripheral competencies; in fact, require it of them!

- begin with targeting and developing the competencies; gradually introduce skills-building.

- include project management skills development for all employees. This set of competencies, more than any other, is required for today's professional/technical job, which is no longer a job but a series of project assignments. The following learning experiences are recommended:

  - Strengthen problem-solving and decision-making skills through working on practical work problems as a training medium (Kemske 1998).

  - Use project assignments that are interesting enough to motivate and challenging enough to provide additional learning to the employee.

  - Provide access and training on how to use self-paced development tools.

  - Provide project management skills development for all employees involved in outsourcing, supplier partnerships, immigration, or exporting of work.

- tap into the older labor force by including them in all of the above. They are too large to ignore, and they offer tremendous potential toward bridging the skills shortage.

- develop a strategy and process to reeducate or provide additional skills for underskilled individuals or older workers who possess the potential to be key contributors, and who are much more readily available and accessible than the already highly skilled candidates.

In summary, you can expect the human resources challenges to remain constant. Dollars are tighter; competition, and therefore mobility, is greater; and the demographics of the workforce are more diverse than ever. Clearly, the skill shortage is worse than ever. The need for education, knowledge, skills, abilities, and talents is at its highest. The door to opportunity is as wide open as it has ever been, for employers and for the workforce. The gap is large. Now is the time to build bridges. The best place to start is at the beginning. Consider how to build a foundation to sustain your company in 2020. Develop a strategy that integrates the untapped workforce sources and develops the competencies needed to sustain our future. The human resources strategy that proactively, aggressively develops its learning capacity will be best-equipped to meet the next decade's toughest challenges. Most of all, a proactive, aggressive human resources strategy will enable individuals to gain further education and skills and begin filling the desperate need for professional, technical, and specialized workers.

Recommended Actions

- Define the essential, primary processes of your business, and the people requirements needed to deliver those processes.
- Offer formal training, specifically skills instruction, to the extent necessary to retain the needed talent. This may include:
    - schools and training facilities.
    - literacy programs such as reading, writing, math, and computer literacy.
    - short courses, certifications, post-secondary education.
    - English as a second language or other languages appropriate to supporting the core business processes.
- Focus learning experiences only on the set of competencies needed for high performance of core processes. Select vendors who provide the peripheral competencies. In fact require it, contractually!
- Begin with targeting and developing the competencies; gradually introduce skills-building.
- Include project management skills development for all employees. This set of competencies, more than any other, is required for today's professional/technical job, which is no longer a job but a series of project assignments. The following learning experiences are recommended:
    - Strengthen problem-solving and decision-making skills through working on practical work problems as a training medium (Kemske 1998).
    - Use project assignments that are interesting enough to motivate and challenging enough to provide additional learning to the employee.
    - Provide access and training on how to use self-paced development tools.

- Provide project management skills development for all employees involved in outsourcing, supplier partnerships, immigration, or exporting of work.

- Tap into the older labor force by including them in all of the above. They are too large to ignore, and they offer tremendous potential toward bridging the skills shortage.

- Develop a strategy and process to reeducate or provide additional skills for underskilled individuals or older workers who possess the potential to be key contributors, and who are much more readily available and accessible than the already highly skilled candidates.

References

America's Job Bank. 1999. [on-line]. Available at http://www.ajb.dni.us.

Coates, J.F. "Emerging HR issues for the twenty-first century." *Employment Relations Today*, 23(4) (1997): 1–9.

D'Amico, C. "Back to the future: A current view of workforce 2000 and projections for 2020." *Employment Relations Today*, 24(3) (1997): 1–12.

Ducci, M.A. "Training for employability." *International Federation of Training & Development Organisations* [on-line]. Available at http://www.iftdo.org/article1.html.

Horne III, J.F. "The chicken wire factor: The shift to encouraging employee initiative." *Employment Relations Today*, 25(1) (1998): 1–9.

Interim Services In Conjunction With Louis Harris & Associates. *1999 emerging workforce*. 1999. [on-line]. Available at http://www.interim.com.

Kemske, F. "HR 2008: A forecast based on our exclusive study." *Workforce*, 77 (1998) [on-line]. Available at http://www.workforceonline.com/research/index.html.

Mower, E. "That was then, this is now: Passage to a new economy." *Employment Relations Today*, 24(3) (1997): 13–20.

Parry, S. B. "Just what is a competency? (and why should you care?)." *Training* 35(6) (1998): 58–64.

Pilot, M.J. "A review of 50 years of change." In *Occupational Outlook Handbook*, 1998–1999. Washington, D.C.: Bureau of Labor Statistics, 1998, table 1.

Sharp, A.G. "Does training keep up with the times?" *Law & Order* 45(12) (1997): 43.

SHRM Workplace Visions. "U.S. education system." *SHRM Issues Management Program*, Alexandria, Virginia: Society for Human Resource Management, May–June 1998.

Verespej, M.A. "The old workforce won't work." *Industry Week* 247 (21 September 1998): 53-62.

USE AND MISUSE OF GENETIC INFORMATION IN THE WORKPLACE[1]

David F. Bush
Workplace, Health, and Safety Committee

Recent developments in genetic research have created a double-edged sword. On the one side we have the promise of new levels of understanding, detection, prevention, and treatment of human disease. On the other we find a new threat of discrimination in the workplace. Where a genetic basis for disease can be established, prevention, early detection, and treatment all become possible. However, such genetic information can be used to unfairly penalize those individuals who have diagnostic indicators of potential health problems. A major concern is the possible exclusion of people from jobs or benefits because they possess a particular genetic characteristic, even though that trait may have no impact on their ability to perform the job and may even be unexpressed in the individual. Furthermore, given the uneven distribution of genetic traits among racial and ethnic groups, it is possible that such discrimination can occur unevenly, affecting some racial/ethnic groups more than others. Gregor Mendel's[2] classic 1866 paper on the laws of genetic inheritance in pea plants has been misused in the past (Markel 1992), and it appears that it could happen again. This chapter will review the current state to which genetic research presents both potential benefit and potential threat to American workers.

The Potential Benefits of Genetic Research

Progress in identifying the many genes that constitute the human genome has allowed scientists to develop techniques for the detection, prevention, and amelioration of the effects of genetic disease. Genetics investigators have demonstrated that inherited genetic errors lead directly to several thousand diseases, including breast and ovarian cancer, cystic fibrosis, sickle cell anemia, and Huntington disease (Asch, Patton, Hershey, and Mennuti 1993; American Society of Human Genetics 1994; Harper 1992; Council on Ethical and Judicial Affairs 1991). Less precise relationships resulting from multiple genetic errors have been shown to contribute to other serious illnesses such as heart disease and cancer. Genetic research has led to technology which has produced tests that have become increasingly available and can be used to identify people who have a susceptibility to certain illnesses.

There are numerous examples of tests that have been developed for detecting genetic disease. The diseases for which such indicators have been developed include colorectal cancers resulting from defects in the APC gene, Huntington disease, sickle cell anemia, and cystic fibrosis. With the rapid expansion of the Human Genome Project, it is expected that many more tests for genetic disease will be available in the near future.

---

[1] The author expresses his appreciation to Amy Nowlin Drummond and David Nocek for their assistance in preparing this manuscript.
[2] Gregor Mendel's classic work on genetics was rediscovered in 1900 and contributed to the eugenics movement popular in the first quarter of the twentieth century.

The Human Genome Project

The Human Genome Project is a federally funded project that is attempting to map the human genome. With a budget of more than $3 billion, this 15-year endeavor seeks to determine the sequential location and protein code for each human gene. It is estimated that more than 4,000 hereditary disorders result from single gene defects, and even more result from the interaction of genetic and environmental factors. After the structural map of the human genome is complete, scientists will continue to struggle to understand the function of all genes and the ways in which they are regulated. This approach is expected to dominate the genetics research agenda for decades, as scientists attempt to create order out of this massive array of complex relationships.

Applications of Genetic Research

The primary application of genetic research has been in the area of genetic testing. Five basic types of genetic testing have been distinguished, with each characterized by a distinct application (Dutton 1995). Each test presents an opportunity for genetic information to enter a family's medical record.

1. **Carrier screening** is used to determine the probability of parents' transmission of genetic disease to their children.
2. **Prenatal diagnostic testing** is used to determine if a fetus has a disease-causing gene.
3. **Predisposition testing** determines genetically based vulnerability to diseases and environmental conditions.
4. When a genetic disease is suspected, **confirmatory diagnostic testing** is conducted to confirm its presence.
5. **Forensic and identity testing** is the application of genetic matching to the establishment of paternity and criminal identification.

Genetic screening in the workplace seems to represent a combination of types 3 and 4, either confirming existing conditions or determining vulnerability. Its rationale is generally based in preventive healthcare, according to clinical laboratory companies developing the technology (Dutton 1995). As a service to employees, such screening would permit the targeting of vulnerable individuals for more frequent monitoring to allow detection of such diseases early, when they are more easily treated. It would also permit the counseling of genetically vulnerable individuals to avoid exposure to industrial chemicals that could create health problems. However, such access to the genetic makeup of employees and job applicants also presents the possibility for reducing future healthcare costs for a corporation through selective discriminatory practices.

A second type of genetic testing that can be used in the workplace is genetic monitoring, the repeated testing of an employee's genetic material to determine if it has changed with the passage of time as a result of exposure to hazardous substances in the workplace. If a population of employees with a specific substance exposure display evidence of above-chance change in genetic materials, appropriate health and safety precautions can be introduced, including a reduction in allowable exposure levels. Genetic monitoring is performed to reduce or eliminate health risk resulting from genetic damage.

Genetic monitoring may hold less threat of employment discrimination than genetic screening, because such monitoring is conducted to determine relationships among hazardous materials, genetic changes, and any subsequent disease processes. Research on the survivors of Hiroshima and Nagasaki demonstrated long delays in the appearance of illness. "Although genetic changes such as chromosomal damage have been associated with exposure to radiation and some chemical mutagens or carcinogens, little is known about which changes are predictive of subsequent disease risk," says a report by four federal agencies (Department of Labor et al. 1998, p. 3).

Genetic Information and Workplace Discrimination

There are several ways in which genetic information can make its way into employment decisions through medical records, some not requiring genetic testing. When employees give family medical histories or make comments during physical examinations, health history data may be recorded that allows physicians to make inferences about possible genetic illness. Another source of such information is the laboratory assessment of a person's output of specific chemical substances, where certain patterns in the results of such tests may suggest genetic characteristics. However, the most direct approach is through an analysis of a person's genetic material, the DNA. This genetic material may reveal indicators of an existing disease, a disease that may develop later in life, or the prospect of having a child with a hereditary illness.

The Sickle Cell Example

In the early 1970s employers used genetic screening to identify carriers of the mutated gene for sickle cell anemia among their African American employees. Even though a cure for sickle cell anemia was not available, federal and state legislation was passed between 1970 and 1972 requiring mandatory screening for African American citizens. While much has been written about this example of genetic screening (Reilly 1975, 1977), three major criticisms have been identified (Markel 1992). First, the screening programs had a racial problem, given that they were applied exclusively to African Americans, even though other groups, such as people of Mediterranean origins, can be carriers. Second, these laws were often characterized by scientific inaccuracy, especially with respect to the way they seemed to equate "carrier status" with "disease status," having the effect of stigmatizing carriers. Third, in their haste to create these laws, legislators omitted several important protective clauses, such as requiring test result confidentiality.

Some companies did learn valuable lessons from their experience with screening for sickle cell anemia. DuPont found itself in hot water with charges from a national newspaper stemming from offering employees the option to refuse the test (Dutton

1995). After the controversy, DuPont changed its policy, giving employees the option to request the test.

Fear of Discrimination

Unfortunately, examples of discrimination and stigmatization related to genetic testing are not limited to the case of sickle cell anemia. Geller (1996) reports on a survey of persons associated with genetic conditions that revealed more than 200 cases of genetic discrimination among the 917 respondents. The surveyed populations contained parents of children with genetic conditions and people at risk of developing such conditions, and about 22 percent reported discrimination by employers, insurance companies, and other organizations using genetic information.

Such negative experiences are consistent with the fears of adverse consequences of genetic testing reported in a number of recent surveys.

1. Many of these were summarized in a government agency report (Department of Labor et al. 1998) that reviewed findings of high percentages of respondents who reported a reluctance to use genetic testing because they feared that the results would be used to justify the denial of jobs or access to health insurance policies.

2. Frieden (1991) cites an interview with Paul Billings in which he revealed having received 40 responses to an ad in the *American Journal of Human Genetics* that asked people to contact him about cases of genetic discrimination.

3. Eighty-five percent of respondents in a 1995 Harris Poll indicated that they were either very or somewhat concerned about the access and use of genetic information by insurers or employers (Department of Labor et al. 1998).

4. Lapham, Kozma, and Weiss (1996) reported that 17 percent of a sample of 332 members of support groups for families with genetic disorders did not reveal genetic information to employers out of fear of discrimination.

5. In a 1997 national telephone survey by the National Center for Genome Resources, 63 percent of more than 1,000 respondents "would not take genetic tests" if employers and health insurance organizations could gain access to the results. Eighty-five percent "felt that employers should be prohibited from obtaining information about an individual's genetic conditions, risks, and predispositions."

6. Kolata (1997) reports that approximately one-third of a sample of women who were at high risk for breast cancer because of gene mutations refused to participate in a study concerned with keeping them healthy because they feared discrimination or loss of privacy.

These studies and data from individual cases (Frieden 1991; Geller 1996), support the idea that Americans do fear adverse consequences from the disclosure of genetic information to employers and insurers, and that these fears are not groundless. Furthermore, it is not comforting to learn that the reason that insurers, HMOs, and employers do not plan to utilize genetic screening is the issue of costs (Frieden

1991). They do not indicate that they will not use such information if they acquire it in a less expensive manner. In fact, says Frieden, "cases of alleged genetic discrimination by insurers stem mostly from insurance companies getting access to results of tests already taken, rather than making their own tests on suspicious applicants and awaiting the results" (Frieden 1991, p. 44). Americans are left with yet another example of "don't ask, don't tell."

Restricting the Use of Genetic Information in the Workplace

The primary justification of using genetic information in employment situations would be empirical evidence of an association between an individual's unexpressed genetic factors and his or her job performance. Because no such evidence exists, most authoritative groups are correct in recommending either a prohibition or a severe restriction on the use of genetic testing and genetic information in the workplace. Two major panels of health care authorities have recently taken such a position.

In an editorial in the *Journal of the American Medical Association* on genetic testing by employers, the Council on Ethical and Judicial Affairs (1991) of the American Medical Association expressed a two-part opinion. The Council stated, "It would generally be inappropriate to exclude workers with genetic risks of disease from the workplace because of their risk" (p. 1830). Genetic testing, it said, lacks sufficient predictive power and would result in unfair discrimination against those with abnormal test results. Furthermore, better means of predicting employee performance are available. However, periodic monitoring of workers exposed to dangerous substances is justified as a means of protecting those individuals who may have greater genetic susceptibility to such agents. The Council concluded, "There may be a very limited role for genetic testing in the exclusion from the workplace of workers who have a genetic susceptibility to occupational illness." It offered a set of conditions that would have to be met to allow such a form of genetic testing.

Members of the Committee on Genetic Information and the Workplace of the National Action Plan on Breast Cancer (NAPBC) and the National Institutes of Health-Department of Energy Working Group on Ethical, Legal, and Social Implications of Human Genome Research (the ELSI Working Group) have published a set of five recommendations for state and federal policymakers regarding discrimination and privacy concerns in the workplace (Rothenberg et al. 1997). These authors also note that although employer-required genetic tests are typically not prohibited, "there is insufficient evidence to justify the use of any existing test for genetic susceptibility as a basis for employment decisions" (p. 1755). They said that even if genetic testing is not used, employers can obtain such information through other means and demonstrate a reluctance to hire or promote those persons whose disease may interfere with work in the future or may cause benefits cost to escalate. Therefore, they urge state and federal policymakers to prohibit employment organizations from using, requesting, or requiring the collection of genetic information. Rothenberg et al. (1997) also want to restrict employer access to genetic information in medical records and to prohibit the disclosure of such information by employers without written authorization. Finally, they urge that strong enforcement mechanisms be applied to violators.

Similarly, The American Society of Human Genetics has issued a statement on genetic testing for breast and ovarian cancer predisposition (American Society of Human Genetics 1994) recommending against mass screening for BRCA1 mutations that are believed to be responsible for about 5 percent of breast cancer cases. The rationale for not engaging in mass screening is based on three practical issues: the probability that a given mutation will result in cancer, the effectiveness and risk of available interventions, and test reliability. Unfortunately, this group's statement is not as clear about direct workplace issues as are the statements by other groups cited above.

Legislative Protection

Even though President Clinton announced that he would support legislation and regulation to protect employees from genetic-based discrimination (Shogren 1998), progress in this area has been slow. The Genetic Privacy and Nondiscrimination Act of 1997 (Colby 1998) would have provided several forms of direct protection, but it has not passed. It's latest version, The Genetic Privacy and Nondiscrimination Act of 1999 has also not passed. Existing protection comes from other laws and regulations at both the federal and state levels, of which most were not written to directly influence genetic testing. In fact, the few federal-level protections that exist result from laws designed to remedy other types of workplace discrimination. These incidental federal protections are limited in scope and not well-established. Clearly they do not provide American citizens with sufficient protection for the abuse of genetic information for discrimination in the workplace. While state legislative bodies have responded to this vacuum, the legislation they have enacted varies in coverage, specific protections, and approaches to enforcement. Given that the largest employers are most likely to utilize genetic information, and given the differences among state laws, federal legislation to provide consistency across all state boundaries is imperative.

Existing Federal Laws

A single federal law directly addresses genetic discrimination: the Health Insurance Portability and Accountability Act (HIPAA) of 1996. As described in the government agencies' report, "HIPAA prohibits group health plans from using any health-related factor, including genetic information, as the basis for denying or limiting eligibility for coverage or for charging an individual more for coverage" (Department of Labor et al. 1998, p. 9). There has also been close collaboration between the Clinton administration and Congress on legislation to prevent disclosure of genetic information or the use of genetic information in the modification of rates by insurance companies. Both HR 2457 and 5132 have been sent to a house subcommittee and senate committee, respectively. However, many of the problems that may arise from the collection or use of genetic information in the workplace are beyond these issues of health insurance.

A better existing source of protection from discrimination based on genetic information are those laws that prohibit discrimination based on disability. While they do not explicitly address genetic information, the Americans with Disabilities Act (ADA) and other laws prohibiting disability-based discrimination, such as the Rehabilitation Act of 1973, offer some protection against discrimination involving genetic-based disability. The ADA offers protection to individuals whose genetic-based disability is symptomatic. However, it does not offer protection from genetic discrimination to those individuals with an unexpressed genetic condition. Genetic testing may reveal a condition in a person that may not express itself for more than a decade, and the ADA leaves such a person vulnerable to genetic discrimination without penalty.

Those who have a genetic disability that is currently asymptomatic lack established protection against discrimination based on genetic information. People who fall into this category include carriers of a disease who may never express the disease, people who have late onset genetic disorders who are identified through genetic screening as being at high risk of developing the illness, and people for whom family history indicates a high probability of presenting the symptoms.

The Equal Employment Opportunity Commission (1995) has developed compliance guidelines that seek to extend ADA protection to such individuals with asymptomatic genetic disorders. These guidelines advise that "an employer who takes adverse action against an individual on the basis of genetic information related to illness, disease, or other disorders regards that individual as having a disability within the meaning of the ADA" (Department of Labor et al. 1998). The ADA prohibits discrimination against a person with a disability, but this EEOC guidance has a limited scope and legal impact. It is less legally binding in court than a law or regulation and is yet to be tested in court.

The ADA does not ensure the privacy of genetic information because it offers no protection for employees from employer requirements or requests to provide genetic information. The ADA generally denies access by employers to the medical records of applicants before a conditional offer of employment. However, during the interval between the conditional offer of employment and the first day of work, the employer may acquire extensive medical information, including genetic information. During this period, the ADA would not prohibit the employer from requiring genetic screening as a condition of employment or from obtaining genetic information from a specialized data bank. Furthermore, after hiring an applicant an employer may request further medical information so long as it is job-related and necessary for conducting business.

Preventing discrimination based on genetic information is difficult. It is difficult to detect such discrimination because it may be based on indicators of disease risk rather than on the manifestation of symptoms. The employer could have a greater awareness of such risk factors than the employee. Under these circumstances, genetic information could be used to deny employment or promotion without regard to job performance or ability. The rapid progress of the research associated with the Human Genome Project increases the probability that genetic data that appear relatively innocuous today may with future research be found to indicate genetic risk. The threat of such research extends to the civil rights of family members because such information may be used to predict their risk of genetic disease for them, presenting the possibility of large-scale discrimination against future generations.

Additional federal law protection against some forms of discrimination based on genetic information is Title VII of the Civil Rights Act of 1964 (Department of Labor et al. 1998). The link to Title VII derives from those cases where racially or ethnically linked genetic disorders serve as the basis for genetic discrimination, making those cases illegal discrimination based on race or ethnicity. Such protection under Title VII would apply only to cases of discrimination where there is an established link between the genetic trait and the particular racial or ethnic group. Such links have been established for few diseases, and therefore Title VII will serve as an effective tool for very few forms of genetic discrimination. Title VII and the other existing federal statutes and regulations offer a less than adequate response to the threat of genetic-based employment discrimination.

State Antidiscrimination Laws

A number of states have passed legislation to regulate the use of genetic information. Arizona, for instance, enacted a detailed genetic testing act in 1997 that applies to both insurance and employer-worker relations in the workplace. The new law amended the Arizona Civil Rights Act making "it an unlawful employment practice for an employer to fail or refuse to hire, to discharge, or to otherwise discriminate against any individual based on the results of a genetic test received by an employer" (Lewis and Roca 1997).

Conclusions

If the health of American citizens is to benefit fully from the knowledge gained from genetic research, it is important that we eliminate the threat of genetic-based discrimination in employment and insurance decisions. The rudimentary research that has been conducted in this area indicates that the threat of discrimination will lead many people to avoid the tests and treatments that have the potential to benefit their health because they perceive the risk of loss as greater than the potential for gain. Federal legislation should be used to ensure that all Americans have a minimum level of protection from genetic-based discrimination. In providing such protection, such laws will eliminate any conflict with the ability of scientists to conduct research related to genetics and health, especially studies investigating occupational health.

Federal legislation designed to satisfy the twin criteria of ensuring that (1) the discoveries from the Human Genome Project are used to promote health and (2) such discoveries are not used to discriminate against either employees or family members should include these three basic protections (Department of Labor et al. 1998):

1. **Condition of employment or benefits**. Employers will not be allowed to request or require genetic tests or disclosure of genetic information from either potential employees or current employees as a prerequisite for either employment or benefits.

2. Deprivation of employment opportunities. Employers will not be allowed to deny any employment opportunities on the basis of genetic information.

3. Obtaining or disclosing genetic information. Employers will not be allowed to obtain or disclose employee genetic information.

There are, however, circumstances under which the use of genetic testing and genetic information may be necessary to ensure health and safety in the workplace or to allow important research. In those circumstances where an employer is in possession of genetic information about employees, such information must be kept in confidential medical files separate from other human resource records. Federal and state laws should reinforce such a critical information firewall.

The circumstances under which employers should be empowered to gather and store such genetic information would include those cases where it would be important to monitor the effects of exposure to a particular agent on genetic damage, or where the employer is a reasonable choice to become involved in the gathering and storing of data for a genetics research project.

The Department of Labor has argued that such restrictions on the collection, dissemination, and use of genetic information in the workplace should apply broadly to employers, both public and private, and labor unions, as well as to other entities created to influence employment and training, including employment agencies, licensing agencies, and certifying institutions.

Provisions should be made for individuals who have experienced genetic information-based discrimination to file complaints with specific existing federal agencies such as the Equal Employment Opportunity Commission or the Department of Labor. If such designated agencies are not able to effect a resolution of such complaints, the new laws and regulations should empower the agencies to file suit on behalf of the complainants in federal court. The courts should be granted the authority to order appropriate relief for the individual complainant, as already provided in similar civil rights laws. Alternative relief should be available through private civil lawsuit. It is important that the agencies charged with the enforcement of such laws be provided with additional resources for the required investigation and enforcement.

Until the appropriate laws and regulations are in place, the potential promise of the Human Genome Project will remain an ominous threat for those concerned about adverse impact in employment and benefits availability. The creation of the appropriate laws and regulations will facilitate the effective application of genetic information for the rapid improvement of public health.

Recommended Actions

The following points are critical in understanding the issues surrounding genetic testing:

- Genetic testing presents a double-edged sword: the potential for better understanding, detection, prevention, and treatment of genetic based disease versus a new threat of discrimination in the workplace.

- Racial and ethnic discrimination may result because genetic traits that lead to disease are unevenly distributed among racial and ethnic groups.
- Employers and insurance carriers could use genetic information to reduce healthcare costs by excluding those found to have genetic potential for disease.
- Genetic tests lack predictive power for the development of symptoms.
- There is no established link between genetic factors and job performance.
- Genetic screening is used to detect existing conditions or vulnerability, while genetic monitoring involves repeated testing to determine if genetic material has changed as a result of repeated exposure to hazardous substances.
- Researchers have found that more that 20 percent of respondents with genetic conditions have reported workplace discrimination.
- Surveys have shown that approximately 85 percent of respondents have some level of opposition to employer access to genetic information.
- Current federal laws and regulations provide limited and indirect protection against discrimination, applying primarily to those who exhibit symptoms.
- State laws constitute an uneven patchwork of coverage, making it imperative that new federal legislation be enacted to provide consistency.

References

American Society of Human Genetics. "Statement of the American Society of Human Genetics on Genetic Testing for Breast and Ovarian Cancer Predisposition." *American Journal of Human Genetics*, 55(5) (1994): i–iv.

Asch, D. A.; Patton, J. P; Hershey, J. C.; and Mennuti, M. T. "Reporting the results of cystic cibrosis carrier screening." *American Journal of Obstetrics and Gynecology*, 168(1) (1993): 1–6.

Colby, J. A. "An analysis of genetic discrimination legislation proposed by the 105th Congress." *American Journal of Law & Medicine* 24 (1998): 444–453.

Council on Ethical and Judicial Affairs, American Medical Association. "Use of genetic testing by employers." *JAMA—The Journal of the American Medical Association* 266 (13) (1991): 1827–1830.

Department of Labor, Department of Health and Human Services, Equal Employment Opportunity Commission, and Department of Justice. "Genetic information and the workplace." (1998). [on-line]. Available at http://www.dol.gov/dol/_sec/public/media/reports/genetics.htm.

Dutton, G. "If the genes fit (genetic testing and employers and insurance firms)." *Management Review* 84 (10) (1995): 25–29.

Equal Employment Opportunity Commission. *Compliance Manual 2*, Section 902, Order 915.002, 902–45 1995.

Frieden, J. "Genetic testing: What will it mean for health insurance." *Business & Health* 9 (3) (1991): 40–46.

Geller, L. "Individual, family and societal dimensions of genetic discrimination: A case study analysis." *Science and Engineering Ethics* 2 (1) (1996): 71–88.

Harper, P. S. "Huntington disease and the abuse of genetics." *American Journal of Human Genetics*, 50(3) (1992): 460–464.

Kolata, G. "Advent of testing for breast cancer genes leads to fears of disclosure and discrimination." *New York Times* 4 January 1997, p. C1.

Lapham, E. V.; Kozma, C.; and Weiss, J. O. "Genetic discrimination: Perspectives of consumers." *Science* 274(5287) (1996): 621–624.

Lewis and Roca, LLP. *Arizona Employment Law Letter* 4 (3) (1997).

Markel, H. "The stigma of disease: Implications of genetic screening." *American Journal of Medicine* 93 (1992): 209–215.

Reilly P. "State supported mass genetic screening programs." In *Genetics and the Law I*. Edited by A. Milunsky and G. J. Annas. New York: Plenum Press, 1975.

Reilly P. *Genetics, Law and Social Policy*. Cambridge: Harvard University Press, 1977.

Rothenberg, K.; Fuller, B.; Rothstein, M.; Duster, T.; Kahn, M. J. E.; Cunningham, R.; Fine, B.; Hudson, K.; King, M.; Murphy, P.: Swergold, G.; and Collins, F. "Genetic information and the workplace: Legislative approaches and policy challenges." *Science* 275(5307) (1997): 1755–1757.

Shogren, E. "Clinton would protect workers from genetic-testing bias." *Nation and World*. 1998 [on-line]. Available at http://www.seattletimes.com/news/nationworld/html98/gene_012098.html.

WORKFORCE CHALLENGES FOR THE TWENTY-FIRST CENTURY

Cornelia G. Gamlem
Workplace Diversity Committee

As we enter the twenty-first century, we see increasing changes within the American workforce. The industrial revolution of the late nineteenth and early twentieth centuries dramatically changed the way people work, with the movement of the workforce from the farm to the factory. This change gave rise to a plethora of laws and regulations designed to redress abuses in the labor market such as use of child labor, lack of protection against injury, layoff for old age and disability, and systemic discrimination against groups of individuals (Anthony, Perrewe, and Kacmar 1999). With the movement now under way from the industrial to the information age, the challenges to human resource professionals increase.

During the early 1960s, the issue of employment discrimination moved to the forefront. While policymakers were beginning to debate models to redress discrimination in employment, racial unrest was giving rise to the civil rights movement. Federal civil rights laws designed to eliminate discrimination resulted. Title VII of the Civil Rights Act of 1964 required most companies and labor unions to grant equal employment opportunity for all. It established the Equal Employment Opportunity Commission (EEOC) to ensure the achievements of Title VII's objectives. Next came Executive Order 11246, in 1965, which prohibited employment discrimination by any employer that has a major contract with the federal government. The Labor Department's Office of Federal Contract Compliance Programs (OFCCP) enforces EO 11246.

Thirty-five years after President Lyndon Johnson signed EO 11246, the use of affirmative action to achieve equal opportunity objectives is still widely debated, particularly in the media. The recent debate has failed to accurately describe affirmative action in the employment context and often confuses it with diversity initiatives. At the same time, there is a growing trend by lawmakers and policymakers to effect social changes via legal and regulatory vehicles rather than by voluntary corporate efforts. For the human resource practitioner, it is important to understand the distinction between federally mandated programs such as affirmative action, and voluntary initiatives to address rapidly changing workforces. This chapter will explain these distinctions and discuss social trends that will affect workplace diversity in the next ten years.

Affirmative action in employment primarily affects companies that receive contracts from the federal government. They are required to comply with the regulations promulgated under Executive Order 11246, the Rehabilitation Act of 1973, and the Vietnam Era Veterans Readjustment Assistance Act of 1974. These laws extend the protections of Title VII to prohibit discrimination and require contractors to exercise outreach efforts so that protected classes have the opportunity to be hired and advance in employment without regard to their race, color, religion, sex, national origin, disability, or veteran status. Rather than providing employment preferences, affirmative action requires companies to actively recruit, interview, and seriously consider a wider variety of candidates. Affirmative action also requires companies to implement policies and programs to help minorities and women advance in employment in those areas of a company's workforce where those groups are not fully represented. Its intention is to remove barriers to employment opportunities and to provide equal employment opportunity for all individuals, not to establish hiring quotas for protected groups. In addition, courts can order companies to establish affirmative action programs to remedy the effects of past discrimination.

In 1987 the Hudson Institute published a study for the Department of Labor entitled *Workforce 2000*. The study reported on workforce changes projected from 1985 to 2000, and documented a shift in labor force demographics with growth in ethnic, racial, and gender groupings (Baytos 1995). These changes would affect not only the workplace, but also external issues such as the changing face of consumers. Demographics were not the only changes affecting companies. Increased competition and entry into global markets were adding demands and pressures. Companies began using a variety of approaches to tap the talent and effectiveness of their workforces, such as high-performance work teams. Important to the success of these teams is the ability of each member to make quality contributions. Companies realized that to be effective they had to manage the diversity of these teams without impeding productivity (Baytos 1995). Driven by these changes, rather than by the legal and regulatory requirements of affirmative action, companies began to implement initiatives that addressed the many dimensions of diversity within their organizations.

Somewhere in the recent debate, the distinction between affirmative action and diversity became blurred and the terms were interchanged, leading to the notion that diversity initiatives are merely affirmative action efforts with a different name. However, if we observe the events along a continuum (see figure 1), society has moved from the golden rule of equal employment opportunity (treating everyone equally as a potential employee), to righting past wrongs that affirmative action is designed to address. Incorporated into affirmative action is the golden rule of equal employment opportunity (EEO) and the principle of nondiscrimination. Moving along the continuum, initiatives have further evolved to emphasize the importance of valuing differences and the importance of including all employees in the workforce, namely workplace diversity. While encompassing the principles of EEO and affirmative action, diversity has a broader reach. Comparing and contrasting these approaches to workplace policies, we see a number of similarities and differences. EEO and affirmative action are constrained by the boundaries of laws and regulations and have a specific mandate, namely, the prohibition of discrimination against defined, protected classes. While EEO offers no guidelines for correcting past discriminatory practices, affirmative action mandates certain efforts to overcome the effects of past practices. Workplace diversity initiatives are not rooted in laws and regulations. They have no defined responsibilities and no constraints. Therefore, they can be broadly defined to address specific issues within a company. While EEO and affirmative action are rigid, workplace diversity is flexible. The point at which the three intersect, however, represents the common goal that they all share, namely respect (see figure 2).

Figure 1 – Diversity Continuum

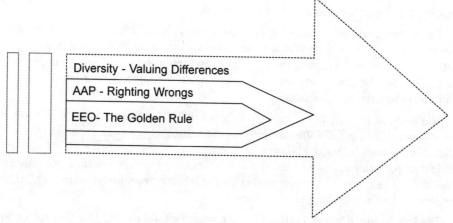

Diversity - Valuing Differences

AAP - Righting Wrongs

EEO- The Golden Rule

Figure 2 – Respect: The Cornerstone

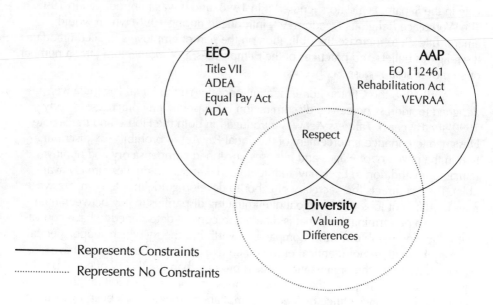

EEO
Title VII
ADEA
Equal Pay Act
ADA

AAP
EO 112461
Rehabilitation Act
VEVRAA

Respect

Diversity
Valuing
Differences

——————— Represents Constraints

.... Represents No Constraints

Corporate diversity initiatives address a wide variety of issues that affect the workplace and the marketplace. Workforce diversity can include tenure with the company, the line of business an individual supports, functional specialty, geographic region, and personal aspects such as age, lifestyle, sexual orientation, education, race, and gender. Globalism, and the differences and similarities in terms of people, culture, politics, technology, priorities, and location, are often core issues within a diversity initiative. Acquisitions and mergers provide mixtures of entities that may be different or similar in the nature of the business, corporate culture, vision, mission, and technology. Cross-functional work teams can present a distinct set of diversity issues as companies manage the similarities and differences regarding tasks, goals, communication patterns, and time orientation (Thomas 1996). In order to design effective diversity initiatives, it is important to understand the issues and challenges shaping the workforce and affecting the workplace.

Lawmakers and policymakers remain concerned about discrimination in employment practices. In fact, the trend appears to be toward more protections and entitlements, and to increasing the regulation and reporting requirements imposed on companies, thereby giving the government more oversight of, and impact on, corporate employment practices.

The Veterans Employment Opportunities Act of 1998 expanded the class of veterans protected by the 1974 Vietnam Veterans law. The Act not only expanded the class of veterans who would be protected (e.g., Gulf War veterans), it also imposed additional reporting requirements. Those requirements include reporting not only the new class of veterans, but also reporting on the minimum and maximum number of employees for the reporting year.

The Employment Nondiscrimination Act, which would extend Title VII protection on the basis of a person's sexual orientation, was considered in 1996 but lost by one vote in the Senate. Legislators ignored it in 1998, and it was reintroduced in 1999. The Workplace Religious Freedom Act, introduced during 1998, which would amend Title VII to increase the obligation on the part of employers to accommodate the religious beliefs and practices of their employees, lost momentum after a number of employer groups raised concerns.

In April 1998 the Clinton administration announced the Equal Pay Initiative, designed to address perceived discrimination in corporate pay practices. In early 1999, the Paycheck Fairness Act was introduced in both the House and the Senate. Designed to enhance enforcement of the Equal Pay Act, it prohibits sex discrimination in the payment of wages and imposes uncapped compensatory and punitive damages (in addition to back pay and liquidated damages remedies already available). The Act directs the Secretary of Labor to develop guidelines to compare wage rates for different jobs with the goal of eliminating disparities in pay between men and women performing work that is different in content determined to have equivalent value (comparable worth). Comparable worth is a theory which supports equal pay for jobs that are not identical or are different in content, but that may have equivalent value to the organization. This is broader than the theory of equal pay for equal work, which requires that jobs be identical in content. In addition, the Department of Labor's Office of Federal Compliance Programs has been rigorous in auditing compensation practices of federal contractors.

As we move into the twenty-first century, an understanding of workforce predictions is necessary in order to address the challenges they present. According to Hattiangadi (1998), skilled labor shortages are expected to continue into the future, placing an increased emphasis on recruitment. This will continue the trend of new employment opportunities for a broader, more diverse, group of job-seekers, including women, older individuals, and people with limited skills and experience. Economic theory suggests that as labor markets tighten the economic costs of discrimination rise. Thus, in the early twenty-first century, with demand outpacing supply, employers are looking to recruit from untapped labor pools, increasing employment opportunities for protected groups.

Additionally, Hattiangadi (1998) asserted that Hispanics are expected to be one of the fastest-growing groups in the population. By 2010, this population may become the second largest ethnic/race group. Despite rapid growth, the Hispanic labor force is predicted to grow to 14 percent of the U.S. workforce by 2020. The representation of African Americans in the labor force is expected to remain constant at the current level of 11 percent into the year 2020. Asian/Pacific Islanders are predicted to represent 6 percent of the labor force by 2020.

The workforce of the twenty-first century will differ significantly in its share of older individuals because the age distribution of the population will shift as workers of the baby boom generation age. Demographers predict that by the year 2010, baby boomers will leave the workplace through retirement, taking with them needed skills and experience. Because the next generation is smaller and fertility rates are declining, workers with the requisite skills and experience to replace these retirees will be scarce. Allowing this group of older workers, who will be healthier and more highly educated than the prior generation of retirees, to continue participating in the labor force will be critical (Kindelan 1998).

The most significant change in the workforce over the past 30 years has been in gender composition. The number of women in the workforce has doubled since 1970, and by 2020 the female share of the labor force is predicted to be about 50 percent. While this change represents only a small increase from 46 percent in 1998, women have considerable opportunity to increase their participation in the workforce. Women work part-time more than men and average only 1,290 annual works hours compared with 1,900 for men. Only about 60 percent of the women in the labor force work full-time year round. (Hattiangadi 1998).

While demographics predictions are significant, it is also important to look at the educational attainment of ethnic and racial groups, as well as the role of immigration. Hispanics and African Americans lag behind both whites and Asian/Pacific Islanders with respect to high school diplomas and higher education degrees. Among Hispanics, this results in large part from strong immigration of relatively low-skilled individuals from Mexico. Most immigrants admitted to the United States during 1996 were from North America, with native-born Mexicans composing almost 50 percent, Asians 34 percent, and Europeans only 16 percent. With respect to educational attainment, today's immigration is a bipolar distribution, consisting of people with college or advanced degrees and highly specialized skills (12 percent have graduate or advanced degrees) and people with little education or few skills (Hattiangadi 1998).

The rise in immigration brings other notable changes to the workplace. For example, the number and diversity of languages spoken in the workplace today presents multiple opportunities for miscommunication and misunderstanding. The barriers are more than those of language, however. They encompass cultural, gender, economic class, ethnic, educational, and religious differences. Success for managers often means feeling comfortable in a multicultural work environment and discovering new ways of communicating and managing conflicts. Managing these changes is the role of human resource professionals (Grimsley 1999).

The Islamic religion is expected to surpass Judaism as the second most commonly practiced religion in the United States. Because many of our country's social customs and mores are rooted in Christian-Judeo beliefs, significant social changes can be expected to emerge, and these changes will affect the workplace. Employers will have to accommodate the daily prayers, washing, dietary requirements, holidays, clothing, and grooming that are part of these religions (Minehan 1998). Human resource professionals face the challenge of educating themselves and their employees about different religions and their impact on the workplace.

This chapter began by discussing affirmative action as a social program designed to address civil unrest three decades ago. Affirmative action was originally designed to remove barriers in employment for African Americans. Issues related to race still confront the nation, as was reported by the Advisory Board of President Clinton's Initiative on Race (White House 1998). Attitudes and behaviors, both organizational and individual, continue to create barriers and give unfair advantages. Other kinds of barriers to employment exist as we enter the twenty-first century. Poor language skills and lack of education are limiting employment opportunities for some workers. External pressures such as competition, skilled labor shortages, globalization, and immigration are driving the need for companies to attract, manage, and retain a continually changing workforce. Human resource professionals should lead the effort within their organizations to respond to these challenges for workers and employers alike. They need to recognize that EEO and affirmative action are still viable tools for overcoming barriers that should be incorporated into diversity initiatives.

A tight labor market has made recruiting high-skilled workers a business priority. Creative sourcing of candidates results in innovative outreach programs, the very heart of affirmative action. When the demand for workers outpaces the supply, moving beyond outreach becomes necessary. Affirmative action requires programs that allow employees to advance in employment. Emphasizing programs for training individuals lacking skills is one example. Education as an enhancement to employment advancement will likely result in the growth of partnerships between educational institutions and corporations.

Many social and corporate policies in existence today were designed for workplaces that no longer exist. These rigid policies are a barrier to employment in workplaces that need to be flexible to compete. A number of social initiatives being debated today, while not traditionally thought of as components of affirmative action programs, do address barriers. For example, Social Security reform will affect the role that the older worker will play in the workforce of the future. Employers will want to keep valued older workers on the job by offering alternative working arrangements such as consulting assignments and phased retirement programs (Kindelan 1998). The contingent workforce will continue to grow by choice, providing greater flexibility in the workforce. A 1999 study by the Bureau of Labor Statistics confirms that a large margin of contingent workers prefer their status to traditional, full-time employment (Bureau of Labor Statistics 1998). The greater flexibility that contingent working arrangements provide will be attractive to the older worker. Companies are introducing policies supporting flexible hours and work spaces, and these programs can assist with the retention of working parents, especially mothers, who need help balancing work and family responsibilities. By retaining women within its workforce, a company also supports affirmative action. The range of work/family issues continues to grow, and companies are challenged to address their employees' work/life balance needs and lifestyle differences.

Human resources professionals can be on the cutting edge of social and organizational change. They can influence the challenges discussed in this chapter by raising organizational awareness about the myths and misrepresentations of affirmative action and educating managers that EEO and affirmative action are components of diversity initiatives. Shifting beyond affirmative action to workplace diversity initiatives, organizations can build inclusive workplaces and change cultures to reflect the current social trends. In doing so, organizations can address workplace changes before social changes are imposed through legislation.

For diversity initiatives to be successful, they must be built on the cornerstones of inclusion and respect. Inclusive workplaces promote respect by encouraging effective communication, setting a climate for learning, and removing barriers to employment and to external factors such as customer and investor interests. Fostering respect increases productivity and builds a competitive advantage for the organization. Diversity initiatives must also be integrated into the organization's overall business strategy and not be limited to human resources and people management strategies. Diversity must be woven into all of the organization's components, including marketing, public relations, and investor relations. A well-integrated, skillfully crafted workplace diversity initiative will position organizations to respond to social changes, create richer corporate environments, and meet organizational goals and objectives.

Recommended Actions

- Build your diversity initiative on the cornerstone of inclusion and respect.
- Recognize that your workplace diversity initiative is a process and not an event.
- Ensure that your workplace diversity initiative supports your organization's business goal and is integrated throughout the organization.
- Understand the changing nature of the workforce, and develop programs, strategies, and processes that reflect these changes in your workplace diversity initiative.
- Recognize that the changing nature of the marketplace affects your customers and clients, and address these changes in your workplace diversity initiative.
- Monitor and understand changing legal and regulatory constraints and audit these changes against your workplace diversity initiative to ensure that compliance is maintained.

- Challenge impending government changes that will increase your burden and limit your flexibility to respond to changing workforce and market trends.

- Recognize that equal employment opportunity and affirmative action requirements continue to exist and that they can complement your diversity efforts.

- Partner with schools and outreach agencies to narrow the skills gap and address language barriers.

- Assess the diversity issues within your organization with respect to societal issues such as race, gender, and socioeconomic status, as well as with respect to organizational issues such as line of business, geographic region, or functional specialty.

References

Anthony, W. P.; Perrewe, P. L.; and Kacmar, K. M. *Human Resource Management*. 3d ed. Orlando, Florida: Dryden Press, 1999.

Baytos, L. M. *Designing and Implementing Successful Diversity Programs*. Englewood Cliffs: Prentice-Hall, 1995.

Bureau of Labor Statistics. "Workers in alternative employment arrangements: A second look." 1998. [on-line]. Available at http://www.bls.gov/opub/mir/1998/11/art2full.pdf.

Grimsley, K. D. "The world comes to the American workplace." *Washington Post*, 20 March 1999, p. A12.

Hattiangadi, A.U. "The changing face of the 21st century workforce: Trends in ethnicity, race and gender." Washington, D.C.: Employment Policy Foundation, 1998.

Kindelan, A. "Older workers can alleviate labor shortages." *HR Magazine* 43(10) (1998): 200.

Minehan, M. "Islam's growth affects workplace policies." *HR Magazine* 43(12) (1998): 216.

Thomas, R. R., Jr. *Redefining Diversity*. New York: AMACOM, 1996.

White House Commission on Race. "One America in the 21st century: forging a new Future." 1998. [on-line]. Available at http://www.whitehouse.gov/Initiatives/OneAmerica/cevent.html.

THE CHALLENGE: EMPLOYEES FOR THE FUTURE*

Phyllis G. Hartman
School-to-Work Committee

Current Shortages of Skilled/Knowledgeable Workers

As U.S. business moves into the new millennium, companies are struggling to find workers with skills needed to do today's jobs. It came as no surprise to most businesses when the U.S. Department of Labor (DOL) announced a new twenty-four-year low in the unemployment rate—4.3 percent in December 1998, a figure that was still holding as the twentieth century ended (Bureau of Labor Statistics 1999). Besides not having many workers to choose from in an expanding economy, companies are finding that those who are applying for open positions do not have the skills to do the jobs. Sixty-nine percent of North American businesses surveyed by the William Olsten Center for Workforce Strategies in 1998 were facing a lack of applicants with proper skills, up from 41 percent in 1993 (William Olsten Center 1998).

The lack of skills is not limited to the so-called soft skills required by leaner management groups brought on by the total quality management (TQM) programs and downsizing of the 1990s. A vice president of administration for a Michigan manufacturer was quoted as saying, "We are emphasizing the improvement of supervisors' 'people' skills to improve our retention odds," and at the same time "industry is faced with rapidly changing technologies, and greater demand than supply of unique technical skills" (William Olsten Center 1998, p. 6). In addition, many current workers often do not even possess basic literacy skills. A 1997 study of 4,500 National Association of Manufacturers members revealed that 30 percent of their job applicants had inadequate reading and math skills. Six out of ten applicants also had deficiencies in employability areas such as attendance (Kirrane 1998).

Global capital, production, and markets, instantaneous transfer of information, and mass production of "customized" products are all affecting work and life in the United States. In the past, reliance on more natural resources, capital, technologies, and skills kept the American worker on top. Today, only quickly changing skills will bring that result. Secretaries are now information managers, forklift operators control inventory records, auto mechanics are repairing with computer chips rather than with wrenches.

Projections About Future Needs

The current lack of skilled workers is not likely to improve in the near future. The government is predicting that by 2006, 32 percent of all job openings resulting from growth or replacement will require more than a high school diploma. The DOL's December 1998 figures also predict that of the top ten occupations with the largest job growth, only three (cashiers, retail salespeople, and receptionists/information

* The author would like to thank Janet Simon, Steve Saylor, and the members of the School-to-Work Committee for their assistance with this manuscript.

clerks) are likely to be ones where on-the-job training alone might be enough (Yu 1998). These numbers become important in light of the increasing numbers of minority workers, specifically African Americans and Hispanics, who traditionally get less education and represent a disproportionately high percentage of the 1 million high school dropouts (Graham 1997). A 50 percent increase in the number of young minorities available for work (those who will reach age sixteen by 2006) could mean that the United States will face an even greater shortage of skilled workers as the current white, baby boomer age group retires (Yu 1998).

A March 1997 article in *Business Week* acknowledged that as the baby boomer workforce ages, there are limited opportunities for younger workers to obtain higher-level skills because the older employees are still working. When the boomers retire, the country may face the prospect of a "shrinking, less skilled workforce after 2020—a phenomenon that would dampen economic growth." Cummins Engine Company in Columbus, Indiana, was cited as experiencing a 29 percent drop in profits in 1996 in the competitive world of engine manufacturing. This drop raised concerns about standing up to continuing competition with an aging workforce whose skills are not increasing at an adequate rate, coupled with no infusion of younger workers because of a 1993 no-layoff union agreement. The young people in the area are moving out in search of better opportunities elsewhere (Stodghill 1997).

While the number of educated/skilled future workers is in jeopardy, the dependence on the people in any organization, whether it be manufacturing or service-focused, seems to be even greater. The Secretary of Labor for the State of Washington, former Boeing Company director, has said, "Today knowledge has become the only source of sustainable, long-term, competitive advantage, but knowledge can be derived only through the skills of individuals. A primary way we will continue to be competitive in the world economy now and twenty years from now is to ensure we have a highly skilled and motivated workforce" (Gayton 1997, p. 26).

Facts That Make Us Face Reality

Even now, businesses are facing shortages in skilled workers. The demand for even greater skills will continue. Knowledge is power in the world of the future, and with the explosion of the use of computers and the Internet, information and its management are keys to success. The greatest increases in population are in those groups who have not had the opportunity to gain strong educational backgrounds. The highest growth in occupations is predicted in jobs like systems analysts, general managers and top executives, nurses, and teacher aides/educational assistants, all of which require more than a traditional high school education.

Younger workers are less likely to get on-the-job experience because of the large number of baby boomers who will not be retired until 2020. Where will they gain the skills and experience necessary to replace the boomers and keep the future economy stable or growing?

Ever-increasing, rapid change in technology, global competition, and the amount of information people are expected to deal with means that new skills are needed for future workers. How can we deal with these new skill needs that we do not even know about, when we are not coping now? Whose problem is it anyway, and who is going to solve it?

Whose Problem Is It Anyway?

Society is suffering. A 1997 *Wall Street Journal* article reported, "In 1979 a 30-year-old male high school graduate earned the equivalent of about $28,000, expressed in today's dollars. Today (1997), a 30-year-old male high school graduate earns about $21,000" (Graham 1997). The ratio of education to earning has declined. Unemployment is at an all-time low. More people are employed in the United States today than in the past twenty-four years. Their pay levels are much lower, however. The two-wage household is more the norm today. Quality of life has not increased for many, even when opportunity for employment has increased. Crime, poverty, and missed opportunity are still prevalent in a society that is experiencing a healthy economic growth.

There are further dangers for society. Manufacturing jobs are moving off shore at an ever-increasing pace. Lower standards of living in other countries offer employers lower-cost employees. Manufacturing, not service, actually creates wealth within an economy. If the trend continues, and U.S. workers are not prepared to take the higher-level/higher paying jobs or those that require technical literacy skills, the United States may lose its place as a world economic leader.

Employers are struggling with responsibility and accountability. The need to turn a profit dominates the philosophy of many business enterprises. The old workplace of the past that "took care" of the employee is all but gone. The loyal employer finds her/himself held down and unable to respond to quickly changing market needs and trends. On the other hand, assuming that knowledge is the power of the future and that only people can have and apply knowledge, employees are the most important resources. Human resources can hold and apply the knowledge effectively. How does management/business meet the needs of the worker in terms of support and loyalty and still make the fast moves and changes dictated by global competition and changing technology? Companies continue to lose out to global competitors when they need to spend financial resources on retraining people on basic skills. They must pass on the costs of this retraining in the cost of their products.

Educators are finding themselves caught in the middle. Traditionally tied since the 1930s to producing people who could succeed in an industrial setting, they feel they are being asked to abandon their well-defined role without the information or the resources to define a new role. Faced with increasing social ills, changes in the family structure, and decreased funds, they are being asked to solve all of the problems. Teachers are expected to educate about conflict management, environmental dangers and issues, and the dangers of drugs and AIDS; improve team-building and communication skills; provide before and after school care; and oh, by the way, still teach reading, writing, math, and social studies. Businesses, often well-meaning but ill-informed, have tried to intervene in education. Efforts to blame or fix schools have been met by resistance from the educational community. It feels the effects of business pointing the finger of blame while they struggle with a crisis of shrinking financial and human resources.

In a *Wall Street Journal*/NBC News poll in March 1997, fifty-nine percent of adults surveyed said that education was essential to success. In the same poll, fifty-eight percent believed that some essential/fundamental changes are necessary in the education systems (Graham 1997).

A significant difficulty faced by schools is the lack of a clear definition for future skill needs. Businesses can't offer future work skills projections. Everyone is aiming at a moving target. In addition, the structure, processes, and available financial and information resources in education today make it difficult to provide timely responses to changing conditions.

What Is the Answer?

Seeking solutions to the problem is only possible by including all stakeholders. Partnership of business, education, and community, as well as parents and students, holds the greatest potential. The need in the workplace is for employees who have a balanced education. They need not only reading, writing, and math skills, but an interdisciplinary application of all three. "Most real-world problems do not fit neatly within the bounds of any one subject area" (Stern and Rahn 1995, p. 39).

The current approach in most schools, and the one most teachers were educated under, was designed around an age-graded, assembly-line pattern, derived from the factory model of the last century (Stern and Rahn 1995). In the traditional assembly line, people were taught to do one function all day, without thinking, like machines. In today's world, change is the key, and learning how to make decisions, work with teams, and solve problems are the components that separate the worker from the machine.

Only by combining the efforts of the total community can U.S. students prepare to be the workforce of the future. Successful programs throughout the country give testimony to the effectiveness of such an approach. "There is plenty of justification for expanding opportunities for work-based learning" (Stern and Rahn 1995, p. 40). For those programs to be most beneficial, they need to be tied to an interdisciplinary curriculum where academics and occupational content go hand-in-hand. Teachers, both academic and vocational, cannot do this alone. They need the resources, both financial and knowledge-based, that businesses possess. Parents need to support schools in this effort, and taxpayers who are not parents need to become involved, often as subject matter experts who can provide volunteer time and information to educators.

What Is the HR Role?

What is the role of the human resources professional in all of this? HR can become a catalyst, a link between business and the community. The emerging role of the HR professional has been as a strategic force in shaping the business of the future by keeping the balance between workers and the organization. This role is a natural fit in re-creating our school and work connections for the future.

As staffing and training professionals, HR is a customer of the community. HR's stake is in helping to develop a strong supply of individuals who can meet future employment needs. By working with businesses, communities, and schools HR professionals become an even more strategic force in everyone's success.

Helping Business and Education Find Each Other

HR professionals have a unique opportunity to use their communication expertise to reach out to local schools and help them link with the resources available in business. Approaching their organizations as employment professionals, they can justify business's investment of time and equipment in support for schools. As community leaders, they can approach schools with the outstretched hand of partnership as opposed to the closed hand and pointing finger of blame.

Examples of successful programs are many and varied, and they go beyond the traditional work-study programs of the past in which vocational students attended school for half a day and worked in local businesses the other half. In Pueblo, Colorado, fifty-three teachers participated in a summer internship program called "Worksite Experiences for Teachers." The program included an employment selection process, an assessment, a one-week internship or shadowing experience, and a curriculum integration workshop. The teachers reported a better understanding of what their students will be facing upon graduation. As a result, new curriculum programs were set up at the schools. In addition, a shared language was established between the educators and the businesses (School-to-Career Resource Center 1998).

School-based enterprises, where teachers and students team with businesses and higher education to create "laboratory" businesses and community projects, have been established. These programs provide students with experience and opportunities to apply learning. One example is Pennsylvania State University's agricultural extension program. The program gets students in inner-city schools in Pennsylvania involved in planting gardens to beautify their school property and often surrounding vacant lots. The students learn about biology and agriculture, the college service provides the plants/seedlings, and the community benefits from an enhanced environment.

Students in school in Eagle County, Colorado, are engaged in a "fish" venture; they built the building and now raise salmon and trout in an ecological system. This raises about $18,000 a year for the school and encourages students to contribute to the ecology of the region. At the same time, the students are learning about biology, ecology, and business, along with problem-solving, cooperation, and teamwork (School-to-Career Resource Center 1998).

Other programs involve workforce development projects combining business leaders, local governments, and professional associations. An example is the YouthWorks program in Pittsburgh, Pennsylvania. Inner-city high school students are employed for the summer through a partnership of local government, economic development advocates, private businesses, and the Pittsburgh Human Relations

Association. A Lehigh Valley, Pennsylvania, Cityworks program brings together city government, a federally funded Private Industry Council, and the local SHRM chapter for a four-day workforce development program that includes local underemployed and hard-to-employ young people each year.

Still other programs include use of community-accepted skill standards, academic passport, or certification programs, use of high school records as standard hiring documents, and community service built into academic or extra-curricular programs.

There are opponents of school-to-work initiatives. Some claim that efforts to set national standards for education will hurt minorities and disadvantaged kids. Others fear standards that will hurt religion. Some believe that school-to-work means that kids will be buttonholed into low-paying manufacturing or service jobs and not encouraged to go on to higher education (Graham 1997). These fears are often unfounded. For instance, most school-to-work programs are based on strong educational principles of "learner-centered" education (National Center for Research in Vocational Education 1997). It would appear that the real danger here lies in limiting the solution of the problem to the control of only one segment of the community. If business, educators, taxpayers, parents, or students try to solve the problem alone, then the doomsayers' predictions could be realized.

HR professionals have an opportunity to create initiatives and establish links that can lead to successful programs within their communities. Working with their own businesses or local SHRM chapters, they can become recognized leaders in an effort to prepare the future workers. They can:

- Initiate programs.
- Participate as advisers to programs.
- Provide input into school curriculum.
- Recruit other employers to participate.
- Assist in screening student or teacher applicants for programs.
- Create work-based staff development opportunities for teachers.
- Provide work-based learning opportunities for students (Kazis and Gittleman 1995)

As developers of workplace policies, HR professionals can contribute in another way. With the number of working parents increasing and the impact of laws like the Family and Medical Leave Act (FMLA), the HR professional can be proactive in development of family-friendly policies. These policies, which can support workplace attendance while supporting community involvement, can contribute to citizen support of local schools. Policies that allow, even encourage, parents to attend school functions will provide support for schools and educators. They represent an outstretched hand to the value of schools. Policies should not be limited to those that affect parents alone. Encouraging employees to become involved in their local schools through time off or flexible scheduling is an investment in the community and the future workforce. HR professionals can help businesses see these links and the ultimate paybacks.

Where Can HR Professionals Start?

SHRM's School-to-Work Committee is one resource for the HR professional. The committee's program, "Educators and Business—Partnership for a Successful Future," available on-line, provides a PowerPoint/slide and script presentation that will help HR professionals in approaching local schools. The program outlines the challenges, the need for a partnered approach among business, education, and the community, a model for school-to-work initiatives, and guided discussion format (SHRM School-to-Work Committee 1998). The Committee also has a reference manual, available by calling SHRM headquarters at 800-283-7476.

In addition, SHRM's home page contains links to many school-to-work sites. Examples of organizations, resources, successful programs, and contacts can be found there. The Web site address is http://www.shrm.org/committees/stw.

The real key to realizing the potential for school-to-work activities from an HR professional's perspective is acknowledging the critical nature of the efforts of every individual. Preparing the future workforce is not in the hands of any one group or individual. HR professionals can be an important catalyst to these efforts by using their already established understanding of business and strategic planning, and by building partnerships among the community, business, and the profession. Taking a step to make these networks a reality will help HR stand out once again as a strategic force in a successful future.

Recommended Actions

- Initiate school-to-work partnerships in your own community.
- Participate as advisers to existing programs.
- Provide input into school curriculum.
- Assist in screening student or teacher applicants for programs.
- Create work-based staff development opportunities for teachers.
- Provide work-based learning opportunities for students.
- As developers of workplace policies, be proactive in development of family-friendly policies that encourage parent/community involvement in local schools.
- Encourage employees to become involved in their local schools through time off or flexible scheduling as an investment in the community and the future workforce.
- Explore SHRM's school-to-work links through the Web site: http://www.shrm.org/committees/stw.

- Be an important catalyst by using already established understanding of business and strategic planning, and by building partnerships in the community, business, and the HR profession.

References

Bureau of Labor Statistics. Press release. Department of Labor, 1999 [on-line]. Available at http://stats.bls.gov/newsrelease/empsit.toc.htm.

Gayton, C. C. "Getting into the education business." *Techniques* 72(5) (1997): 26–28.

Graham, E. "Education becomes the paramount issue." *Wall Street Journal*, 14 March 1997, p. R4.

Kazis, R., and Gittleman, M. "School-to-work programs." *Info-Line* Issue 9509, (September 1995).

Kirrane, D. E. "Good help is harder to find." *Association Management* 50(3) (March 1998): 33.

National Center for Research in Vocational Education. "School to work for the college bound." *Centerfocus* 16 (March 1997): 1.

School-to-Career Resource Center. "Effective examples in Colorado." August 1998 [on-line]. Available at http://ccdweb.ccd.cccoes.edu/stcresource.

SHRM School-to-Work Committee. *Educators and Business—Partnership for a Successful Future.* 1998 [on-line]. Available at http://www.shrm.org/committees/699stwpost.pdf.

Stern, D. and Rahn, M. "Work-based learning." *Educational Leadership* 52(8) (1995): 37–38.

Stodghill, R. "The coming bottleneck." *Business Week* 35 (49) (1997): 184.

William Olsten Center for Workforce Strategies. *Staffing strategies: 1998 Olsten Forum on Human Resource Issues and Trends.* Melville, New York: William Olsten Center, pp. 1–6.

Yu, J. L. Bureau of Labor Statistics of the Department of Labor. December 1998 [on-line]. Available at http://stats.bls.gov/blshome.html.

Suggested Readings

SHRM School-to-Work Committee. School to work reference manual. Alexandria, Virginia: Society for Human Resource Management, 1999.

School-to-Work Resources. Examples of organizations, resources, successful programs, and contacts. SHRM March 2000 [on-line]. Available at http://www.shrm.org/committees/stw.

PROTECTING A COMPANY'S VALUABLE INTANGIBLE ASSETS IN THE INFORMATION AGE*

Linda S. Johnson
Employment Committee

Whether a company is large or small, chances are pretty high that some form of information is among its most valuable assets. From customer lists to marketing plans, from product formulation to pricing information, data and information are increasingly becoming the commodities of the future. This phenomenon has been coupled with the increased use of technology by businesses to collect, store, and distribute information. As a result, never before have businesses been so vulnerable to unauthorized access to and use of company information. And never before has the need to maintain the confidentiality of such information been as vital to keeping a competitive edge in our fast-paced, rapidly changing global marketplace.

Some companies, especially those in the high technology industry, have wisely recognized the need to protect company information and already require some employees to sign employment agreements that include nondisclosure and noncompetition provisions. Other companies have adopted specific policies governing the use of e-mail or the Internet. But these employment agreements and focused information security policies frequently fall short of providing a company with the full security it should have for protecting itself against inappropriate use or disclosure of important company information. For whatever reason, companies are often lax in uniformly or consistently adopting protective employment agreements. And even when there is an information security policy in place, it typically addresses only a certain technology such as e-mail rather than the information that needs to be protected regardless of the format in which it is maintained.

Why Does a Company Need a Comprehensive Information Security Policy?

The failure to appropriately secure a company's intangible assets can result in numerous problems. The most typical situation involves the employee who leaves his or her employer, goes to work for a competitor, and solicits the customers or vendors of the former employer. Or a company discovers that an ex-employee or soon-to-be ex-employee has deleted software, and that the employee intends to start a competing business to market that software. Sometimes, companies altogether fail to consider that even with current employees, maintaining the security of company information is critical. For instance, certain types of information, such as personnel and employee health records, may carry a legal obligation of confidentiality. Inappropriate disclosure of this information can lead to lawsuits and financial damages. Without proper precautions, anyone with access to company-maintained data (i.e., employees, independent contractors, interns, or even building maintenance or janitorial crews) can discover and download vast amounts of company data with

---

* The author would like to thank David Wolowitz, Esq., and Sarah B. Knowlton, Esq., for their assistance with this manuscript.

minimal effort. Even office recycling bins can pose a threat to information security if nonshredded documents are recycled without consideration of their content.

As we start into the new century, every company should take the time to evaluate its need to adopt a comprehensive information security policy. By doing so, any business that expends significant resources in developing its customer lists, specialized software, unique marketing strategies, and the like will help to ensure that these valuable intangible assets are protected to the greatest extent possible from abuse, both from its existing workforce and from departed employees.

What Should a Company Do First?

The starting point for developing an effective information security system is to create an information security team or committee whose task it is to develop a draft information security policy. The policy itself will have two main components: a statement of general principles and a listing of the means by which the general goals will be achieved. How the team is constituted will be critical to determining the likelihood of its success. Most organizations, especially larger ones, are composed of various constituencies. Successful implementation of a comprehensive information security policy will require acceptance by all of the key constituencies.

No system will succeed without the support of management. Therefore, management must be involved with the drafting of the information security policy from the outset. If the organization is large enough to have an information systems department, the team should include a member of the department. It should also include a member of the human resource department. Selection of other team members will depend on the nature and the makeup of the organization.

The first step, for the team developing the information security policy, is to conduct an audit of all the ways in which information flows into and out of the company. The purpose of the audit is to determine the company's vulnerability to accidental or intentional access or disclosure, as well as to identify the kinds of information developed or maintained by the company. It should evaluate how information is developed, shared, and utilized within the organization. The audit team should find out which documents, if any, are recycled and how the recycled paper is handled. The team should create an audit trail for sensitive computer files so that there is a record of who is accessing company information, and this record should be reviewed periodically. If some levels of employees are not represented on the audit team, the team should involve those employees, asking them to identify areas of concern. With the knowledge it acquires, the audit team can do a risk assessment to determine what weaknesses need to be addressed and what strengths need to be reinforced.

What Should Be Included in the Statement of General Principles?

Following the audit and risk assessment, the information security committee will be ready to prepare its initial draft of the general principles for the information security policy. This statement should include goals, objectives, and responsibilities for information security. The general principles section should be broadly focused so that it will not have to be constantly revised as a result of rapid changes in technology or in how the company itself handles information. It should also be tailored to reflect the ideology and culture of the specific organization.

Although each organization's information security policy will differ, some common elements should be included in any such policy. For example, the policy should clearly state that it governs all information in the company's possession, regardless of the format in which it is maintained. The cornerstone of the policy should be a statement reflecting the fact that the company owns all information within its possession and/or control. Establishing ownership of the information is critical to the company's ability to obtain legal recourse if information is stolen, altered, or inappropriately disclosed. The policy should also clearly define the company's organizational policy for protecting information so that anyone with legitimate access to it understands his or her responsibility as an "information safe-keeper." It should specify who has access to particular information and the purposes for which it can be used. The policy should make clear that employees may not use company information for nonbusiness purposes and may not remove it without authorization. Many companies have failed to implement policies that make clear their proprietary interest in the business information and the technology or systems that support it. A policy that is developed after an employee removes critical information may be too late to protect the company's interests.

An information security policy should define what types of confidential or proprietary information are covered by the policy. While there are already laws, such as state and federal trade secret laws, that generally prevent an employee or other individual from inappropriately using proprietary information of a current or former employer, what qualifies as a trade secret or protectable proprietary information may be open to questions. Such questions can be greatly minimized or even eliminated through the information security policy. For certain types of information such as sensitive computer files, the company will want to limit the people who have access to the information and restrict the opportunity to obtain or duplicate information.

The information security policy should also include procedures for how information should be protected, such as through passwords or lock and key for hard copies, and ensure that these procedures are followed. If a company seeks court assistance in protecting its information, one of the first questions the court will ask is "Did you actually treat the information confidentially?" A court will be less likely to provide the company with a legal remedy if there is evidence that so-called "confidential information" has not been maintained confidentially because of inappropriate disclosures or sloppy or inadequate security procedures.

An information security policy should make clear the need for security and the significance of failure to comply with its requirements. A policy without enforcement will be ineffective. Education and awareness should not be overlooked. The general policy should create a permanent information security team whose responsibility is to maintain awareness of information security issues throughout the organization.

Finally, another common element in the general principles of most information security policies will be a statement that employees do not have an absolute expectation of privacy in information generated in the workplace. It should explain that there may be legitimate business reasons or instances, such as investigations of theft or discrimination, or even as simple a reason as an employee's absence, when the company will need to access an employee's e-mail, voice mail, or other company equipment. It should be clear that the use of technology or any information medium for harassment, or any other inappropriate intrusion, will not be tolerated.

After the draft statement of general principles for an information security policy has been created, the team should submit it to top management for review. It is crucial that management buy into the general goals and objectives of any information security policy before it is implemented. Moreover, before the team can complete the policy by developing procedures and controls relating to specific technologies, events, and behaviors, it needs to know that its general statement of principles is acceptable to management.

An example of the statement of general principles of a comprehensive information security policy follows:

Information and the systems that create, store, and transmit it are critical and sensitive assets of the ABC Company (the "Company") which must be protected. Any information owned by or in the custody of the Company, including personal employee information for which there is an established business, regulatory, or legal need, whether generated internally or received from external sources, is considered the property of the Company. In addition, the Company is the custodian and caretaker of countless pieces of confidential information belonging to and pertaining to our clients and their affairs. This information is often not in the public domain and it is highly sensitive. It has been entrusted to the Company with an expectation that it will be maintained in confidence.

The Company has a responsibility to protect its information and information systems in an appropriate manner from unauthorized or unintended use, disclosure, destruction, alteration, or violation. The security of information must be maintained regardless of how the information is stored (e.g., computer, voice mail, paper). It is the responsibility of every employee and subcontractor to be vigilant in protecting the integrity of Company information and information systems from violation by internal as well as external sources. The degree of sensitivity of information will determine the appropriate level of security to be utilized. Every employee and subcontractor shall acknowledge receipt and review of the Company's information security policy by signing and dating the attached acknowledgment and returning it to the Human Resource Department for inclusion in the employee's personnel file. All references to "employees" herein shall include subcontractors, interns, and any other person who is authorized to be on Company premises for business reasons. New employees or those who have not been trained on information security procedures must receive such training before they access or utilize any Company information. Any incident with respect to a breach of security or concerns about the integrity of information systems should be reported immediately to the Director of Information Systems. Internal security audits will be conducted by the Company from time to time to evaluate the effectiveness and adequacy of security measures.

Information and information systems are intended to be used for Company business. Sending messages that may be considered offensive, harassing, intimidating, or discriminatory is prohibited, as is use of such information or systems for personal gain. Occasional personal use is permitted as long as the use does not affect the Company's productivity or interfere with the Company's business operations. Employees should keep in mind, however, that even personal files and information may be accessed by the Company if there is a legitimate business, regulatory, or legal need for doing so. Any unauthorized use will be considered a misappropriation and may subject the employee to disciplinary action, including dismissal.

Personal codes and devices, such as passwords, alarm codes, keys, access cards, and voice mail identifiers, have been provided to employees to enhance the security of information and systems and to facilitate access to Company premises at times when the building may not be open to the public. These passwords, codes, and devices should never be shared with others, even within the Company. Passwords for all programs should be changed routinely to safeguard the security of the Company's assets, even if the change is not automatically prompted.

Each administrative department within the Company is responsible for identifying security needs that are specific to its operations and functions. Employees in each department will be responsible for familiarity with particular policies that supplement the general security policy.

The foregoing is a statement of the Company's general policy on information security. It applies to all of the Company's employees, subcontractors, information, systems, and technologies, whether or not they are specifically mentioned herein. Upon termination of employment for any reason, each employee will be expected to return any property belonging to the Company, including computer disks, documents, copies, notes and personal identifiers.

How to Achieve the Goals Set Forth in the General Principles

After the information security policy's general principles have been approved by management, the team must shift its focus to developing the procedures and controls necessary to achieve the general goals. It may be wise at this point to alter the makeup of the team to include employees who utilize certain technologies on a daily basis. There are certain systems and technologies that will require more definitive directives for proper security. Among the items that a company should consider having are specific sections on physical files and hard copies of information, facsimile transmissions, laptop computers and disks, Internet and e-mail, telephones and voice mail, computer workstations, and special precautions for telecommuters. These narrower procedures and controls will be more technologically focused and will need to be revised more often than the general goals as technology changes and as problems with the procedures become evident. In addition to sections on specific technologies, some of the specific procedures and controls will focus on events such as hiring and firing. Still others will focus on certain behaviors such as use of technology for personal purposes or sharing of passwords.

Examples of specific technology-based and other types of policies that should be in a comprehensive information security system are the "Internet and E-mail" and "Computer Workstations" sections that follow:

Internet and E-mail

Internal and external e-mail systems are available to employees to assist with the conduct of business. The electronic mail system hardware and software are assets of the Company, as are all messages composed, sent, or received on the e-mail system. Employees should remember that the Company may access e-mail messages for any business, regulatory, or legal purpose.

Each user of the e-mail system has a personal password, which should not be shared and which should be changed frequently to avoid unauthorized access. Even when passwords are properly used, confidentiality of messages should not be assumed. E-mail messages placed in "trash" are retained for a period of sixty days by the Company. Messages not placed in "trash" will be retained indefinitely until deleted by the employee. Each employee should treat each other person's messages as strictly confidential and should not attempt to gain access to someone else's messages without that person's permission.

Caution should be exercised when using external e-mail via the Internet. Although intentional interception of external e-mail is prohibited by law, e-mail over the Internet is not as secure as standard telephone service. Remember that e-mail messages, as any electronically stored data, may be discoverable in litigation. Finally, no information may be posted to a Web site or otherwise disseminated on the Internet on behalf of the Company without the permission of the Executive Director of the Company or the Company's Director of Information Systems.

Computer Workstations

Each employee must have a personal password in order to gain access to the computer network and to certain programs. Passwords must be changed routinely and should be kept strictly confidential. Each user should log out of the system and switch off his or her terminal at the end of the day.

Receptionists and others working in public areas that are visible or accessible to nonemployees should not leave information on the monitor when away from the work station and should utilize password-protected screen savers. During extended breaks or lunch, employees in public areas should log out of the system.

An information security system should also inform employees that their rights to access and use company information terminate when they are no longer employed by the Company. Companies should create a post-termination checklist to ensure that employees return all company property, including copies of all information, before they leave and that computer and other access is terminated on that day. The policy itself should provide penalties for violations so that there is an incentive to comply with the policy. An important precaution is to create and test a disaster recovery plan to recover the information if it is lost, destroyed, or stolen.

How Should a Company Implement the Policy?

Implementation of an Information Security Policy should begin with educating and training employees and others subject to the policy and seeking their input on how to ensure that the policy is followed. Every covered individual, from employees to interns to independent contractors, should be required to sign and date an acknowledgment form stating that the individual understands his or her responsibility to safeguard all company information in accordance with the policy and further understands the ramifications (e.g., discharge or termination) of noncompliance.

In developing and implementing a policy, companies should keep in mind that no set of procedures and controls can ever be complete. No organization will ever be able to fully anticipate every information management problem that might arise. Indeed, the very purpose of having an information security policy—with broad statements of principles supported and monitored by a continuingly operating information security team that emphasizes education and, when necessary, enforcement—is to demonstrate that the company is diligent with regard to the protection of sensitive information. A well-constructed information security policy will provide a good faith defense. In the event of disclosure of confidential information, it will also provide an organization with legal recourse if information has been misappropriated. Policies that focus merely on specific technologies, such as e-mail, faxes, and the Internet, run the very real risk of being perceived as incomplete and therefore inadequate. No company can anticipate every point of vulnerability with regard to access to information. But every company can articulate general policies regarding the need to protect confidential and sensitive information. Every company can educate its employees and maintain awareness. And every company can develop a track record of enforcement to demonstrate that it takes its policies seriously. A company that enacts these measures is much more likely to defend itself successfully in the event of an accidental disclosure or theft of information that it has a fiduciary obligation to protect. Companies that discover that crucial information has been misappropriated will be in a better position to recover it if they have a clear policy that provides evidence of their control and ownership of the information.

We are living in the information age. The way we handle information today is different from the way we handled it even 10 years ago, in large part because of dramatic advances in technology. These advances continue to take new shape, seemingly on a daily basis. The years 2000 and beyond will bring about new ways in which we develop, use, and store the vast quantities of information on which most modern businesses rely. The risks are very high that the old methods for dealing with information storage are grossly inadequate. Despite these risks, few companies have taken the proactive measure of developing a comprehensive information

Developing an Information Security Policy

1. Create an information security team or committee.
- Involvement management.
- Involve a member of the information systems department, if any.
- Involve human resources.
- Select other team members depending on nature and makeup of company.

2. Conduct an audit of all ways in which information flows into and out of the company.
- Evaluate how information is developed, shared, and utilized within the company.
- Find out how documents or computers are recycled or destroyed.
- Involve all levels of employees.

3. Prepare a statement of general principles of the policy.
- Include goals, objectives, and responsibilities for information security.
- Define what types of information are covered and who is covered by policy.
- Explain expectations regarding privacy, security, maintenance, and destruction of information.
- Reflect the ideology and the culture of the organization.
- Submit the statement to management for acceptance.

4. Develop procedures and controls relating to specific technologies and behaviors.
- Include, for example, physical files, facsimiles, laptop computers, Internet and e-mail, telephone, voice mail, computers and telecommuters.
- State possible penalties for noncompliance.

5. Implement the policy.
- Disseminate the policy and require a signed acknowledgment by every employee.
- Educate and train all employees about the policy and its implementation.
- Follow up to keep the policy and training current.

security policy. Instead, many have gone only so far as to implement isolated technology-specific policies such as an e-mail or Internet policy. This simply is not enough. As we move into the twenty-first century, all companies should evaluate their need for implementing a comprehensive information security policy. Only by doing so will companies take the necessary risk management steps for securing their valuable intangible assets to the greatest extent possible. Being proactive is always the best defense.

Recommended Actions

- Create an information security team composed of all levels of employee groups.
- Conduct an information security audit of risk assessment to determine the company's vulnerability to accidental or intentional access or disclosure, as well as to identify the kinds of information developed or maintained by the company.
- Develop a comprehensive information security policy that addresses all forms of company information, including e-mail and Internet, voice mail, paper, or computer.
- Educate and train employees and others subject to the policy regarding its provisions.
- Monitor compliance with the policy. Conduct random security audits.
- Review the policy periodically to ensure that it continues to meet the company's needs and is effective.

Suggested Readings

Behar, R. "Who's reading your mail." Fortune, 3 February 1997, 57–70.

Lewis, P. H. "Threat to computers is often the enemy within." New York Times, 2 March 1998, p. B1.

Remnitz, D. and Breed, R. "Network security audits keep the hackers at bay." National Law Journal, 2 February 1998, pp. C9–10.

Rotenberg, M. The Privacy Law Sourcebook: United States Law, International Law, and Recent Developments. Washington, D.C.: Electronic Privacy Information Center, 1998.

Wood, C. C. Information Security Policies Made Easy. Sausalito, California: Baseline Software, 1996.

Young, L. F., and Christenson, G. A. "Guidelines for company policies on employee privacy in the electronic workplace: a report of sample policies and analysis." Cincinnati, Ohio: Center for Information and Technology and Law, College of Business Administration and College of Law, University of Cincinnati, August 1994.

THE FUTURE OF UNIONS

James A. Laumeyer
Employee and Labor Relations Committee

Ever since the enactment of the National Labor Relations Act in 1935, labor unions have been a powerful influence in the United States. In the decades immediately following World War II, unions effectively bargained the terms and conditions afforded all American workers. They were able to influence the election of sympathetic policymakers who would successfully sponsor favorable legislation and regulations. During most of the twentieth century, labor unions enjoyed, and took advantage of, a position of significant power. At the start of this millennium, however, both the future and the vitality of unions are in question. Contemporary articles present conflicting positions as to whether organized labor is a dinosaur on the verge of extinction or whether it will persevere and evolve in response to changes in the political and cultural environment (Hurd 1998; Rosenthal 1998). At the core of this debate is the decline of union membership, best illustrated by the following graph (Bureau of Labor Statistics 1999).

Union Density, 1930–1997
Membership as Percentage of Payrolls

For the human resource professional, the discussion is not theoretical. It represents the basis for previewing human resource jobs in the future. More specifically, the existence of a union in a particular workplace will continue to require additional skills and responsibilities of human resource professionals. Each human resource professional will have a critical role in the determination of the union status of the organization. This chapter provides an accurate projection of labor unions into the next two decades. To understand the current and future status of unions, it is necessary to understand the transformation of unions from a major national power to the current weakened state. Unions do not exist in a vacuum. They have been somewhat decimated by external change forces. The decline is due, in part, to the failure of unions to adjust or adapt, but such contention does not take into account the extent of the forces for change that have dramatically affected labor unions. Further, although unions in general have experienced hardships, unions also have had some successes—for example, significant growth in the public sector and in some specific industries.

This chapter addresses the future of unions in selected industries and workplaces in order to offer insight into the general implications of the winds of change relating to unions. Human resource professionals will recognize the power of personal influence as a primary determinate of the result of union organization efforts in their workplaces. The most appropriate analysis and discussion of the current and future status of unions will not center upon unions themselves, but will focus on the significant forces or drivers of change external to unions. Human resource professionals are fully aware of these significant drivers of change: workforce and employment. Analysis of these drivers is based on statistical information, projections of the data, and the opinion of respected sources. Great care was taken to avoid the trap of simplistic extrapolation. The projections of influential data are represented only by information that has been supported by "expert testimony." Simple extraction certainly would support the perception that labor unions will be nonexistent or meaningless in the near future. But this chapter shows that labor unions will continue to be influential in the future, especially in specific workplaces and under specific conditions.

Workforce Considerations

In today's vigorous economy, many workers have little need for what unions have traditionally offered: competitive compensation, job security, and equitable grievance procedures. Unions continue to tout higher wages for their membership, but surveys show that, in general, higher wages are a lesser concern of workers. Most workers today regard adequate compensation as a given, and this view will continue in the tight labor markets of the early decades of the millennium (Adams 1998). Although some categories of workers do find the prospects of higher pay more attractive, many regard job satisfaction as their primary interest. Unions, however, have demonstrated little or no influence on job satisfaction. Studies have indicated that unionized employees experience less job satisfaction than their nonunion counterparts (Kleiman 1997). Human resource professionals can play a critical role in the delivery of increased job satisfaction to employees.

While unions cannot deliver the workers' premier need, they do have two offerings that are very attractive to certain groups of workers. First is job security (Holley and Jennings 1997). In previous decades, job security was held as sacred only by those employees whose security was threatened. It is ironic that increased numbers of workers are concerned about job security in this tight labor market. Anxiety has increased in the wake of such significant events, such as the passage of the North

American Free Trade Agreement (NAFTA), corporate downsizing, and the growth of outsourcing.

Some concerns of blue-collar workers relating to NAFTA have been justified. The Labor Department reports that more than 210,000 blue-collar jobs (primarily in the manufacturing sector) were lost in the five years after the legislation was enacted. At the same time, NAFTA is reported to have "boosted export-related U.S. economic growth" and created more American jobs (primarily white-collar and service jobs) in a single month than were created in the year before its enactment (Wildavsky 1999). Consequently, Congress will enact new treaties, such as Fast Track, that will have similar results: a loss of blue-collar jobs and a significant gain of other jobs.

Similarly, the concerns of both blue-collar and white-collar workers have been justified relative to downsizing and outsourcing, which have become common strategies for organizations looking for ways to cut costs in highly competitive markets. It has become a common occurrence to find media stories on the corporation that announces the layoffs of thousands of workers. Additionally, the outsourcing of work continues to grow, particularly in the public sector. The Outsourcing Institute in New York "reports that spending on outsourcing has grown fivefold this decade" (the 1990s) (Overman 1997, p. 112). Therefore, it is understandable that workers in search of protection from downsizing and outsourcing will turn to unions. And unions have been responsive to these concerns. Howard A. Sieber, partner and principle consultant for HR Intervention Associates, as cited by Overman, stated:

> Unions work hard to create more language that inserts them into the decision-making process, and they have been successful. I see a resurgence of unions' willingness to exercise strike power to stop, slow or otherwise change management's position, relative to outsourcing or subcontracting (Overman 1997, p. 112).

The second offering used by unions to attract workers builds on employees' strong expectation of fair and respectful treatment. The federal government's propensity for legislating employee rights has reduced the need for unions. But employees still recognize unions as the guardian of fair and respectful treatment in the workplace, and the perception of unfair or disrespectful treatment by management can create an opportunity for a union to organize. The implications for the human resource professional are obvious. Fair treatment of employees is a fundamental objective of human resource management. Therefore, our influence in the positive treatment of employees will aid productivity and retention and perhaps diminish the need for unions in organizations. In his influential study of personnel practices in nonunion companies, Foulkes (1980) found that companies that successfully remained nonunion were more likely to promote management philosophies emphasizing employees as stakeholders and good employee relations. At the level of practice, Foulkes and others (e.g., Fiorito, Lowman, and Nelson 1987) have found that formalized, consistent, and progressive human resource policies substantially reduce employee interest in unionization. According to this analysis, workers' needs will not be the basis for seeking union representation. However, in cases of anxiety over job security or the perception of unfair treatment, groups of employees will seek union representation. The progressive actions of human resource professionals will improve conditions in most organizations, resulting in increased job satisfaction for most workers.

In addition to the worker's wants and needs as cited above, two other conditions positively influence union organization. First, workers tend to favor unions if their companies have a "directive" (chain of command) rather than participative or open culture (Mathis and Jackson 1997). It appears that unionization is perceived as the worker's vehicle for input and participation. This finding is a "call to action" for human resource professionals who perceive that the culture within their companies is directive in nature. While more participative cultures are perceived as conducive to higher productivity, a culture shift can also be justified on the basis of filling this apparent desire of workers to participate. Second, workers who have been union members in the past are more likely to favor union representation (Mathis and Jackson 1997). Accordingly, human resource professionals who work in industries or geographical locations that are heavily unionized should be acutely aware of the inclination. This inclination could have significant implications in the merger of organizations when one or more are organized.

Finally, a very different union leadership is emerging that will create a new appeal to workers. Emergent leaders within labor can be characterized as the "Ivy League Leaders." Highly educated leaders have assumed the helms of labor unions such as the Teamsters, Service Employees, and Hotel Workers. In addition to creating a more "professional image," these leaders are attempting to interest workers in terms of ideology and social issues, in addition to the traditional union offerings. While such offers may not appeal to all workers, it may be very effective in attracting professional workers such as physicians. In essence, this is an evolution of union offerings that has not been fully tested in the workplace until this decade.

Worker Demographics

The demographic profile of the workforce will continue to change dramatically in future decades (Mathis and Jackson 1997). It is very likely that benefit to unions will be slight to moderate. The change in the workforce will continue in the groupings of women and minorities.

Women

It is clear that women will constitute the vast majority of the labor supply for the next two decades. Two out of three applicants for jobs will be female (Mathis and Jackson 1997). Historically, unions have not actively recruited women for membership. Such complaints as the lack of female labor leaders and the lack of sensitivity to women's issues have been common barriers between women and unions in the past. However, the AFL-CIO has now recognized that "Working women absolutely are the future of this labor movement" (Outwater 1997, p. 1).

While not conclusive, studies and surveys have indicated that women are more likely than men to join unions, 49 percent to 40 percent (*Wall Street Journal* 1998). The rationale for the inclination of women to organize is obvious. Though women represent the majority of the workforce, compensation of female workers is collectively lower than that of male workers (Mathis and Jackson 1997). Women continue to dominate low-paying occupations such as clerical jobs and are more likely to work part-time. Women are also likely to be the sole provider for their family. Accordingly, many female workers are more concerned about compensation than the workforce as a whole. Women bring significant needs to the workplace that are unique (Mathis and Jackson 1997)—for example, a greater need to balance family and work demands, and needs for additional flexibility in hours and affordable day care. Often they perceive unions as the vehicle for satisfying these needs.

These inclinations of the largest group of tomorrow's workers should be encouraging for unions. Unions will have a greater opportunity to organize female workers, provided that women find unions more appealing than in the past. Because of the feminization of the workforce and the expressed inclination of women to join unions, human resource professionals should ensure that the needs and preferences of women are addressed within their organizations. By avoiding conditions such as poor treatment or the failure to listen to women, organizations can effectively eliminate the impetus for female employees to seek unionization.

Minorities

Similarly, studies indicate that African American workers have more favorable attitudes toward unions than white workers do. Further, African American workers have a higher percentage of union members (17.7 percent) than white members (13.5 percent) do. While African American workers will not represent a large percentage of the future workforce, this inclination has significant implications for unions and for organizations in many urban areas in this country (Amber 1999).

It is clear that Hispanic workers will constitute a growing percentage of the future U.S. labor force, especially in the Southwest. Attitudes of Hispanic workers have been less favorable toward unions. Hispanics represent the lowest percentage (11.9 percent) of union membership in terms of racial categories. Hispanic females have the lowest percentage (10.8 percent) of union membership (Amber 1999). This is not to say that human resource professionals should consider nonunion status as a given if their workforce is predominantly Hispanic. Progressive human resource practices will still be the most effective factor in workers' consideration of the need for a union in their workplace.

Contingent Workers

One of the fastest-growing sections of the labor force is the contingent worker. Approximately 20 percent of today's workers are parttime or temporary. Because of the nature of their employment, few temporary workers belong to a union (Bureau of Labor Statistics 1984, 1998). Only 7 percent of parttime workers are union members. One of the temporary employment firms is currently the largest employer in the United States, yet unions have not been able to represent this large group of workers. The transient nature of temporary positions is not consistent with traditional union representation; in the private sector there are actually legal barriers to the unionization of temporary workers. While unions have been able to organize large numbers of parttime workers in huge organizations (e.g., United Parcel Service), unions have not been able, presumably for logistical reasons, to organize the vast majority of these workers in smaller organizations. Therefore, it appears that this large group of workers will continue to be nonunion members in the future. Unions appear to have a major misunderstanding of the plight of the contingent workers. Unions characterize contingent workers as victims, or workers trapped in the undesirable fate of a contingent worker. Yet analysis of the composition of these workers indicates that contingent work is a choice, predicated upon personal reasons. More specifically, many of these workers are students, working mothers, or workers between more permanent employment. The demographics of the future workforce provide some encouragement to unions. Clearly, female and black workers have more favorable attitudes toward unions than the white, male workers who have represented the majority of the workforce in the past. The apparent challenge to the human resource profession will be consideration of the sensitive and responsive needs of a diverse workforce.

Private Sector

The private sector has historically been the strength of the labor movement. In the future, however, most unions in the private sector will fight for survival. Much of this twist of fate is a result of the external winds of change and the evolution of the U.S. economy. The most significant changes have been the changes in the nature and the geographical locations of U.S. jobs. These changes have a significant adverse impact on the traditional core unions of the labor movement, and they account for the declining numbers in union membership. These impacts are most noticeable in the analysis of major industries.

Manufacturing

Manufacturing represents the largest occupational group of private sector union members, at 3.2 million members (Bureau of Labor Statistics 1996). Manufacturing jobs continue to be jobs that will be exported as a result of U.S. trade agreements and global competition. Although many manufacturing jobs will be created, the majority will be created in states that have low union membership. For example, *Time* magazine has reported that Arizona and Texas are the "hottest places" for manufacturing jobs in the future (Greenwald 1997). Both of these states have low union membership rates (7% and 6%) (Bureau of National Affairs 1999a) and will not be fertile ground for unionization in the future.

While the outlook for labor is adversely affected by the relocation of a large number of jobs essentially out of unions, there is the potential for unions to replace some lost manufacturing jobs. According to Philip Simon (1999), small companies are now dominating the manufacturing industry. This change is encouraging to unions for two primary reasons. First, unions have demonstrated a higher success rate in organizing small organizations. Second, small organizations do not usually have a full-time human resource professional to ensure the proper treatment of employees and to counsel the company during the organizing activities.

Another potential for union organization relates to industry efforts to streamline processes for purposes of efficiencies. Many large manufacturing companies are consolidating supply, service, and distribution centers. These efforts generally accomplish the stated objective of efficiencies. But some employees may be disgruntled with the company about the consolidation efforts if they have been forced to relocate or to accept jobs that are lower-paying or not to their liking. Therefore, one result of these consolidations is to increase the likelihood of union organizing. In fact, some of these centers have become bigger targets for union organizing. They create the possibility of gaining a large number of new members. Human resource directors in these companies should make every effort to address these issues throughout the planning and implementation of such efforts. These efforts could decrease the chances of union organization.

It is apparent that unions will experience significant losses in membership as a result of the geographical location or relocation of manufacturing jobs in the future. It is also apparent that unions will have more opportunity to add some members in small businesses. It is probable that there will be fewer unionized manufacturing workers in the future and that manufacturing will not be the industry of the greatest union numbers.

Services

The services industry employs the most workers (30.7 million) in the country and represents one of the lowest rates of union membership (5.4%), 1.6 million (Bureau of Labor Statistics 1999b). In general, unions have had very little success in organizing service workers. There are several factors that could assist unions in their organizing efforts. First, it is possible, but unlikely, that Congress will legislate single-site bargaining units. Because most service companies are small and comprised of stores or service centers, single-site legislation would be a major boon for union organization. Second, the use of Internet organizing could facilitate the organization of service stores or centers that are geographically scattered. Although Internet organizing will become a major tool for labor organizations, unions will not make significant inroads into most service organizations. Unions could make significant gains in one service area—health care services. Health care, now approximately fifteen percent unionized (Bureau of National Affairs 1999b), represents a huge opportunity for union organization. JoAnn Shaw, vice president and chief human resource officer of the University of Chicago Hospitals and Health Systems, says union-organizing activities have increased in number semiannually between 1996 and 1998 from 11.5 percent to 16.6 percent (ASHHRA 1998).

There are some underlying factors that may result in the increase of unionization in the health care industry. First, most health care facilities employ a significant number of employees. Second, many health care companies have continued directive cultures, which cause employees increasing dissatisfaction. Third, unions in this industry have developed some momentum. Employees in a nonunion company may be more susceptible when aware of other organization activities in other health care facilities. In addition, physicians have recently become very interested in unionization. To date approximately 2 percent of the 1.4 million physicians have organized

(Stilwell 1998). While the rationale for physicians to organize is not apparent, the uncertainties of this industry and the new ideological offering of unions appear to be two significant reasons.

The implications and challenges for human resource professionals in health care are enormous. HR personnel should be fully aware that their industry is a hotbed of union-organization activities. It would be prudent to scrutinize company programs, culture, and practices aggressively for causes of employee dissatisfaction in order to anticipate or prevent union-organizing activities. Although unions will not establish significant gains in the service industry as a whole, unions will continue to target all health care workers and will be successful in gaining significant membership.

Transportation

With 1 million union members, and the highest concentration of union members (26.5%) (Bureau of Labor Statistics 1999b), the transportation industry will grow during the next two decades. For example, Julie Showers (1999), managing director-labor relations for Northwest Airlines, states: "Unionization within the airline industry is on the increase, not the decrease. Of the major national carriers, four out of five are heavily unionized." The transportation industry also provides the labor movement with greater visibility. For example, who could not be aware of a strike action against a major carrier? Unlike other unions, organizers of transportation workers will not face significant challenges such as the relocation of jobs or the challenge of organizing scattered groups of workers. Therefore, the transportation industry will provide additional union membership and will establish a stronger and more visible leadership role in the labor movement.

Wholesale and Retail Trade

Like to the service industry, the sales industry has a large number of workers (second to the service industry) and a low union member percentage (5.6%) (Bureau of Labor Statistics 1999b). The challenges for unions are the same in other "scattered employee" groups. In addition, the sales industry has a high concentration of contingent workers, such as students who do not perceive their employment relationship as long term.

Some large retail companies, like some manufacturing companies, will consolidate distribution centers, which could create additional probability of union organization. As discussed for the manufacturing industry, human resource professionals should be diligent in such consolidation efforts in order not to cause unionization. In general, this industry offers unions little opportunity to gain significant membership from the enormous pool of workers.

Construction

The construction industry is a well-recognized bastion of the labor movement. The industry has 1 million union members and a union member concentration of 18.6 percent. There will be some growth in construction jobs, and construction companies will continue to "double breast" or maintain nonunion entities for opportunities of highly competitive bidding (Greenwald 1997). In contrast to other traditional union strongholds, such as manufacturing, unions will experience slight gains in construction union members in the future.

In summary, the future of unions in the private sector presents more challenge than opportunity. The most fertile industry, manufacturing, will decline in union membership. Unions will not be effective at gaining significant numbers of new members in the two huge industries of service and sales. The bright spots for private sector unions will be transportation and health care workers.

Public Sector

In contrast to the private sector, the future of public sector unions is much more optimistic. Public sector union membership is approaching fifty percent of all union membership (Bureau of Labor Statistics 1999b). The unions representing teachers (National Education Association) and government employees (American Federal of State, County, and Municipal Employees) are two of the largest unions in the labor movement. Public sector union membership rate is a lofty 37.2 percent (Bureau of Labor Statistics 1999b). There will be slight growth in the number of government jobs in the future, especially in area of education, although it is apparent that factors such as charter schools and vouchers could result in some erosion of union membership.

Similar to their colleagues in the private sector, public sector employees perceive significant threats from government outsourcing and from privatization. This reduced influence is aggravated by the tendency of public employers to have directive or autocratic cultures. Unions are considered an ally in the minimization of both of these significant threats. In addition, public sector human resource professionals have less influence than their private sector counterparts in the implementation and administration of the programs and processes that directly affect the employees.

Labor legislation is a paramount consideration in the public sector. Consequently, some public sector employees continue to be prohibited from union representation. But legislative limitations will continue to affect only a minority of government employees in the future. Accordingly, private sector unions will gain considerable numbers of members in the future, and public sector unions will dominate the labor movement after experiencing significant growth. The public sector presents few barriers to labor organizations and offers a very large pool of workers attracted to unions.

Conclusion

The future of unions is slightly more favorable than their current state. Unions will continue to represent a substantial number of workers. Based upon this analysis, union membership can be expected to include between 20 and 25 percent of the workforce.

The labor movement will continue to have considerable political clout, and union-sponsored strike actions will continue to have significant impact on the employment climate in this country. Current trends forecast a major shift of power and prominence within the labor movement. Unions representing transportation workers and health workers will rise in influence in the private sector. Public sector employees, including teachers, will comprise the new majority of union membership.

There are several significant implications for human resource professionals, who have a most critical role in providing and nurturing work environments of care, concern, and appreciation for the employees. First, this analysis provides a preview of future union representation in various industries. Each human resource professional should carefully examine the trends and predict the extent to which experience with labor relations will be necessary in their own organizations. Second, and most significant, human resource professionals should have a better understanding of their own individual influence and involvement in the determination of the union status of their particular organizations. Third, human resource professionals should recognize that unionization is not necessarily evidence of deficiencies on the part of either management or the human resource department. Rather, unionization can be systemic or the result of the inclinations and concerns of the workforce. For example, the anxiety and fear of public employees about privatization is not in response to any evidence in their current workplaces. This analysis of historical and current trends is offered to give human resource professionals the opportunity to visualize and shape their futures.

Recommended Actions

- Nurture employee job satisfaction through proper selection, performance feedback, recognition, and job design.
- Provide training and clear expectations for supervisors and managers to ensure fair, respectful, and appropriate treatment of all employees.
- Provide proper communication and equity when implementing employee reductions.
- Provide methods for fostering employee involvement, internal communication, and a sense of personal ownership in the company.

References

Adams, M. "The stream of labor slows to a trickle." *HR Magazine,* 43(10) (1998): 84–89.

Amber, M. "Union membership numbers." *Daily Labor Report.* Bureau of National Affairs, Inc. 4 February 1999 [on-line]. Available at http://www.newsstand.k-link.com/nwsstnd.

ASHHRA/OMNI Semi-Annual Labor Activity Report. 1 January–30 June, 1998). 13th report, 1–8.

Bureau of Labor Statistics Census. *Employment and Earnings.* Bureau of Labor Statistics, Washington, D.C.: U.S. Government Printing Office, January 1984 and January 1998.

Bureau of Labor Statistics. "Union affiliation of employed wage and salary workers by occupation and industry." Bureau of Labor Statistics Table 3, 29 January 1996 [on-line]. Available at http://stats.bls.gov:80/news.release/union2.t03htm.

Bureau of Labor Statistics. "Unions and part-time workers." AFL-CIO, 12 January 1999a [on-line]. Available at http://www.aflcio.org.

Bureau of Labor Statistics. "Union Membership Trends." AFL-CIO, 12 November 1999. [on-line]. Available at http://www.aflcio.org/uniondifference/uniondiff11.htm.

Bureau of National Affairs. Union members by state, 1997. AFL-CIO, 12 January 1999a [on-line]. Available at http:/www.aflcio.org/org/uniondifference/uniondiff16.htm.

Bureau of National Affairs. Union Labor Report: Reference File. BNA. 4 February 1999b [on-line]. Available at http://www.newsstand.k-link.com/nwsstnd.

Department of Labor. "Employment and earnings." AFL-CIO 12 January 1999 [on-line]. Available at http://www.aflcio.org/uniondifference.

Fiorito, J., Lowman, C., and Nelson, F. "The impact of human resource policies on union organizing." *Industrial Relations*, 26(2) (Spring 1987): 113–126.

Foulkes, F. *Personnel Policies in Large Nonunion Companies*. Englewood Cliffs, NJ: Prentice-Hall 1980.

Greenwald, J. "Where the jobs are." *Time*, 149(3) 20 January 1997 [on-line]. Available at http:wysiwyg://cgi.pathfinder.com/time/magazine/1997/dom/97012cover.html.

Holley, W. and Jennings, K. *The Labor Relations Process*. 6th Ed., Orlando, Florida: Harcourt Brace College Publishers, 1997.

Hurd, R. "Contesting the dinosaur image: The labor movement's search for a future." *Labor Studies Journal*, 22(4) (1998):5–42.

Kaufman, B.E. "The future of the labor movement: A look at the fundamentals." *Labor Law Journal*, 48(8) (August 1997):474–484.

Kleiman, L.S. *Human Resource Management*. 8th ed. Minneapolis/St. Paul: West Publishing, 1997.

Mathis, R. and Jackson, J. *Human Resource Management*. 8th ed., Minneapolis/St. Paul: West Publishing, 1997.

Outwater, L. *Daily Labor Report*, Bureau of National Affairs, 9 September 1997, p. 1.

Overman, S. "Unions demand a voice." *HR Magazine* 42(7) (1997)112–118.

Rosenthal, M. "Leadership is critical to resurgence." *Labor Studies Journal* 22(4) (1998):43–46.

Showers, Julie (julie.showers@nwa.com). "Future of unions." E-mail to J. Laumeyer (jim.laumeyer@dot.state.mn.us), 29 January 1999.

Simon, P. Input for the future of unions. In Letter to Jim Laumeyer, 4 January 1999.

Stilwell, E. "Hearing opens on doctor's bid to unionize." Cherry Hill, New Jersey, *Courier-Post*. 5 November 1998, p. 13D.

Wall Street Journal "Women to women." 24 March 1998, p. A1.

Wildavsky, B. "Not happy after NAFTA." *U.S. News and World Report*, 126 (11 January 1999):49.

MEASURING HR'S FUTURE

Raymond B. Weinberg
Research Committee

Folk musician Bob Dylan's hit "The Times They Are A-Changin'" could easily apply to both the last decade and the next for the field of human resource management. Turbulent change presents both challenges and opportunities for human resource practitioners. How HR responds to these challenges and opportunities determines its credibility and ultimately its very survival.

The challenges faced by HR are many. Its critics are widespread, as evidenced by Thomas A. Stewart, who proclaimed in a *Fortune* magazine editorial: "Nestling warm and sleepy in your company like the asp in Cleopatra's bosom is a department whose employees spend 80% of their time on routine administrative tasks. Nearly every function of this department can be done more expertly for less by others. Chances are, its leaders are unable to describe their contribution to value added except in trendy, unquantifiable and wannabe terms—yet, like the serpent unaffected by its own venom, the department frequently dispenses to others advice on how to eliminate work that does not add value" (Stewart 1996, p. 105).

Stewart's criticism, although exaggerated, is not without some degree of merit. HR must be able to measure, in quantifiable terms, the value it adds to organizations. It must learn to forsake HR fads, many of which are cross-dressed as strategic initiatives. It must have an impact and be able to measure that impact on the organization's bottom line. The failure of human resources to measure its contribution has led to its own credibility problem. David Ulrich summed it up well in his appropriately titled article, "Judge Me More by My Future Than by My Past," when he stated, "While the HR as we know it (with images of policy police, regulations and administrative guardians) has passed, a new HR is emerging" (Ulrich 1997b, p. 5). This new HR he proposes must focus on deliverables and impact.

The purpose of this chapter is twofold. First, the chapter examines changes in the workplace that will affect the delivery of HR in the next decade. Robotics, information age technology, and telecommunications will have a profound effect on jobs and organizations. The virtual workplace is close upon us. HR in this workplace may have little resemblance to the HR of today. Second, this chapter will examine measurement of the value added by HR in the next decade's workplace—what will be measured and how it will be measured. Only through measurement can the human resource field regain its credibility.

Measurement—HR's Achilles' Heel

Although the HR function, in one form or another, has been around since before 1900, measurement of HR contributions is a fairly recent development. It wasn't until the mid-1960s that the proponents of a concept called human resource accounting made initial attempts at quantifying the value of human resources (Brummet, Flamholtz, and Pyle 1968). These proponents advocated that the value of human resources be treated as an asset rather than an expense on financial accounting statements. Although not addressing the value of the contribution of the HR function per se, these early pioneers challenged the belief that human resources couldn't be quantified.

Later approaches in measuring the value of the human resource function were primarily activity- and cost-based (Fitz-enz 1984; Cascio 1991). These approaches emphasized cost-effectiveness in justifying HR activities and initiatives.

Today's approaches have focused on measuring the relationship of HR's contribution to the organization. Using objective, quantifiable organizational effectiveness criteria and qualitative measures of HR deliverables, the focus of these approaches has been on drawing a clear line of sight between the quality of HR practices and productivity, sales, earnings per share, profitability, and other measures of an organization's success (Huselid and Becker 1995; Huselid and Becker 1996; Becker et al. 1997; Welbourne and Andrews 1996). Some researchers have even used the list of most admired companies from *Fortune, Inc.*, and *Business Week* in an index (much like the Dow Jones), comparing performance of those firms on the list and comparable firms not on the list, with significant findings (Callette and Hadden 1998). This research justifies the value contributed by HR to the bottom line. Unfortunately, for the typical HR practitioner these measurement methodologies have escaped use. Clearly, the measurement of HR contribution must find its way out of the ivory towers and down to the level of the individual firm if HR is to truly become a business partner.

The New Workplace

The previous decade brought about significant changes to the workplace, creating many challenges for the HR field. The decade gave rise to economic and employment shifts, global competition, organizational restructuring, demographic/workforce diversity changes, work/family considerations, skill shortages, education and training deficits, and expanding employee rights (Mathis and Jackson 1997). For the most part, these changes were driven in response to pressures from outside of the organization. The challenges that were posed to HR in the 1990s may pale in comparison with the projected challenges over the next ten years.

The next set of challenges will arise from three fundamental transformations in the workplace—the changing nature and structure of jobs, the evolving new relationship between employee and employer, and the new fluid structures that organizations need to be competitive in the dynamic marketplace of the twenty-first century. For the most part, these changes will arise from within the organization. Each of these transformations must be examined in relationship to its impact on HR. With an understanding of the magnitude of these changes, an analysis of how HR's future contribution will be measured can be made.

Jobs

The next decade's workplace will be fundamentally different from today's workplace because jobs will be different. Human resources has long relied on the concept of the job to base many of its activities. Jobs were analyzed by systematically gathering information on their content, requirements, and context. Job analysis and resultant job descriptions were the heart of most HR activities, including recruitment and selection, compensation, training and development, performance appraisal, and legal compliance (Mathis and Jackson 1997). Jobs were highly defined, and human resource activities for the most part derived themselves from the concept of the specialized job.

Both the structure of jobs and the skills required to perform them will undergo a major transformation. Jobs used to be based upon the high-volume industrial model. New information age technology will have a profound effect on these jobs and the very nature of work. In fact, jobs as they are known today may cease to exist in the postindustrial world (Rifkin 1995).

Previously, new technologies have had a trickle-down effect, reducing product costs, increasing consumer demand, and putting more people to work in new information age jobs and industries (Rifkin 1995). In the 1990s, organizations reengineered, productivity grew, profits increased, and all was well for shareholders (Mishel and Bernstein 1992). In all likelihood, the next wave of technological advances will render many jobs obsolete. Premiums will be paid for certain highly skilled jobs in the next decade's workplace. Some analysts have envisioned only three types of jobs in this new era—routine production services, in-person services, and symbolic/analytic services (Reich 1991). Only the skilled symbolic/analytical jobs will be in high demand. HR will have to adjust to these new jobs.

The twenty-first century will also give way to jobs where knowledge and intellectual capabilities are what differentiates one employee from another (Bahrami and Evans 1997). Focus will change from what is done to what one is capable of doing. Instead of compartmentalized, narrow jobs defined by functional or occupational domains, broader, more expansive roles will evolve (Crandall and Wallace 1998). Work is envisioned to move from position-based to person-based systems, where intellectual capital and competencies will constitute the new competitive advantage. As a result, emerging new trends such as virtual workplaces, "anytime/anyplace" work, contingent work, and cyberlinked work will become more commonplace. Human resource practitioners will have to play a pivotal role in adapting HR systems to this new work.

The New Employment Relationship

The euphemism that past behavior is the best predictor of future behavior does not bode well for human resources. The past decade has seen organizations alter the relationship between employer and employee in many ways. Restructuring, reengineering, zero-based staffing, outsourcing, rightsizing, and downsizing have characterized this period. As a result, the commitment of even the most loyal employees has been tested by the psychological contract—an unwritten understanding based upon mutual trust that defines what the employee and the organization expect to give to and receive from each other during their relationship. Before the 1990s the psychological contract was very stable. Employees went to work for employers with reliable expectations for rewards and long-term employment

(Sims 1994). This mutual relationship was based upon employers protecting the interest of employees in return for dedication, hard work, loyalty, and commitment. As organizations' external environments become more chaotic, the psychological contract began to be reshaped.

This altered employment relationship has given way to what has been described as the "new psychological contract" between employees and employers (Rousseau and Geller 1994). As Rousseau and Geller allude, a major function of a human resource manager is to foster an appropriate psychological contract. Human resources officers will be faced with the challenge of redefining expectations under the new psychological contract. They must find means of strengthening the likelihood of mutually satisfying exchange relationship between employees and organizations. The concept of job security, so long sought after by employees, will give way to career security, where competencies and capabilities become the new workplace currency. The workplace that evolves will require flexibility on the part of employees in order to attain this new form of security. As rules of the game change, HR must work harder in making sense out of the new employment relationship.

The New Organization

If the changing nature of jobs and the employment relationship didn't pose enough issues for HR, the organization of the next decade will create a more fluid environment for the delivery of HR services. In the past, organizations were highly structured, with clearly defined boundaries. Organizational success was determined by four factors: size, role clarity, specialization, and control (Ashkenas et al. 1995). The organizational structure determined by these factors tended to be very rigid and departmentalized. Every person had a job and a function, and performance was measured against standards. In the new organization, those historical success factors have been replaced by speed, flexibility, integration, and innovation (Ashkenas et al. 1995). Organizations are moving from fixed boundaries to more fluid boundaries. Lines on the organizational chart have become blurred. The organization of the new workplace will reformulate external, loosen horizontal, and flatten vertical and cross-geographic boundaries. What this means for HR is that its constituency or consumer group will expand far beyond employees. These blurred boundaries will result in former competitors forming strategic alliances and new entities developing that represent the entire length of the value chain (Crandall and Wallace 1998). HR will have a whole new constituency.

These blurred boundaries will spawn the emergence of the virtual organization, one not bounded by visual and physical proximity. Employees will remote-work using telecommunications and technology to fulfill their new roles. HR will also be virtual, with services instantaneous, on demand, and at a place most convenient to its customers. HR administrative functions will be shed, and the focus will be on service and strategic deliverables. Multimedia kiosks, paperless HR, desktop learning, and distance supervision and learning will be commonplace. HR measurement in the new organization will be more difficult.

Measuring Human Resources Value-Added Contribution

Effective human resource practices will be necessary for organizational success and growth. Current research has already verified this relationship (Huselid and Becker 1995). The question becomes what and how do you measure to determine the value-added contribution of HR practices in the workplace of the future. Most economics textbooks define value-added as the incremental addition to profit that results from transformational activity. Numerous terms have been used or misused to describe valued-added, including accountability, return on investment (ROI), effectiveness, worth, impact, cost versus benefit, and bottom line contribution. These terms have in common the emphasis on measuring HR's practices link to tangible business goals. As Ulrich has stated, "These terms focus on results and not activities, deliverables not doables" (Ulrich 1997a, p. 24).

What should be measured? The HR practices of the new workplace have not yet been defined. New practices and tools will be forthcoming. Ulrich says, "These tools will focus on such areas as: global HR (learning to manage HR issues and global competition), culture change (defining tools for crafting and changing corporate culture), technology (adapting HR to the ever-changing information highway), leader of the future (defining the competencies of the future, not past leader) and knowledge transfer (understanding how to generate and generalize knowledge)" (Ulrich 1997b, p. 6).

How can HR measure its value-added for tools and practices not yet defined? Changes in jobs, the employment relationship, and organizations point to measures of HR's value-added contributions in the areas of:

Intellectual capital assessment and investment. This will be the currency of the new workplace. The unmapped and untapped knowledge of an organization will have profound economic impact by creating competitive advantage. HR's role in assessing and developing intellectual capital will affect the bottom line and be a key area for measuring of value-added (Stewart 1997).

Extended value chain enhancement. With new customers beyond the walls of the traditional organization—suppliers, competitors and communities—participating in the value chain, HR will need to collaborate with this extended group in adding value. The measures of HR contribution will go beyond traditional boundaries of the organization to a larger constituency. Broader measures may be needed.

Values stewardship. One way for HR to redefine expectations of its new employment relationship will be through a strengthening of culture. HR must measure the impact of its practices on the shared beliefs and values of the organization, and in turn the impact on the financial goals of the enterprise values redefinition will reshape the psychological contract.

Action learning development. Learning about learning, solving problems in real time will reduce the lag between learning and application and bridge the gap between process and outcomes will have to be measured. (Burke 1995, p. 166).

HR will lead the way in action learning development by calculating translating theory who practice and measuring the return.

Competency-based system application. HR's emphasis on what really affects performance in the organization will help shape the HR tools and practices of the next decade. Competency-based staffing, development, and rewards will become commonplace. Measuring competency development and payoff will be a priority.

The tools and practices of the past give way to these tools and practices of future. These future tools and practices, although still undefined, will have characteristics of adaptability, quick delivery, and measurable impact.

A Word of Caution

In the virtual HR organization of the future, these tools and practices may not rest in the human resource department or function. They very well could be disbursed through line management. The HR department may actually disappear. The question becomes how you measure the contribution of HR practices independent of the HR function (Ulrich 1997b).

Although HR has been accountable for HR practices, in reality the entire organization is responsible for their implementation. HR practices are embodied in organizational practices. They cannot be separated. No matter where HR is performed, effective HR practices will need to be present.

Traditionally, HR measurement and evaluation has had three levels. These are measures of perceived effectiveness (feedback from stakeholders), measures of performance (indicators of HR performance), and measures of return on investment (monetary value of program benefits compared with cost) (Phillips 1996). The movement will be toward return on investment where important business outcomes can be measured—where value-added can be seen.

Conclusion

Measuring HR's contribution has certain payoffs to organizations. Measuring value-added makes good economic sense. Every HR practice should provide a return on investment. Measuring value-added contributions also provides proof of results. By keeping a scorecard of how HR practices affect important organizational outcomes, line management appreciates the value of these practices. By measuring value-added, it encourages the organization to focus on important HR deliverables. It will tie practice outcomes to bottom line contribution. Measuring the value-added HR services increases the function's credibility. By measuring value-added contributions, HR will be viewed not as a staff function, but as a true business partner. "The Times They Are A-Changin'."

Recommended Actions

- Measure HR deliverables rather than activities.

- Calculate ROI for each and every HR program and for the HR function as a whole.
- Change the measurement focus from cost to value.
- In ROI, focus on specifically quantifying the numerator (value) rather than the denominator (cost).
- Build measurement into the design of HR programs in the beginning, rather than after the program has been implemented.

References

Ashkenas, R.; Ulrich, D.; Jick, T.; and Kerr, S. *The Boundaryless Organization.* San Francisco. Jossey-Bass, 1995.

Bahrami, H., and Evans, S. "Human resource leadership in knowledge-based entities: Shaping the context of work." *Human Resource Management* 36(1) (1997):23–28.

Becker, B.; Huselid, M.; Pickus, P.; and Spratt, M. "HR as a source of shareholder value: Research and recommendations." *Human Resource Management* 36(1) (1997):39–47.

Brummet, R.; Flamholtz, E.; and Pyle, W. "Human resource measurement—a challenge for accountants." *Accounting Review* 47(2) (1968):217–227.

Burke, W. "Organizational change: What we know and what we need to know." *Journal of Management Inquiry* 4 (1995):158-171.

Callette, B., and Hadden, R. *Contented Cows Give Better Milk.* Germantown, TN: Saltillo Press, 1998.

Cascio, W. *Costing human resources: The Financial Impact of Behavior in Organizations.* Boston: Kent Publishing, 1991.

Crandall, N. F., and Wallace, M. *Work and Rewards in the Virtual Workplace.* New York: AMACOM, 1998.

Fitz-enz, J. *How to Measure Human Resources Management.* New York: McGraw-Hill, 1984.

Huselid, M., and Becker, B. *High Performance Work Systems and Organizational Performances.* Paper presented at the Academy of Management Annual Conference, Vancouver, British Columbia, 1995.

Huselid, M., and Becker, B. "Methodological issues in cross-sectional and panel estimates of HR-firm performance link." *Industrial Relations* 35(3) (1996):400–422.

Mathis, R., and Jackson, J. *Human Resource Management.* St. Paul: West Publishing Company, 1997.

Mishel, L., and Bernstein, J. *The State of Working America 1992–1993.* Washington, D.C.: Economic Policy Institute, 1992.

Phillips, J. A*ccountability in Human Resource Management.* Houston: Gulf Publishing, 1996.

Reich, R. *The Work of Nations.* New York: Random House, 1991.

Rifkin, J. *The End of Work.* New York: G. P. Putnam's Sons, 1995.

Rousseau, D., and Geller, M. "Human resources practices: Administrative contract makers." *Human Resource Management* 33(3), (1994):385–406.

Sims, R. "Human resource management's role in clarifying the new psychological contract." *Human Resource Management* 33(3) (1994):373–382.

Stewart T. *Intellectual Capital: The New Wealth of Organizations.* New York: Doubleday/Currency, 1997.

Stewart, T. "Taking on the last bureaucracy. " *Fortune,* 15 January (1996):105–106, 108.

Ulrich, D. *Human Resource Champions: The Next Agenda for Adding Value and Delivering Results.* Boston: Harvard Business School Press, 1997a.

Ulrich, D. "Judge me more by my future than by my past." *Human Resource Management* 36(1) (1997b):3–8.

Welbourne, T., and Andrews, A. "Predicting performance of initial public offering firms: Should human resource management be in the equation?" *Academy of Management Journal* 39(4) (1996):891–919.

ABOUT THE SOCIETY

Michael R. Losey
Society for Human Resource Management

In reading this book, it becomes obvious that the human resource profession, born less than a century ago, has already undergone enormous change, evolving from essentially a personnel clerk to a senior-level strategic business partner. In the twenty-first century, the human resource profession will truly come of age.

The Society for Human Resource Management has long anticipated these changes in the profession and has endeavored to meet them. For decades the Society has supported functional committees to stay abreast and anticipate changes and issues in such areas as compensation and benefits, labor and employee relations, health, safety and security, training and development, and management practices. Their expertise is reflected in these chapters.

In 1976 the Human Resource Certification Institute (HRCI), an affiliate of the Society, was established to certify the knowledge of those in the human resource profession. To develop the test for certification, the Society and HRCI identified a body of knowledge. That body of knowledge has been growing, and it will continue to expand at exponential rates. Each year HRCI breaks its own records in the number of human resource professionals who take the exams. And, more and more companies are seeking human resource professionals who are certified through the Institute. These companies realize that the human resource profession has a quantifiable body of knowledge that requires study and mastery. They recognize that just as you cannot "sell from an empty wagon" you cannot expect someone to do human resource work "with an empty head." Higher barriers of entrance to the profession are developing.

In discussing the future of the workplace and the human resource profession, the urgency for better education and lifelong learning opportunities for human resource professionals becomes apparent. As the field comes of age, colleges and universities must establish human resource management majors that emphasize strategic business planning in their curricula. The Society has long encouraged the formal study of human resource management and fosters such study through its student and adult education programming.

As previously discussed, the future will require that federal and state laws and regulations change to allow organizations to meet the needs of their workers. The Society has an active governmental affairs department and an award-winning grassroots program to help effect these changes. But these laws and regulations must not be altered without the leadership and input of human resource professionals. Members of Congress and state legislators *must* hear from human resource professionals if these laws are to be amended fairly. It is certainly gratifying to be asked to testify before a federal or state legislative body because it speaks to the importance of the profession in the United States. If the human resource profession is to truly move into its strategic business role, however, human resource professionals must become more active in legislative and regulatory affairs, serving as strategic partners to Congress, state legislators, and regulatory agencies.

Early on, the Society recognized that the world would become a much smaller place in the twenty-first century and that human resource professionals would have to be prepared to cope with increased globalization. So, in 1991, SHRM established the Institute for International Human Resources (IIHR), a division of SHRM that helps educate human resource professionals about the challenges associated with a global economy and to generate solutions. Today, IIHR represents more than 5,300 members in more than forty countries.

SHRM is also a founding member (and currently president) of both the North American Human Resource Management Association (NAHRMA) and the World Federation of Personnel Management Associations (WFPMA). Because of the Society's foresight, it is deeply involved in global issues, with members in more than 100 countries, and therefore it is prepared to assist human resource professionals whose organizations are entering international waters.

ABOUT THE EDITOR

Marc G. Singer is professor of management at Middle Tennessee State University and president of Emadjen Management Consulting. He received his B.B.A. in 1968 from the City College of New York, his M.B.A. in 1971 from Baruch College, and his Ph.D. in 1973 from the University of Tennessee. An active consultant, trainer, and researcher, Dr. Singer specializes in staffing, performance appraisal, and government rules and regulations, particularly as they relate to equal employment opportunity and labor relations. Dr. Singer is widely published in professional journals, he is the author of a textbook on human resource management, and he co-edited the second edition of SHRM's *Effective Human Resource Measurement Techniques* that was sponsored by the SHRM Foundation. From 1997–1999, Dr. Singer served as chair of the SHRM research committee and as a director on the SHRM Foundation Board.

ABOUT THE AUTHORS

Raylana S. Anderson, CEBS, SPHR, a human resource and employee benefits consultant, is the proprietor of Anderson Consulting in Peoria, Illinois. She received her B.A. in 1981 and her M.B.A. in 1988 from Bradley University. In addition to assisting companies in the development of comprehensive employee relations programs and total compensation practices and policies, Ms. Anderson has authored or co-authored several widely used HR compliance guidebooks. Ms. Anderson served as the 1998–1999 chair of the SHRM Compensation and Benefits Committee.

Debbra M. Buerkle, CCP, SPHR, is managing partner with Human Resources & Management Solutions, specializing in employee relations consulting services. She received a B.A. in 1977 from Thiel College and completed master's studies in Applied Communication and Alternative Dispute Resolution at the University of Denver. Actively involved with the SHRM since the mid-1980s, Ms. Buerkle currently serves on the SHRM's Legislative Action Committee. She also has served as Colorado's state legislative affairs director and as the Colorado Springs chapter's legislative affairs liaison.

Robyn Burke, SPHR, is a human resource service delivery executive with Computer Sciences Corporation. She received her B.S. in 1987 and her M.Ed. in 1991 from Vanderbilt University. Over the past several years, Ms. Burke has delivered workshops and training programs on a variety of HR topics; she has designed and implemented performance management, succession planning, and organizational/individual development tools; and she has recently authored a SHRM white paper on managing the careers of high performers. Ms. Burke is a member of the SHRM Human Resource Development Committee.

David F. Bush, is professor of Industrial/Organizational Psychology and coordinator of the graduate program in HRD at Villanova University. He received his B.A. in 1965 from the University of South Florida, his M.A. in 1968 from the University of Wyoming, and his Ph.D. in 1972 from Purdue University. An active researcher and consultant, Dr. Bush has in excess of sixty publications, is the originator of the *Alligator Syndrome*, has developed several assessment instruments, and serves as an editor of the *Journal of Systems Improvement*. An active SHRM member, Dr. Bush has served as president of the Philadelphia regional chapter of the SHRM, and he is currently the professional development chair of the Pennsylvania State Council of the SHRM and a member of the SHRM Workplace Health and Safety Committee.

Cornelia G. Gamlem, SPHR, is corporate manager, employee relations, for Computer Sciences Corporation. She received her B.S. in 1983 from California State University, Sacramento, and her M.A. in 1995 from Marymount University. Ms. Gamlem has extensive experience in the areas of policy-setting and program management, specifically in areas involving equal employment opportunity, affirmative action, employee relations, and workplace diversity. An active writer, Ms. Gamlem has authored several SHRM white papers on topics such as affirmative action, alternative dispute resolution, workplace diversity, and the Family and Medical Leave Act. Ms. Gamlem joined the SHRM Workplace Diversity Committee in 1993 and served as chair in 1997–1999. She served as an at-large member of the 1996 board of directors for the Institute for International Human Resources, and she currently serves as a vice president at-large on the SHRM's 2000 Board of Directors.

Phyllis G. Hartman, SPHR, is director of human resources for Stylette Plastics in Oakdale, Pennsylvania, and an instructor at LaRoche College . She received her B.S. in 1971 from Edinboro State University, and her M.S. in 1990 from LaRoche College. Before her current position, Ms. Hartman worked at SAE International, where she managed staff training and development, and recruiting functions. An active speaker and writer, Ms. Hartman has delivered presentations to various HR associations, and she co-authored a 1994 book chapter on recruitment and staffing for the American Society of Association Executives (ASAE). Ms. Hartman is a former president and member of the board of directors of the Pittsburgh Human Resources Association, she served as the 1998–1999 treasurer of the SHRM Pennsylvania State Council, and she is a member of the SHRM School-to-Work Committee.

Linda S. Johnson is a partner with the law firm of McLane, Graf, Raulerson & Middleton, P.A. She received her B.S. in 1981 from Rivier College and her J.D. in 1984 from Boston University School of Law. In addition to her practice focusing on employment law defense and corporate management, Ms. Johnson has written numerous articles for local publications. Recently she authored "The Employee Handbook: Careful Drafting Makes the Difference Between Having a Sword or a Shield," published in the 1997 edition of the Defense Research Institute's *Employment Law Basics*. Ms. Johnson is a member of the SHRM Employment Committee.

James A. Laumeyer is the director of administration for the Minnesota Department of Transportation, Northeastern Minnesota. He received his B.A. degree in 1973 from Macalester College, and his M.B.A. in 1978 from the University of Minnesota–Duluth. A prolific speaker and writer on topics relating to employer and labor relations, Mr. Laumeyer also serves as an adjunct faculty member at the University of Minnesota–Duluth, the University of Minnesota–Carlson School, and the College of St. Scholastica. Mr. Laumeyer is the past president of the Minnesota Public Employer Labor Relations Association, and the past chair of the SHRM Employee and Labor Relations Committee.

Michael R. Losey, SPHR, CAE, is president and CEO of the SHRM. He received both his B.B.A. and his M.B.A. from the University of Michigan. With more than 40 years of HR experience, Mr. Losey is a frequent spokesperson and writer on HR issues, and he recently co-edited the book *Tomorrow's HR Management*. Mr. Losey currently serves as president of the World Federation of Personnel Management Associations (WFPMA), as president of the North American Human Resource Management Association (NAHRMA), and as a fellow and director of the National Academy of Human Resources (NAHR).

Raymond B. Weinberg, CCP, SPHR, is a principal and senior consultant for the Silverstone Group, Inc. He received his B.S.B.A. in 1973 and his M.B.A. in 1977 from the University of Nebraska at Omaha. Before his current assignment, Mr. Weinberg was human resources director at Father Flanagan's Boys Home, where he was directly responsible for administering all phases of HR for a 1,700-employee youth care organization operating in seventeen cities and eleven states. In addition to his workplace experience, Mr. Weinberg has taught HR-related courses for the past twenty-five years at colleges and universities including Buena Vista University, Metropolitan Community College, and the University of Nebraska at Omaha. Mr. Weinberg is an active member of many professional associations, a member of the SHRM Research Committee, a director on the SHRM Foundation Board, and a past president of the Human Resource Certification Institute. In recognition of his expertise in, and contributions to, the field of HR, Mr. Weinberg was presented with the SHRM 1993 "Award for Professional Excellence."